GRAPHIS RECORD COVERS

GRAPHIS

Graphis/Record Covers

Edited by Walter Herdeg $ 21.50

This comprehensive survey of album art presents a fascinating cross-section from the early stages of record cover design up to the most recent achievements in this field. Arranged in seven sections — the pioneers; the work done in the 1950s; and five music categories: classical music; jazz; light music (songs, folk and country, sound tracks); pop/rock/beat; miscellaneous records (children's, literary recordings, educational records, special presentations, Japanese projects).
Preface by Robert Cato, Vice President of United Artists Records. Introductory texts to the music sections by Colman Andrews, editor of *Coast* magazine; Stefan Böhle of Deutsche Grammophon Gesellschaft, Hamburg; and Stanley Mason, assistant editor of *Graphis*. Detailed captions and indexes of artists, designers, art directors and publishers.

A COMPANION VOLUME IN THIS SERIES:

GRAPHIS/DIAGRAMS

The Graphic Visualization of Abstract Data
Edited by Walter Herdeg

Selected with the graphic designer in mind, who is often faced with the difficult task of having to present a body of information in diagrammatic form, this international review will serve as an abundant source of inspiration. It also demonstrates convincingly that statistical and diagrammatic graphics do not necessarily have to be dull, that the creative designer can introduce an imaginative touch without loss of "legibility".
There are six sections: (1) statistical, comparative diagrams; (2) flow diagrams, organization and time charts; (3) diagrams visualizing functions, processes; (4) tabulations, timetables; (5) cartographic diagrams, decorative maps; (6) diagrams used as design elements. Introductory text by Leslie A. Segal, creative director of Corporate Annual Reports, Inc., New York. A subject index facilitates finding items of particular interest. There are also indexes of designers, artists, art directors, agencies, studios, clients, publishers.
184 pages, 9¼" × 9³/₈", 268 illustrations, with 86 in color.

Write for a complete catalogue to:
VISUAL COMMUNICATION BOOKS

Hastings House, Publishers
10 East 40th Street, New York 10016

RECORD COVERS

The evolution of graphics reflected
in record packaging

Die Schallplattenhülle als Spiegel
der graphischen Entwicklung

L'évolution de l'art graphique vue
à travers la chemise de disque

Edited by: / Herausgegeben von: / Réalisé par:

Walter Herdeg

The Graphis Press, 8008 Zürich (Switzerland)

Editor, Art Director, Designer: Walter Herdeg
Assistant Editor: Stanley Mason
Project Manager: Vreni Monnier
Cover Design: Walter Herdeg

160093

Distributed in the United States by

Hastings House

Publishers

10 East 40th Street, New York, N. Y. 10016

PUBLICATION No. 135   [ISBN   8038–2669–9]

Contents   Inhalt   Sommaire

Editor's Foreword

A book on the design of record covers would be incomplete, to say the least, if it did not contain some account of the beginnings and the early stages of development of an art form whose total evolution up to date is in any case limited to a few decades. We have therefore included in this book sections dealing with the pioneers of record-cover design and with the work done in the nineteen-fifties, but have restricted our examples to the outstanding achievements and to those artists who really succeeded in setting a trend.

From the early nineteen-sixties onwards the material has been divided not into chronological but into musical categories. While this was necessary to bring a measure of system and clarity into our arrangement, the divisions cannot lay claim to any absolute validity. There are many borderline cases where a different classification would have been possible, and there is inevitably a certain amount of overlapping.

Although this book deals specifically with record-cover design, it also mirrors, in a wider frame of reference, the general trends of the graphic design and the photography produced in the periods under review and thus constitutes an interesting retrospect over the changing tastes and the main directions of advance manifested in these two areas.

We have been fortunate in obtaining, for our introductory texts, the services of writers who are recognized authorities in their various fields. We should like to express our thanks to these authors, as well as to all the artists and photographers, and particularly the record companies, who have given us the benefit of their expertise and assistance. We hope that the finished work will seem to them, at least in some measure, to repay their efforts.

Vorwort des Herausgebers

Eine Publikation über die Gestaltung von Plattenhüllen wäre sicher unvollständig, wenn sie nicht einen Überblick über die Anfänge und die frühen Entwicklungsstadien einer Kunstform vermitteln würde, die eigentlich erst einige Jahrzehnte als solche anerkannt ist. Wir haben dem allgemeinen Teil deshalb zwei Kapitel vorangestellt, die den Pionieren in der Gestaltung von Plattenhüllen und den Arbeiten aus den fünfziger Jahren gewidmet sind; wir mussten unsere Auswahl jedoch auf die hervorragendsten Beispiele und diejenigen Künstler beschränken, die auf diesem Gebiet wegweisend waren.

Die abgebildeten Plattenhüllen von den frühen sechziger Jahren bis heute wurden im Hinblick auf eine klarere Übersicht nicht chronologisch unterteilt, sondern nach Musikkategorien. Es wird jedoch nicht der Anspruch auf absolute Gültigkeit erhoben, denn es gibt Grenzfälle, bei welchen eine andere Einordnung durchaus vertretbar wäre, und so waren gewisse Überschneidungen nicht zu vermeiden.

Obwohl dieses Buch hauptsächlich der Gestaltung von Plattenhüllen gewidmet ist, spiegelt es im weiteren Sinne auch die Entwicklung des graphischen Designs und der Photographie in diesem Zeitabschnitt wider. Es ist gleichzeitig ein interessantes Dokument über den sich ändernden Geschmack des Publikums und die auf diesen zwei Gebieten erzielten Fortschritte.

Wir hatten das Glück, für unsere Einführungstexte Autoren zu finden, die auf diesem Gebiet anerkannte Autoritäten sind. Ihnen möchten wir herzlich danken, wie auch allen Künstlern und Photographen und speziell den Plattenfirmen, die mit Rat und Tat am Gelingen dieser Publikation mithalfen. Wir hoffen, dass sie durch das vorliegende Werk wenigstens teilweise für ihre Bemühungen entschädigt werden.

Avant-Propos de l'Editeur

The Authors of Introductory Texts
Die Autoren der Einführungstexte
Les Auteurs des textes d'introduction

Un ouvrage consacré à la conception des pochettes de disques serait pour le moins incomplet si l'on n'y trouvait un rappel des origines et l'illustration des premiers stades de développement de cette forme d'art, dont l'évolution ne s'étend en tout cas que sur quelques décennies. Nous avons donc inclus dans ce livre des chapitres sur les pionniers de l'art de la pochette de disque, ainsi que sur les années 1950, tout en nous limitant aux faits importants et aux créateurs qui ont fait date.

Du début des années 1960 jusqu'à présent, les exemples n'ont pas été classés par chronologie, mais par catégories musicales. Commode pour la clarté de l'exposé, ce classement ne saurait prétendre à une validité absolue. Dans nombre de cas limites, la répartition catégorielle aurait pu être différente, sans compter les chevauchements inévitables.

Quoique le sujet de l'ouvrage soit la conception des pochettes de disques, il n'en reflète pas moins, dans un contexte élargi, les grandes orientations graphiques et photographiques des périodes examinées et constitue ainsi une rétrospective intéressante des goûts changeants et des grandes voies d'évolution qui se manifestent dans ces deux domaines.

Nous avons pu bénéficier, pour nos textes d'introduction, de la contribution d'experts de renom que nous remercions chaleureusement. Nous voudrions associer à ces remerciements tous les artistes et photographes, et en particulier les éditeurs de disques, qui nous ont fait profiter de leur connaissance spécialisée en la matière et de leur amicale assistance. Nous formulons le vœu que l'œuvre achevée puisse, dans une certaine mesure, répondre à leur attente et justifier ainsi l'effort fourni en faveur d'un portrait, que nous voudrions vivant et stimulant, de l'art subtil d'habiller le disque.

BOB CATO, who studied under such celebrities as Moholy-Nagy, Gyorgy Kepes and Alexey Brodovitch, has worked as a painter, sculptor, photographer and designer, and as art director of various magazines, including *Harper's Bazaar* and *McCall's*. He has had several one-man exhibitions and has directed the design departments of Columbia Records and Revlon. He is now Vice President of United Artists Records, where he heads the Creative Services.

COLMAN ANDREWS is at present editor of *Coast* magazine, an attractive monthly published in Beverly Hills. He is a freelance writer and photographer and one of the most sought-after authors of liner notes for the covers of jazz and blues records.

STEFAN BÖHLE studied graphic design and typography in Brunswick, Germany. In 1969 he became art director for record covers in the Deutsche Grammophon Gesellschaft in Hamburg, where since 1972 he has been in charge of design and advertising for the company's special productions.

STANLEY MASON was born in Canada and took a language degree at Oxford. A freelance writer and magazine editor, he has been associated for many years with The Graphis Press and its publications on art and design.

BOB CATO, der unter Berühmtheiten wie Moholy-Nagy, Gyorgy Kepes und Alexey Brodovitch studierte, arbeitete als Maler, Bildhauer, Photograph und Designer, später als Art Director für verschiedene Zeitschriften, darunter *Harper's Bazaar* und *McCall's*. Seine Arbeiten wurden verschiedentlich in Einmann-Ausstellungen gezeigt. Er leitete die Design-Abteilungen von Columbia Records und Revlon und wurde vor einiger Zeit zum Vizepräsidenten von United Artists Records ernannt, wo er den Creative Services vorsteht.

COLMAN ANDREWS ist Chefredakteur der Zeitschrift *Coast*, eine gestalterisch und inhaltlich anspruchsvolle Monatsschrift, die in Beverly Hills herauskommt. Daneben arbeitet er als freischaffender Schriftsteller und Photograph und gilt als einer der gesuchtesten Autoren für Liner-Texte von Jazz- und Bluesplatten.

STEFAN BÖHLE studierte Graphic Design und Typographie in Braunschweig. 1969 wurde er künstlerischer Leiter der Schallplattenabteilung der Deutschen Grammophon Gesellschaft in Hamburg, wo er seit 1972 im Bereich der Spezialausgaben dieser Gesellschaft für Gestaltung und Werbung verantwortlich ist.

STANLEY MASON wurde in Canada geboren und graduierte in Sprachen an der Universität Oxford. Heute arbeitet er als freischaffender Schriftsteller und Zeitschriftenredakteur. Als Mitglied der Graphis-Redaktion befasst er sich seit vielen Jahren mit Graphik und angewandter Kunst.

BOB CATO, qui a fait ses études sous l'égide de célèbres artistes tels que Moholy-Nagy, Gyorgy Kepes et Alexey Brodovitch, a travaillé ensuite comme peintre, sculpteur, photographe et designer et comme directeur artistique de divers magazines, entre eux *Harper's Bazaar* et *McCall's*. Il a plusieurs expositions individuelles. Il a dirigé le département de design de Columbia Records et Revlon. Depuis quelques temps il est Vice-Président de United Artists Records, où il a sous sa direction les services de création.

COLMAN ANDREWS est à présent éditeur du magazine *Coast*, une publication mensuelle très soignée qui parait à Beverly Hills. Ecrivain et photographe indépendant, il est un des auteurs les plus recherchés pour les textes au verso des pochettes, surtout pour les disques de jazz et de blues.

STEFAN BÖHLE a étudié le design graphique et la typographie à Brunswick en Allemagne. Directeur artistique pour les pochettes de disques de la Deutsche Grammophon Gesellschaft à Hambourg de 1969 à 1972, il est chargé depuis lors du design et de la publicité des productions spéciales de cette maison.

STANLEY MASON est né au Canada et a pris ses grades en langues à l'Université d'Oxford. Journaliste indépendant et rédacteur de magazine, il s'occupe depuis des années des publications d'arts graphiques et d'arts appliqués des Editions Graphis.

The art of the twelve-inch square

"Good morning, Mr. Dylan, how do you want to package your rock 'n' roll?"

After World War II there was a graphic renaissance that was felt in the fields of magazine and book publishing, television, architecture, industrial and packaging design and advertising, to name but a few. All participated in the creative uses of graphics, design, typography and photography. Only the recording industry was a late bloomer. Not because there was a dearth of concerned, tasteful and knowledgeable record people to guide their companies to good designers. The problem was that there was no creative impetus within the industry itself to propel the companies out of their pre-conditioned attitudes to packaging and design.

But it happened… *The Beatles* and *rock 'n' roll.*

So, here at last was the impetus, the sources of pure inspiration. The music and its extra-ordinary thrust of power, the inspired packaging all wrapped up for the incredible, insatiable audience of young people that responded with such joy and devotion.

At the same time the new music brought into focus the roots that had given it so much of its life… jazz, country and Western music, the blues, the classics and even the guy who *played* his nose.

So, instead of the can of soup, the silk stocking, the super-duper car, the thirst-killer coke and the never-ending streak of lipstick to give belief and credibility to, the designer of the record cover had to deal with a "real and human" product that was just as concerned, if not more so, about its own image, its own message on its own package! It really was the beginning of a new consciousness about the dialogue that had to exist between the designer and the music-maker.

One of the most moving and possibly the most individualistic and interesting examples of this dialogue developed between the art and the music that grew out of the exotic thunder of the San Francisco "sound" during the middle and late sixties. Album art, posters, light shows and magazines all reflected a cohesiveness and sense of identity that was the San Francisco scene. For me it remains the only "area-oriented folk art" that truly embodied the synthesis of art and music of this renaissance I speak of.

As for the state of the art today, all of us have been privy to the growing sophistication of the album package: the new papers, the new board innovations and of course the impact of the "concept package". The package that has more to offer than just the record and the outside graphics.

One of the most interesting of the conceptual packaging approaches was that of the series produced by the president of Columbia Records, Goddard Lieberson. With these innovative packages we can experience the synthesis between literature, art, music, the spoken word and the package. The Columbia Literary Series (twelve contemporary authors reading their own works), The Union and The Confederacy albums, The American Revolution (with a marvellous essay from the English point of view, by Robert Graves!), The Art and Music of Mexico, The Badman (a classic album about the outlaws of the early West), The Irish Rebellion and Doctors and Medicine—all examples of very astute, loving and concerned musical journalism and packaging.

The album covers reproduced on the following pages have been divided up into various categories of music. For instance, a light tracing has been made of the graphic history of jazz album art and design. Jazz has always had its own power and magic, and here the designer/ photographer/artist is offered a rare opportunity to couple his powers with the magic of jazz.

The light music area of album design was in many ways one of the most demanding until the rock explosion took place. It was only then that the sales-oriented people and the recording artists themselves began to understand the "commercial value" of a well-designed cover for the marketplace. When pedantic graphic thinking replaced "middle-of-the-road" thinking, the album stood a fine chance of first-rate exposure. It is here, I can assure you, that the designer works the hardest to make a meaningful piece of graphics for his "client".

Designing for the pop/rock album is the one area that undoubtedly demands the most commitment and involvement on the part of the designer/photographer/artist. So, it is here that we have the ultimate problem and it is here we can witness some of the answers.

I hope this book will be the beginning of a more regular and detailed reporting of the development of this truly interesting "folk art". A positive response will perhaps encourage the editors of GRAPHIS to continue their interest in the art of Record Cover Design.

Bob Cato

Die Kunst auf dem «Zwölf-Zoll-Quadrat»

«Guten Morgen, Mr. Dylan, wie wollen Sie Ihren Rock 'n' Roll verpacken?»

Nach dem 2. Weltkrieg kam es zu einer graphischen Erneuerung, die sich unter anderem in den Bereichen Zeitschrift und Buch, Fernsehen, Architektur, Industrie- und Verpackungsdesign bemerkbar machte. Sie alle hatten an der schöpferischen Nutzung von Graphik, Design, Typographie und Photographie teil. Nur die Schallplattenindustrie war ein Nachzügler. Nicht weil es an interessierten, geschmackssicheren Schallplattenleuten gefehlt hätte, die die Gesellschaften zu guten Designern geführt hätten, sondern weil kein herausfordernder Anstoss aus der Industrie kam, vorgeprägte Vorstellungen von Verpackung und Design zu ändern.

Aber da kamen… die *Beatles* und der *Rock 'n' Roll.*

Und endlich war die Anregung da, die Quelle reiner Inspiration. Die Musik mit ihrem aussergewöhnlichen Drive und die wirkungsvolle Verpackung warteten nur auf das begeisterte, unersättliche jugendliche Publikum, das mit Freude und Hingabe reagierte.

Gleichzeitig rückte dadurch diejenige Musik wieder ins Rampenlicht, auf die sie zurückgriff und der sie so viel Leben verdankte… auf Jazz, Country & Western Music, den Blues, die Klassiker und sogar den Mann, der seine Nase als Instrument *spielte.*

Statt mit Suppendosen, Seidenstrümpfen, Super-de-Luxe-Autos, durstlöschendem Cola und dem nie versiegenden Lippenstift, die mit Glaubwürdigkeit zu versehen sind, hatte es der Designer der Schallplattenhülle mit einem «echten und menschlichen» Produkt zu tun, das ebensosehr, wenn nicht noch stärker, um sein Image, seine Botschaft und seine Verpackung besorgt war. Es war dies der Ausgangspunkt einer neuen Erkenntnis über den Dialog, der zwischen Designer und Musiker entstehen musste.

Eines der bewegendsten und vielleicht individuellsten und interessantesten Beispiele dieses Dialogs entwickelte sich aus der Kunst und der Musik, die während und gegen Ende der sechziger Jahre aus dem exotischen Klang des San Francisco «Sound» erwuchs. Plattenhüllen, Poster, Light Shows und Zeitschriften reflektierten gemeinsam einen Zusammenhalt und ein Identitätsgefühl, das als San-Francisco-Szene bekannt wurde. Für mich bleibt das die einzige «gebietsorientierte Folk Art», die wirklich die Synthese von Kunst und Musik in der von mir angesprochenen Erneuerung verkörperte.

Was den heutigen Stand der Kunst angeht, hatten wir alle Gelegenheit, die zunehmende

Verbesserung der Plattenalbenverpackung mitzuerleben: die neuen Papiersorten, die Neuerungen der Seitenaufteilung und natürlich die Wirkung des «Konzeptpakets», das mehr zu bieten hat als nur die Schallplatte und die graphische Gestaltung der Hülle.

Eine der interessantesten Bemühungen der Konzeptverpackung war eine von Goddard Lieberson, dem Präsidenten von Columbia Records, produzierte Serie. Anhand dieser fortschrittlichen Hüllen können wir die Synthese aus Literatur, Kunst, Musik, dem gesprochenen Wort und der Verpackung erfahren. Die Columbia Literaturserie (zwölf Autoren lesen ihre eigenen Werke), die Alben über die Union, Konföderation, die amerikanische Revolution (mit einem grossartigen Essay aus englischer Sicht von Robert Graves!), Kunst und Musik Mexikos, der Badman (ein klassisches Album über die Banditen des Wilden Westens), die irische Revolution und Ärzte und Medizin – all das sind Beispiele für scharfsinnigen, liebevollen und engagierten Musikjournalismus und Verpackung.

Die auf den folgenden Seiten wiedergegebenen Schallplattenhüllen sind nach verschiedenen Musikkategorien unterteilt. So ist z. B. die Geschichte von Graphik und Design von Jazz-Plattenhüllen nachgezeichnet. Der Jazz hat immer seine eigene Kraft und Magie gehabt. Deshalb hat hier der Designer/Photograph/Künstler die seltene Gelegenheit, sein Können mit der Magie des Jazz zu koppeln.

Bis zum Beginn der Rock-Explosion war der Entwurf von Alben für Unterhaltungsmusik einer der schwierigsten Bereiche. Erst dann verstanden die Geschäftsleute und die Schallplattenkünstler allmählich den «kommerziellen Wert» eines gut entworfenen Covers auf dem Markt. Als konsequentes graphisches Konzept das «neutrale» Denken ersetzte, bekamen Plattenalben eine gute Chance, besonders beachtet zu werden. In diesem Bereich, so viel ist sicher, leistet der Designer Schwerstarbeit, um seinem «Kunden» sinnvolle Graphik zu fertigen.

Der Entwurf eines Pop- oder Rock-Albums fordert seitens des Designers, des Photographen oder Künstlers zweifelsohne stärkstes Engagement. Deshalb stellt sich hier das grösste Problem, und wir können hier auch einige der Antworten sehen.

Ich hoffe, dass dieses Buch der Anfang einer regelmässigeren, detaillierteren Berichterstattung über die Entwicklung dieser wahrhaft interessanten «Folk Art» ist. Eine positive Reaktion ermutigt vielleicht die Herausgeber von GRAPHIS, sich auch weiterhin für die Kunst des Schallplattencovers zu interessieren.

Bob Cato

L'art du microsillon

«Bonjour, M. Dylan, on vous l'emballe comment, votre rock 'n' roll?»

Au lendemain de la Seconde Guerre mondiale, les arts appliqués ont connu une véritable renaissance, particulièrement sensible dans l'édition de livres et de magazines, la télévision, l'architecture, l'esthétique industrielle, le design d'emballage et la publicité. Une créativité nouvelle s'est exprimée dans l'art graphique, le design, la typographie et la photo. Or, l'industrie du disque a fait figure de lanterne rouge, non pas faute d'experts du disque apportant à leur tâche goût, intérêt et connaissances et capables de mobiliser de bons artistes pour la présentation des disques, mais en raison d'une tradition figée de l'emballage et du design qui a longtemps exclu toute velléité novatrice.

Alors survinrent les *Beatles*... le *rock 'n' roll.*

Qui déclenchèrent une véritable vague de fond de créativité, d'inspiration à laquelle la présentation des disques ne put se soustraire. Il fallut l'adapter au courant nouveau qui électrifiait une jeunesse ivre de musique, satisfaire par des pochettes créatrices l'ardeur insatiable de toute une génération de fans.

La nouvelle musique éclairait en même temps ses sources d'inspiration... le jazz, la musique populaire, la musique de l'Ouest, le blues, la musique classique et jusqu'au gars qui joue de la trompette avec son nez.

Le designer pouvait enfin mordre sur autre chose que les boîtes de soupe, les bas de soie, les super-voitures, le coca tuant la soif, la gamme interminable des rouges à lèvres. Il devait s'expliquer avec un produit «réel et humain» qui attachait autant, sinon plus d'importance à son image et à son message sur l'emballage. Il en résulta une prise de conscience nouvelle quant au dialogue à instaurer entre le designer et le créateur musical.

L'un des exemples les plus saisissants de ce dialogue art-musique, peut-être même le plus individualiste et le plus intéressant de tous, est la production son-image tonitruante et exotique à la fois du «sound» de San Francisco du milieu à la fin des années 60. Les albums, le design, les posters, les spectacles de lumière, les magazines, tous reflétaient une identité de conception étonnante et constituent à mes yeux le seul «art populaire régional» qui ait vraiment incarné la synthèse art-musique durant cette renaissance.

Où en est l'album de disques aujourd'hui? Nous l'avons vu devenir de plus en plus sophistiqué en faisant appel aux nouveaux matériaux et à la nouvelle notion de «concept» dans l'emballage, qui aboutit à une conception intégrée englobant non seulement le disque, donc la musique, et la photo ou le dessin de la pochette, mais tous les éléments en jeu, littérature, art, musique, parole et emballage. Un excellent exemple d'emballage conceptuel nous est fourni par les séries produites par le président de Columbia Records, Goddard Lieberson: la Série Littéraire de Columbia (douze auteurs contemporains lisant leurs œuvres), les albums de l'Union et de la Confédération, la Révolution Américaine (avec un essai merveilleux du point de vue anglais, par Robert Graves), L'Art et la Musique du Mexique, Le Hors-la-loi (The Badman), un album classique sur les premiers hors-la-loi de l'Ouest américain, La Rébellion Irlandaise, Les Docteurs et la Médecine, autant d'exemples d'un art avisé, attachant et passionné du journalisme musical et de l'emballage.

Les couvertures d'albums reproduites sur les pages qui suivent ont été réparties d'après les différentes catégories musicales. C'est ainsi qu'a été évoquée l'histoire graphique de l'art et du design des albums de jazz. Le jazz possède une puissance et magie propres que le designer/photographe/artiste est appelé à rejoindre par sa création.

Le secteur de la musique légère a toujours posé des problèmes ardus à l'artiste jusqu'à l'avènement du rock. C'est seulement lorsque les spécialistes de la vente et les musiciens eux-mêmes se sont mis à réaliser la «valeur commerciale» d'une couverture bien faite, en pleine révolution rock, et que l'on a accepté d'abandonner la prudente tactique du juste milieu en matière de design que l'album de musique légère, qui s'étiolait, a pris vie et vigueur. Je pense que c'est là le domaine qui en demande le plus à l'artiste s'il veut réaliser une présentation graphique ou photographique qui colle au désir de son «client».

Quant à l'album pop et rock, il exige que le designer/photographe/artiste s'engage à fond. C'est donc ici que nous trouvons des réponses au problème crucial de notre art.

J'espère que la présente publication fera fonction de *primum mobile* dans le domaine de l'information sur le design de pochettes et d'albums de disques et contribuera à son progrès.

Bob Cato

Index to Artists and Photographers
Verzeichnis der Künstler und Photographen
Index des artistes et photographes

15

Index to Designers
Verzeichnis der Gestalter
Index des maquettistes

Index to Art Directors
Verzeichnis der künstlerischen Leiter
Index des directeurs artistiques

Index to Publishers
Verzeichnis der Verleger
Index des éditeurs

GRAPHIS publications

GRAPHIS ANNUAL, The international annual of advertising and editorial graphics
PHOTOGRAPHIS, The international annual of advertising and editorial photography
GRAPHIS POSTERS, The international annual of poster art
ANNUAL REPORTS, Conception and design of annual reports
GRAPHIS/PACKAGING 2, An international survey of package design
FILM & TV GRAPHICS, An international survey of film and television graphics
THE SUN IN ART, Sun symbolism of past and present, in popular art, fine and applied art
THE ARTIST IN THE SERVICE OF SCIENCE, Scientific and semi-scientific art

GRAPHIS Publikationen

GRAPHIS ANNUAL, Das internationale Jahrbuch der Werbegraphik und der redaktionellen Graphik
PHOTOGRAPHIS, Das internationale Jahrbuch der Werbephotographie und der redaktionellen Photographie
GRAPHIS POSTERS, Das internationale Jahrbuch der Plakatkunst
ANNUAL REPORTS, Konzeption und Gestaltung von Jahresberichten
GRAPHIS/PACKUNGEN 2, Internationales Handbuch der Packungsgestaltung
FILM & TV GRAPHICS, Eine internationale Übersicht über Film- und Fernsehgraphik
DIE SONNE IN DER KUNST, Sonnensymbole aus Vergangenheit und Gegenwart
DER KÜNSTLER IM DIENST DER WISSENSCHAFT, Wissenschaftliche und populärwissenschaftliche Kunst

GRAPHIS publications

GRAPHIS ANNUAL, L'art publicitaire et rédactionnel graphique international
PHOTOGRAPHIS, Le répertoire international de la photographie publicitaire et rédactionnelle
GRAPHIS POSTERS, Le répertoire international de l'art de l'affiche
ANNUAL REPORTS, Conception et design de rapports annuels
GRAPHIS/EMBALLAGES 2, Répertoire international des formes de l'emballage
FILM & TV GRAPHICS, Répertoire international de l'art graphique au cinéma et à la télévision
LE SOLEIL DANS L'ART, Symboles du soleil du passé à nos jours, tirés du folklore et des beaux-arts
L'ARTISTE DU SERVICE DE LA SCIENE, L'illustration scientifique et scientifique vulgarisée

Colman Andrews

The advent of the long-playing record, c. 1949, did not immediately change the graphic scope of the designer of record packaging, but when the change did come it was dramatic and important.

Collections of 78-rpm records had been presented frequently as "albums", of course (and were, in a sense, more genuinely definable as such than are today's single-record lps), but with occasional exceptions these earlier albums never really encouraged the development of sophisticated packaging. For one thing, they were rectangularly shaped, but had a square picture area (usually approximately ten by ten inches), because the left-hand side of the album was covered with a one- or two-inch strip of monochromatic binding tape—an unfortunate visual handicap for any designer. The first long-playing record albums, on the other hand, were simply ten inches square; later, the widespread adoption of the 12-inch-square format made the design surface even more attractive. (The square format, incidentally, is considered by some photographers to have been influential in the rise in popularity of the single-lens, square-format, reflex camera—a tool obviously perfectly suited to record-jacket illustration.)

The simple, physical bulk of 78-rpm albums indicated a different display style in record stores, too. Walls of stores today are lined with rows of flat, attractive packages; 78-rpm albums took much more space, and were seldom displayed frontally. Cover art, then, was almost incidental, and remained so even into the beginnings of the lp era, when most record stores had sample copies of albums available for customer play. When this practice stopped, the cover of an album suddenly became its most important—perhaps its only—selling point.

A new medium appeared, in other words, challenging graphic creators to generate concepts of design and illustration that would relate intelligently to another highly-developed art form (music), and that might successfully stimulate visual interest among potential record-buyers.

There was really no precedent in commercial illustration or design. Packaging of most consumer products stresses brand-name identification and presupposes disposability. Book-jacket design, for the most part, is limited from a practical point of view to the arrangement of type on the book's side or spine. Perhaps the closest parallel to the unique design opportunities offered by the long-playing record jacket is in the design of magazine covers, for like record covers they must both contain and advertise what is inside.

Die Einführung der Langspielplatte um 1949 hat für den Designer nicht sofort die graphischen Möglichkeiten der Plattenverpackung verändert, aber als die Änderung kam, war sie dramatisch und wichtig.

Sammlungen von Platten mit 78 UpM waren oft als «Alben» präsentiert worden (und im Gegensatz zu den Ein-Platten-LPs von heute konnte man sie auch tatsächlich so bezeichnen), aber diese frühen Alben — mit gelegentlichen Ausnahmen wie Pin Koreys Cover für «Innovations by Boyd Raeburn» für die Marke Jewel — trugen nie besonders zur Entwicklung raffinierter Verpackungen bei. Zum einen waren sie rechteckig, hatten aber eine quadratische Bildfläche von gewöhnlich etwa 25×25 cm, weil das Album links mit einem drei bis fünf cm breiten einfarbigen Bindestreifen abgedeckt war, was für jeden Designer ein unglückliches visuelles Handicap darstellt. Die ersten Langspielplatten-Alben waren dagegen einfach zehn Zoll im Quadrat (25,5×25,5 cm). Später machte die weite Verbreitung des 12-Zoll-Quadrats (30,5× 30,5 cm) die Designfläche sogar noch attraktiver. (Das quadratische Format wird übrigens von einigen Photographen als wesentlicher Faktor für den rapiden Popularitätsgewinn der einäugigen, quadratförmige Bilder liefernden Spiegelreflexkamera angesehen, die für Plattenhüllenillustrationen sehr geeignet ist.)

Durch den Umfang der platzraubenden 78er Alben drängte sich eine bestimmte Einordnung auf — selten frontal —, während sich heute an den Wänden der Geschäfte flache, attraktive Packungen reihen. Eine illustrierte Frontseite war deshalb fast nebensächlich. Das blieb so bis in die Anfänge der LP-Ära hinein, als die meisten Plattengeschäfte noch Vorführexemplare der Alben hatten. Als dieser Brauch aufhörte, wurde die Albenhülle plötzlich zum wichtigsten — vielleicht einzigen — Verkaufsanreiz.

Ein neues Medium forderte den Graphiker heraus, Konzepte zu entwickeln, die in intelligenter Beziehung zu einer anderen hochentwickelten Kunstform (der Musik) stehen und Käuferinteresse wecken sollte.

Es gab dafür in Werbung und Design eigentlich keinen Präzedenzfall. Bei Konsumgütern wird meist der Markenname betont, nicht die Bestandteile des Produkts, und die Verpackung wird weggeworfen. Das Design von Schutzumschlägen für Bücher beschränkt sich aus praktischen Erwägungen auf die Anordnung der Schrift auf Vorderseite und Rücken. Am ehesten ist noch eine Parallele zum Design eines Zeitschriftentitelblattes zu sehen. Wie eine Plattenhülle muss es den Inhalt aufzeigen und für ihn werben.

Si l'avènement du microsillon vers 1949 n'a pas signifié d'emblée des opportunités créatrices nouvelles, il n'en a pas moins préparé un bouleversement qui, une fois intervenu, a été lourd de conséquences.

Les collections de disques 78 tours se présentaient la plupart du temps sous forme d'«albums» – le terme étant plus adéquat alors que pour les mono-disques lp d'aujourd'hui. Pourtant, à quelques exceptions près ces premiers albums n'ont jamais stimulé l'art de l'emballage dans le sens d'une sophistication du design. Il y avait à cela des raisons matérielles, ainsi le format rectangulaire opposé à la surface utile qui, elle, était carrée (environ 25×25 cm) pour laisser la place au mors de reliure, une bande monochrome de 2 à 5 cm de large sur la gauche. On imagine le handicap visuel que cela représentait pour le créateur de la pochette. Les premiers albums de microsillons, par contre, ont adopté d'emblée le format carré de 25×25 cm pour passer par la suite à celui, encore plus attrayant, de 30×30 cm. Notons en passant que certains photographes considèrent ce format carré comme un facteur essentiel de la popularité de l'appareil reflex de format carré, parfaitement adapté au travail de l'illustrateur de pochettes lp.

Le volume et le poids des albums 78 tours imposaient une présentation en magasin différente de ce qu'elle est aujourd'hui pour les emballages légers, de faible épaisseur, qui ont envahi les rayons et se prêtent aussi à la disposition face au client. On imagine aisément que l'empilage systématique des albums 78 tours n'incitait guère les designers à un gros effort d'imagination. Cet état de choses se perpétua jusque fort avant dans l'ère du microsillon, où le client continuait de passer un disque spécimen avant de faire son choix. Lorsque le jeune public se mit à acheter sur titre, ou sur simple impulsion, la pochette du disque se révéla vite être son majeur argument de vente, sinon le seul. Et il fallut la soigner en conséquence.

Un nouveau mode d'expression vit le jour, où des artistes de talent s'efforçaient de créer en parallèle à la musique des illustrations vraiment créatrices et accrochantes. L'art publicitaire traditionnel ne put leur être de grand secours, puisqu'il se contentait de souligner la marque de préférence au contenu du produit et visait l'élimination rapide de l'emballage. Quant au design des jaquettes de livres, il était surtout axé sur la typo du dos, et son support était également éphémère. Il n'y a que le design de couvertures de magazines que l'on puisse comparer à celui des pochettes, car elles sont à la fois contenant et élément promotionnel.

Pioneers
Pioniere
Pionniers

Pioneers / Pioniere
Pionniers

ARTIST/KÜNSTLER/ARTISTE:

1) 2) David Stone Martin
3) 4) Joseph Low
5) 6) Ben Shahn

PUBLISHER/VERLEGER/EDITEUR:

1) Mercury Record Prod., Chicago
2) 5) Disc Company of America
3) 4) The Haydn Society, Boston
6) Capitol Records, Hollywood

1) 2) Among the artists and designers of repute who left their mark on the record album cover after the Second World War was David Stone Martin. Born in Chicago in 1913, Martin set up as a freelance after the war, doing a wide variety of design work but also acting as art director—from 1945 onwards—for the Disc Company of America. Our two examples show how he lent his strong yet sensitive line to simply conceived yet highly effective covers for *Disc* and *Mercury* records. His album covers finally ran into the hundreds. That shown in fig. 1 won an award of distinctive merit at the 1951 show of the New York Art Directors Club. See also fig. 16.

3) 4) Joseph Low, born in Pennsylvania in 1911, is a typographer and graphic artist perhaps best known for the fact that he set up his own hand press, the Quattrocchi Press, in Morristown, N.J., at the outset of his career and used it as the instrument of most of his design work. Primarily a typographer and a printmaker using both woodcut and linocut, Low did a striking series of record covers in three-colour linocut for the Haydn Society, Boston. Two of them are shown here.

5) 6) Even an artist of the calibre of Ben Shahn did not hesitate to bring his talents to bear on the record cover. Born in Russia in 1898, Shahn was first and foremost a painter whose art was passionately involved in social and human issues. Fig. 5 is an early design for the Disc Company of America; in the classic record cover shown in fig. 6 the subject of death and transfiguration has suggested the motif of the phoenix.

1) 2) David Stone Martin zählt zweifellos zu denjenigen bekannten Künstlern und Designern, die nach dem 2. Weltkrieg die Gestaltung von Plattenhüllen nachhaltig beeinflussten. Martin, 1913 in Chicago geboren, arbeitete nach dem Krieg als freier Graphiker auf allen Gebieten der Gebrauchsgraphik und war von 1945 an Art Director der Disc Company of America. Die beiden Beispiele für *Disc* und *Mercury* zeigen, wie er durch strenge Linienführung, doch starke Sensibilität einfache, aber sehr effektvolle Hüllen entwarf. Die von ihm gestalteten Plattenhüllen gehen in die Hunderte. Die Hülle in Abb. 1 wurde 1951 an der Ausstellung des Art Directors Club von New York ausgezeichnet. Siehe auch Abb. 16.

3) 4) Joseph Low, 1911 in Pennsylvania geboren, ist Typograph und Graphiker. In weiten Kreisen ist er vielleicht dafür am besten bekannt, dass er seit Beginn seiner Karriere eine eigene Handpresse, die Quattrocchi Press, in Morristown, N.J., betrieb und sie für den Druck seiner Arbeiten brauchte. Als eigentlicher Typograph und Graveur, vor allem von Holz- und Linolschnitten, entwarf er eine eindrucksvolle Serie von Hüllen mit dreifarbigen Linolschnitten für die Haydn Society in Boston. Zwei Beispiele aus dieser Serie sind hier abgebildet.

5) 6) Sogar ein Künstler vom Format eines Ben Shahn setzte sein künstlerisches Talent auf dem Gebiet der Plattenhüllen ein. Shahn, 1898 in Russland geboren, war ein Maler, dessen Kunst sich vor allem mit sozialen und gesellschaftlichen Themen auseinandersetzte. Abb. 5 ist eine frühe Plattenhülle für die Disc Company of America; für die klassische Hülle in Abb. 6 wurde das Phönix-Motiv als Symbol für Tod und Transfiguration verwendet.

1) 2) David Stone Martin est du nombre des artistes et designers renommés qui ont fortement marqué la présentation des albums de disques au lendemain de la Seconde Guerre mondiale. Né à Chicago en 1913, designer indépendant après la guerre, Martin fut aussi directeur artistique de la Disc Company of America dès 1945. Nos deux exemples révèlent le trait vigoureux et pourtant sensible qu'il sut mettre au service de conceptions aussi simples qu'efficaces lors de la réalisation d'albums *Disc* et *Mercury*. Il a conçu des centaines d'albums de disques. Celui de la fig. 1 lui a valu un Award of Distinctive Merit à l'exposition de 1951 du New York Art Directors Club. Cf. aussi la fig. 16.

3) 4) Joseph Low, né en Pennsylvanie en 1911, est un typographe et artiste graphique connu pour avoir dès le début de sa carrière utilisé sa propre presse à bras, la Quattrocchi Press, à Morristown, N.J., d'où sont sortis la plupart de ses travaux. Au bénéfice d'une formation de typo et de graveur (bois et lino), il a réalisé entre autres une série impressionnante de pochettes de disques en linogravure trichrome pour la Haydn Society de Boston, dont deux figurent dans notre sélection.

5) 6) Même un artiste comme Ben Shahn n'a pas hésité à appliquer son talent à la création de pochettes de disques. Né en Russie en 1898, Shahn était avant tout un peintre passionnément engagé dans les affaires sociales et humaines. La fig. 5 représente une de ses premières créations pour la Disc Company of America; la pochette du disque classique de la fig. 6 fait appel au symbole du phénix pour traiter le thème de la mort.

1

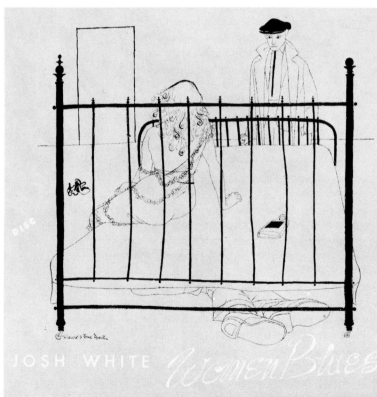

2

3

5

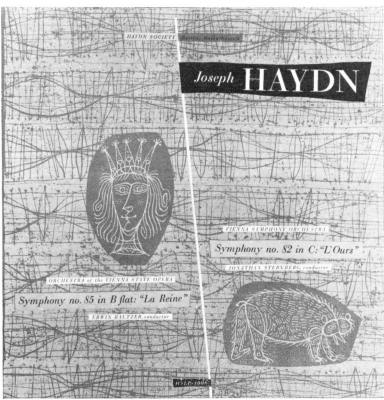

4

6

7)–9) Columbia Records made Alex Steinweiss their art director in 1939, and by 1947 he had done over 350 album covers for them. A New Yorker, born in 1917, Steinweiss proved to be an unusually able designer who broke with tradition and gave the music interpretations on his covers a powerful point-of-sale appeal. He was at home with all types of music, as these examples show. In all he designed over 2000 covers.

10)–12) Eric Nitsche, a Swiss born in 1908 who went to America in 1934, is perhaps best remembered for some brilliant industrial posters, but he also did highly attractive work in many other fields. Thus he designed over 300 record covers for *Decca* which are outstanding for their crisp clarity and for the immediacy of their impact.

13) Robert M. Jones was art director of Columbia Records and later of RCA Victor Records. In these capacities he helped to create a new and more exciting face for the album cover.

14) Record covers now attempted to suggest or interpret the music they contained, as in this example for an RCA Victor recording of Respighi.

15) George Maas did some pleasingly decorative covers for *Keynote* records.

16) A striking design for songs by the Byzantine Singers by David Stone Martin (see figs. 1 and 2).

7)–9) Alex Steinweiss, 1917 in New York geboren, wurde 1939 Art Director von Columbia Records. Es zeigte sich, dass Steinweiss ein ausserordentlich befähigter Designer war, der mit der Tradition brach und seinen musikalischen Interpretationen als Umschlagillustration einen starken absatzfördernden Anstrich gab. Wie diese Beispiele zeigen, war er in jeder Musikart zu Hause. Er entwarf über 2000 Plattenhüllen für verschiedene Firmen.

10)–12) Eric Nitsche wurde 1908 in der Schweiz geboren und wanderte 1934 nach Amerika aus. Am besten in Erinnerung sind vielleicht seine brillianten industriellen Plakate, obwohl er auf allen Gebieten der Gebrauchsgraphik Hervorragendes leistete. Für *Decca* entwarf er über 300 Hüllen, die durch ihre Klarheit und Unmittelbarkeit beeindrucken.

13) Robert M. Jones war Art Director von Columbia Records und später von RCA Victor. In dieser Eigenschaft war er bemüht, der Schallplattenhülle durch augenfällige Gestaltung ein neues Gesicht zu geben.

14) Wie dieses Beispiel von RCA Victor für eine Aufnahme von Respighi zeigt, wurde versucht, das musikalische Werk graphisch zu interpretieren.

15) George Maas entwarf einige sehr dekorative Plattenhüllen für *Keynote* Records.

16) Eine effektvolle Umschlagillustration von David Stone Martin für Songs der Byzantine Singers (s. Abb. 1 und 2).

7)–9) Columbia Records fit d'Alex Steinweiss son directeur artistique en 1939. Né à New York en 1917, Steinweiss s'affirma comme designer de grand talent et novateur résolu. Ses interprétations musicales sur des pochettes de disques s'avérèrent extrêmement efficaces sur le lieu de vente. Comme le montrent nos exemples, il connaissait la musique sur le bout de ses doigts. On lui doit plus de 2000 pochettes.

10)–12) Eric Nitsche, d'origine suisse, né en 1908, émigra aux USA en 1934 et s'y fit connaître par de brillantes affiches industrielles. Il fut actif dans bien d'autres domaines et réalisa plus de 300 pochettes pour *Decca* dans un style net, concis et direct.

13) Robert M. Jones fut directeur artistique de Columbia Records, par la suite de RCA Victor Records. Grâces à son influence et ses propres réalisations, il contribua à rénover la présentation des albums de disques dans le sens d'une plus grande stimulation visuelle.

14) Les sujets des pochettes cherchèrent désormais à suggérer ou à interpréter la musique du disque; cet enregistrement de Respighi sur disque RCA Victor est un bon exemple pour illustrer cette tendance.

15) George Maas fit quelques belles pochettes décoratives pour les disques *Keynote*.

16) Un design percutant pour les chansons des Byzantine Singers, par David Stone Martin (cf. les fig. 1 et 2).

7

8

10

11

13

14

9

12

15

ARTIST/KÜNSTLER/ARTISTE:

7)–9) Alex Steinweiss
10)–12) Erik Nitsche
13) Robert M. Jones
14) Stahlhut
15) George Maas
16) David Stone Martin

PUBLISHER/VERLEGER/EDITEUR:

7)–9) 13) Columbia Records, New York
10)–12) Decca Records, New York
14) RCA/Victor, New York
15) Keynote Records
16) Disc Company of America

16

Colman Andrews

Just as the development of the long-playing record encouraged the development of a new graphic medium with its own unique set of problems and challenges, so did the improvement of these records technologically encourage a new sort of growth and experimentation in the record industry itself.

The fifties were in many ways (as pioneer record-company veterans will gladly confirm) the golden age of the record business. Multi-million-dollar artist contracts, cut-throat sales and promotion techniques, and huge conglomerated holding companies had not yet been visited upon the industry. Individuals, whether producers or company presidents, could still—for better or for worse—impose their own artistic preferences, their own stylistic parameters, on the artists in their employ—both the musical and graphic artists. In many cases, this was fortunate (the happy proclivity of Norman Granz, among others, for the strong but gracefully evocative drawings of David Stone Martin, the Weiss brothers' penchant for the works of Arnold Roth, etc.). But it is impossible to neglect the fact that all too many record jackets of the fifties (now thankfully forgotten) were decorated with illustration that was simply unprofessional, in quite a literal sense: more than one record executive's wife supplied a craft-class collage, more than one art-student son moonlighted as a design director.

Of the many good album jackets that were produced during the fifties, it is interesting to note two things: First, photography was used comparatively rarely, and, when it was used, it was rather seldom colour photography. (There was, to go along with this lack, a very highly developed sense of non-photographic texture in album jackets, it should be noted. Most record covers of the fifties were reasonably complex in terms of the graphic elements they involved, and representations of paper, cloth and wood were commonly included.) Second, the musical form which was to truly revolutionize the record business in all of its aspects (including, most certainly, its graphic ones), and which can be said to have been born in the middle of the fifties, made virtually no impact at all on the state of record-album art in the early years of its life. This form, of course, was rock-and-roll, and it did not influence album-jacket design simply because there were very, very few rock-and-roll albums produced until the early sixties, and those which did appear were merely collections of single records, not works conceived of and executed as long-playing albums.

So wie sich aus der Einführung der Langspielplatte ein neues graphisches Medium mit eigenen Problemen und Anforderungen entwickelt hat, so hat die Verbesserung dieser Schallplatten technologisch eine neue Art von Wachstum und Experimentieren in der Plattenindustrie selbst bewirkt.

Die fünfziger Jahre waren (wie die Veteranen unter den Plattenfirmen gerne bestätigen werden) in vielerlei Hinsicht das Goldene Zeitalter des Plattengeschäfts. Künstlerverträge über viele Millionen Dollar, halsabschneiderische Verkaufs- und Werbepraktiken und riesige Konglomerate hatten die Industrie noch nicht heimgesucht. Individuen, ob Produzenten oder Firmeninhaber, konnten noch auf Gedeih und Verderb ihre künstlerischen Präferenzen und ihre stilistischen Parameter den von ihnen angestellten Künstlern aufzwingen – und zwar den Musikern wie den Graphikern. In vielen Fällen gereichte das zum Vorteil (man denke an die Begeisterung von Norman Granz für die starken aber anmutig evokativen Zeichnungen von David Stone Martin oder etwa die Vorliebe der Gebrüder Weiss für die Werke von Arnold Roth usw.). Aber es ist unmöglich zu übersehen, dass allzu viele Illustrationen auf Plattenhüllen der fünfziger Jahre (die zum Glück in Vergessenheit geraten sind) im wahrsten Sinne des Wortes unprofessionell waren: Mehr als eine Produzentenehefrau lieferte eine Kunstunterricht-Collage, mehr als ein Kunst studierender Sohn dilettierte nebenher als Designdirektor.

Bei den vielen guten Plattenhüllen, die in den Fünfzigern produziert wurden, fallen zwei Dinge besonders auf: Erstens wurden relativ selten Photos und noch seltener Farbphotos verwendet. (Es sei angemerkt, dass für die meisten Plattenhüllen der fünfziger Jahre nicht-photographische Elemente – Papier, Holz, Stoff usw. – sehr raffiniert nachgeahmt wurden.) Zweitens hatte die Musikform, die das Schallplattengeschäft in jeder Hinsicht (selbstverständlich auch in graphischer) verändern sollte und deren Geburtsstunde man in der Mitte der fünfziger Jahre ansetzen kann, während ihrer Anfangsjahre praktisch keinerlei Einfluss auf die künstlerische Gestaltung von Plattenalben. Diese Musikform war der Rock-and-Roll, der das Plattenhüllendesign nur deshalb nicht beeinflusste, weil bis zum Beginn der sechziger Jahre nur wenige Rock-and-Roll-Langspielplatten produziert wurden, und die, die erschienen, waren einfach Zusammenstellungen von Singleplatten, keine als Langspielplatten konzipierte und aufgenommenen Werke.

A l'aube des années 50, l'introduction du micro-sillon a largement contribué au développement d'un nouveau mode d'expression graphique avec son cortège de problèmes et de prouesses, en même temps qu'elle bouleversait l'industrie du disque tout entière, l'orientant résolument dans la voie de l'expérimentation et de l'innovation constantes.

Les années 50 représentent à plus d'un égard l'Age d'or de l'industrie du disque. Tous les vétérans de la fabrication ou de l'édition en conviendront. Les contrats d'artistes portant sur des millions de dollars, la guerre des nerfs impitoyable dans le marketing et la vente, les conglomérats géants, toutes ces plaies d'Egypte ne s'étaient pas encore abattues sur le monde du disque. Les individus, producteurs ou P.D.G. de sociétés, pouvaient encore s'offrir le luxe impénitent d'imposer leurs vues et préférences artistiques pour le meilleur ou pour le pire, d'exiger le respect de leurs propres conceptions stylistiques de la part des artistes qu'ils employaient à titre de musiciens ou de designers. Dans la plupart des cas, ces choix imposés s'avéraient fort heureux — que l'on songe à la faveur dont jouissaient auprès de Norman Granz et de bien d'autres les dessins vigoureux et pourtant pleins de grâce et de pouvoir évocateur d'un David Stone Martin, ou à la prédilection des frères Weiss pour les créations d'Arnold Roth, etc. Pourtant, ne nous abusons pas: bien trop nombreuses ont été durant cette décennie les pochettes aujourd'hui oubliées (et pour cause) qui s'ornaient d'illustrations d'amateurs, le népotisme aidant. C'est ainsi que plus d'une épouse de directeur composait de savants collages sortis tout droit de ses cahiers de collège, et plus d'un jeune Léonard éblouissait son père en jouant au directeur artistique après les cours.

Dans le lot important de bonnes pochettes produit durant les années 50, on note l'emploi restreint de la photo, surtout de la photo couleur, de pair avec une interprétation poussée de la texture non photographique de la surface. Les moyens graphiques les plus variés entraient dans la composition illustrative: papier, tissu, bois, etc. Il est également intéressant d'observer que la musique appelée à révolutionner l'industrie du disque (jusques et y compris la présentation des pochettes), le rock, qui fit son apparition avec les années 50, n'eut pratiquement aucune incidence sur l'habillage des pochettes jusqu'à la fin de la décennie. La raison doit en être cherchée dans le nombre très restreint de productions de longue durée à cette époque. Il fallut attendre le début des années 60 pour voir le rock imposer sa griffe à l'art de la pochette de disque.

The Nineteen-Fifties
Die Fünfziger Jahre
Les Années cinquante

By the nineteen-fifties record collectors were legion and the record industry was going from strength to strength. The period was thus one of consolidation for the record cover as an art form. Recognition of this fact in Europe found striking expression in the sleeves of the *Club Français du Disque*, a record club attached to an even larger book club. The works recorded by this club were selected by a jury and the recordings made with exceptional care on specially manufactured waxes under the direction of the artistic management. This approach offered a unique opportunity to the cover designers—prominent among whom was Pierre M. Comte—to match the uniformly high quality of the recordings in the conception and treatment of their covers. A basic design was chosen with a square in the top left-hand corner bearing the initial of the composer, with a portrait diagonally opposite to it. The title of the work ran across the top of the cover towards the right. The design itself was always photographic and usually abstract. An identifying colour was used for the composers of each century. Many of the cover designs were inspired by the abstract expressionist movement in art. They sought to give an aesthetic impression of the spirit of the work concerned and, apart from paving the way to an appreciation of the music for some, even helped others to understand—this time via the music—an art movement to which they had previously had no access. Examples of other European record covers from the same period are shown at the far right.

In den 50er Jahren stieg die Zahl der Plattensammler rapid an und die Schallplattenfirmen buchten Erfolg nach Erfolg auf ihr Konto. Dies war also auch das Jahrzehnt, in welchem sich die Plattenhülle als Kunstform etablierte. Ein schlagender Beweis dafür sind die Plattenumschläge des *Club Français du Disque*, ein Plattenclub, der zu einem noch grösseren Buchclub gehörte. Die von diesem Grammoclub herausgegebenen Werke wurden von einer Jury begutachtet und unter der künstlerischen Leitung des Clubs mit äusserster Sorgfalt auf speziell hergestellten Kunststoff geprägt. Diese Einstellung dem musikalischen Kunstwerk gegenüber bot auch dem Umschlaggestalter – einer der prominentesten war Pierre M. Comte – einzigartige Möglichkeiten, da seine Umschlagkonzeption die durchwegs hohe Qualität der Platten widerspiegeln sollte. Eine einheitliche Grundkonzeption wurde gewählt: ein Quadrat in der linken obern Ecke mit der Initiale des Komponisten und dessen Portrait diagonal gegenüber; ein Band am obern Rand für den Plattentitel; bestimmte Farben zur Kennzeichnung der Komponisten des selben Jahrhunderts. Häufig wurden abstrakte Photographien als Umschlagillustration verwendet, was auf eine Beeinflussung durch die abstrakte expressionistische Bewegung in der Kunst schliessen lässt. Es wurde versucht, den Geist der Musik auf ästhetische Weise zu interpretieren, womit einigen der Weg zur Musik geöffnet, andern durch die Musik eine Kunstrichtung nähergebracht wurde, die ihnen bis anhin unzugänglich war. – Rechts weitere europäische Plattenhüllen aus dieser Zeit.

Au début des années 1950, les collectionneurs de disques étaient devenus légion, et l'industrie du disque était plus florissante que jamais. C'est ainsi que cette décennie vit s'affirmer définitivement la pochette de disque comme forme d'art. En Europe, cette tendance se vérifia de façon remarquable dans la production de pochettes du *Club Français du Disque*, une guilde du disque fondée par une importante guilde du livre. Les œuvres distribuées par le Club étaient sélectionnées par un jury, puis gravées avec soin dans une cire de fabrication spéciale sous le contrôle de la direction artistique du Club. Il en résulta une qualité exceptionnelle que les artistes travaillant pour le Club – au premier plan, Pierre M. Comte – eurent à cœur d'égaler dans la conception et l'exécution de leurs pochettes. Une maquette de base fut mise au point, qui présentait dans le coin gauche supérieur un carré où était inscrite l'initiale du compositeur, dont le portrait faisait pendant au carré suivant la diagonale. Le titre de l'œuvre figurait au haut de la pochette. Chaque siècle musical était caractérisé par une couleur-code. Un grand nombre des compositions utilisées pour la pochette s'inspirèrent de l'expressionnisme abstrait et cherchèrent à traduire l'esprit de l'œuvre en question par des moyens esthétiques. Ces créations facilitèrent l'approche de la musique à certains et en familiarisèrent d'autres avec un grand courant de l'art moderne. – On trouvera à l'extrême droite de cette double page d'autres exemples de la production européenne hors du Club durant la même période.

Maurice Ohana
Llanto por Ignacio Sanchez Mejias
Sarabande pour clavecin et orchestre

17

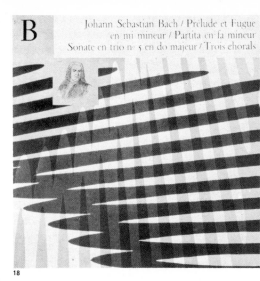

Johann Sebastian Bach / Prélude et Fugue en mi mineur / Partita en fa mineur
Sonate en trio n° 5 en do majeur / Trois chorals

18

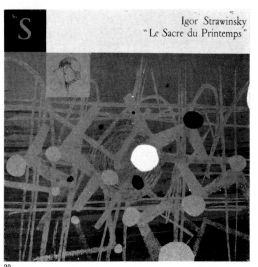

Igor Strawinsky
"Le Sacre du Printemps"

20

Serge Prokofieff
Sonate pour piano n° 2, opus 14 ré mineur Toccata, opus 11
Visions fugitives, opus 22

21

Trailing the Blues

23

Serge Prokofieff
Concerto pour violoncelle
en mi mineur Opus 58

24

Les succès de Django Reinhardt
par Claude Bolling
et son "Grand Club Orchestra"

19

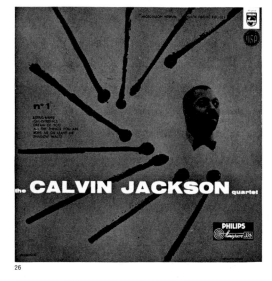

n° 1

the CALVIN JACKSON quartet

PHILIPS

26

The Nineteen-Fifties
Die Fünfziger Jahre
Les Années cinquante

Igor Strawinsky
Petrouchka

22

17)–25) Examples of record covers for the *Club Français du Disque* with a uniform basic layout and the use of photographic abstractions.
26) Cover for a recording by a popular quartet.
27) Cover for a recording by a swing band.
28) Cover for music by a German composer, well-known for his music for Brecht. Black, olive and green.

17)–25) Beispiele aus der Serie einheitlich gestalteter Schallplattenhüllen des *Club Français du Disque* mit abstrakten Photographien als Umschlagillustrationen.
26) Hülle für Aufnahmen eines Quartetts.
27) Für eine Platte der Dutch Swing College Band.
28) Hülle für Lieder des bekannten Deutschen Komponisten Kurt Weill, der unter anderem auch die Songs für Brechts Stücke schrieb. Schwarz, oliv und grün.

17)–25) Exemples de pochettes réalisées pour le *Club Français du Disque* d'après une maquette prédéterminée, en faisant usage d'abstractions photographiques.
26) Pochette pour l'enregistrement d'un quartette populaire.
27) Pochette pour le disque d'un orchestre de swing.
28) Pochette pour la musique d'un compositeur allemand, bien connu par ses chansons pour Brecht. Noir, olive, vert.

ARTIST/KÜNSTLER/ARTISTE:

17) 24) Jacques Darche
18) 23) 25) Pierre M. Comte
19)–22) Jacques Daniel
26) M. Laville
27) Kees van Roemburg
28) Hannes Jaehn

PUBLISHER/VERLEGER/EDITEUR:

17)–25) Club Français du Disque, Paris
26) Phonogram, Paris
27) Phonogram, Baarn
28) CBS/Elektrola Schallplatten Gesellschaft, Köln

Dutch swing college band

Shortwave shuffle
Lulu's back in town
Working man blues
There 'll be some changes made

Recorded at the Kurhaus Scheveningen
September 1955

PHILIPS

27

ERINNERUNGEN AN
KURT WEILL

Columbia

28

N neuf Negro Spirituals
Gospel Songs

25

29) 30) Covers for a recording from a Rachmaninoff opera and for a Bach concerto in a "masterworks" series. Fig. 29 in full colour, fig. 30 in purple and black.
31) Cover for music by Chopin from a series for the Haydn Society of Boston.
32) Cover for a jazz recording.
33) A further cover from the same series as fig. 31, this time for a comic opera by Paisiello.
34) Cover for a jazz record.
35) One of the series of record covers designed by Joseph Low for the Haydn Society (see figs. 3/4).
36) One of five covers without text for songs by George Gershwin, painted by the French artist Bernard Buffet.
37) Cover for an organ recital by the famous founder of the hospital at Lambarene.
38) Cover for a Strauss festival recording.

29) 30) Beispiele aus der Plattenserie «Meisterwerke», hier für eine Oper von Rachmaninow und ein Konzert von Bach. Abb. 29: mehrfarbig; Abb. 30: lila und schwarz.
31) Plattenhülle für verschiedene Klavierstücke von Chopin aus einer Serie der Haydn Society in Boston.
32) Hülle für eine Jazz-Platte.
33) Ein weiteres Beispiel aus der gleichen Serie wie Abb. 31, hier für eine komische Oper von Paisiello.
34) Umschlag für eine Jazz-Platte mit Aufnahmen der bekanntesten Vertreter des Chicago Style.
35) Eine von Joseph Low entworfene Hülle aus der Serie für die Haydn Society (s. auch Abb. 3/4).
36) Eine von fünf Schallplattenhüllen ohne Text für Lieder von George Gershwin, gemalt vom französischen Künstler Bernard Buffet.
37) Hülle für ein Bach-Orgelkonzert, gespielt von Albert Schweitzer, dem Begründer des Spitals in Lambarene.
38) Plattenhülle für Aufnahmen von einem Strauss-Festival.

29) 30) Pochettes pour l'enregistrement d'un opéra de Rachmaninov et d'un concerto de Bach dans une série de «chefs-d'œuvre». 29) Polychromie, 30) pourpre, noir.
31) Pochette pour de la musique de Chopin. Série réalisée pour la Haydn Society de Boston.
32) Pochette pour un disque de jazz.
33) Une autre pochette de la série de la fig. 31, cette fois-ci pour un opéra comique de Paisiello.
34) Pochette d'un disque de jazz.
35) Pochette extraite de la série conçue par Joseph Low pour la Haydn Society (cf. les fig. 3/4).
36) L'une des cinq pochettes sans texte peintes par Bernard Buffet pour des chansons de George Gershwin.
37) Pochette pour un récital d'orgue par le célèbre fondateur de l'hôpital de Lambaréné, le Dr Albert Schweitzer.
38) Pochette pour un festival Strauss.

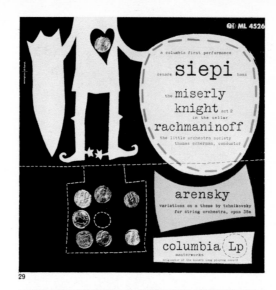

29

30

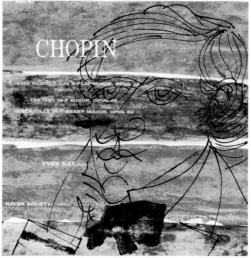

31

32

33

34

ARTIST/KÜNSTLER/ARTISTE:

29) Rudolf de Harak
30) Roy Kuhlmann
31) 33) Jerome Snyder
32) David Stone Martin
34) 37) Ben Shahn
35) Joseph Low
36) Bernard Buffet
38) Bill Bunce

ART DIRECTOR/DIRECTEUR ARTISTIQUE:

34) 37) S. Neil Fujita
36) Sheldon Marks

PUBLISHER/VERLEGER/EDITEUR:

29) 30) 34) 37) Columbia Records, New York
31) 33) 35) The Haydn Society, Boston
32) Mercury Record Prod., New York
36) Verve Records, New York
38) RCA/Victor, New York

40

39

ARTIST/KÜNSTLER/ARTISTE:

39) 40) 44) 45) Antonio Frasconi
41) Saul Bass
42) Art Goodman
43) Henry Markowitz
46) S. Neil Fujita
47) 48) Reid Miles

ART DIRECTOR/DIRECTEUR ARTISTIQUE:

41)–43) Saul Bass
47) 48) Francis Wolf

PUBLISHER/VERLEGER/EDITEUR:

39) Folkways Records, New York
40) 44) 45) Caedmon Records, New York
41) Decca Records, New York
42) 43) Saul Bass & Assoc., Los Angeles
46) Epic/Columbia Records, New York
47) 48) Blue Note/United Artists Records,
Los Angeles

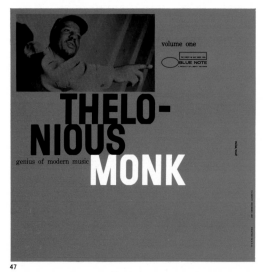

47

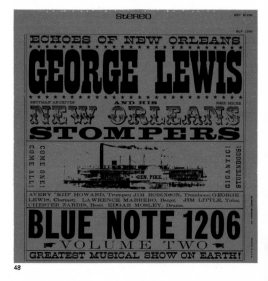

48

41

42

43

44

45

46

39) Cover for a recording of folk songs inspired by the famous trial of Sacco and Vanzetti. Red and black on white background.
40) Record cover from a series of readings of literary texts. See also figs. 44 and 45.
41) Cover for a recording of music from the sound track of a Preminger film.
42) Cover for a recording of film music. Black and white on deep orange ground.
43) Cover for music from a film based on a novel by Françoise Sagan. Blue and black on pale olive.
44) 45) Two covers for records with readings of poetry and drama from the same series as shown in fig. 40.
46) Typographic cover design for a rhythm record.
47) Cover for a recording of music by the famous black pianist Thelonious Monk.
48) Cover creating a nostalgic period atmosphere for music by a New Orleans band.

39) Schallplattenhülle für Volkslieder, deren Texte auf dem berühmten Prozess gegen die Anarchisten Sacco und Vanzetti beruhen. Rot und schwarz auf weissem Hintergrund.
40) Hülle aus einer Serie von literarischen Platten, hier mit Texten aus Werken von Edgar Allen Poe (s. Abb. 44/45).
41) Plattenhülle für Aufnahmen aus Otto Premingers Film «Der Mann mit dem goldenen Arm».
42) Plattenhülle für Filmmusik. Schwarzweiss auf in Dunkelorange gehaltenem Hintergrund.
43) Umschlag für Aufnahmen aus der Verfilmung von Françoise Sagans Roman. Blau und schwarz auf Helloliv.
44) 45) Weitere Beispiele aus der gleichen literarischen Serie wie Abb. 40, hier für Gedichte und Lesungen aus Dramen.
46) Typographische Gestaltung für eine Rhythmusplatte.
47) Plattenhülle für Aufnahmen des bekannten schwarzen Jazz-Pianisten Thelonious Monk.
48) Hülle, die die Atmosphäre aus den Anfängen des Jazz heraufbeschwören soll. Für eine New Orleans Jazz-Band.

39) Pochette pour un enregistrement de chansons populaires inspirées du procès des anarchistes Sacco et Vanzetti. Rouge et noir sur blanc.
40) Pochette d'un disque figurant dans une série d'interprétations de textes littéraires. Cf. aussi les fig. 44 et 45.
41) Pochette pour un disque avec la musique originale d'un film de Preminger.
42) Pochette d'un disque de musique de film. Noir, blanc sur orange foncé.
43) Pochette pour un disque avec la musique d'un film d'après un roman de Françoise Sagan. Bleu, noir sur olive pâle.
44) 45) Deux pochettes de récitations poétiques et dramatiques. Série de la fig. 40.
46) Maquette typo pour une pochette de disque de «rhythm».
47) Pochette pour un enregistrement du célèbre pianiste noir Thelonious Monk.
48) Pochette évoquant le souvenir de la grande période de la Nouvelle-Orleans, pour un orchestre de cette ville.

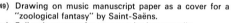

49

50

49) Drawing on music manuscript paper as a cover for a "zoological fantasy" by Saint-Saëns.
50) Full-colour cover for an opera by Leoncavallo.
51) Cover for a recording of "music for nervous people".
52) Full-colour cover for a sampler record of sounds for radio presentation.
53) Cover for a recording of trombone solos.
54) Cover for a record of jazz music by performers from the East Coast.
55) Cover for a "Latin concert". Design chiefly in yellow and orange shades.
56) Cover in collage for a Beethoven symphony.
57) Line drawing used on a cover for music by Schubert and Mozart from a "masterworks" series.
58) Cover for a recording of songs about New York played by a popular dance band.

49) Zeichnung auf einem Notenblatt als Umschlagillustration für Saint-Saëns «Karneval der Tiere».
50) Mehrfarbige Hülle für eine Oper von Leoncavallo.
51) Graphische Interpretation des Plattentitels «Musik für nervöse Leute».
52) Mehrfarbige Hülle für eine Schallplatte mit Geräuscheffekten für Radiosendungen.
53) Plattenhülle für Posaunen-Soli.
54) Umschlag für eine Platte mit Aufnahmen verschiedener Jazz-Musiker von der Ostküste Amerikas.
55) Plattenumschlag für ein «Lateinisches Konzert». Design vorwiegend in Gelb- und Orangetönen.
56) Collage als Umschlagillustration für Beethovens 3. Symphonie, Eroica.
57) Strichzeichnung für eine Hülle aus der Serie «Meisterwerke» mit Musik von Schubert und Mozart.
58) Hülle für Aufnahmen von Songs über New York, begleitet von einem bekannten Tanzorchester.

49) Dessin sur papier à musique en guise de pochette pour une «fantaisie zoologique» de Saint-Saëns.
50) Pochette polychrome pour un opéra de Leoncavallo.
51) Pochette d'un disque de «musique pour nerveux».
52) Pochette polychrome d'un disque spécimen de sons divers pour présentation radio.
53) Pochette pour un disque de solos de trombone.
54) Pochette d'un disque de jazz enregistré par des musiciens de la côte atlantique des Etats-Unis.
55) Pochette pour un «concert latin». Maquette aux tons jaunes et orange prédominants.
56) Collage pour pochette d'une symphonie de Beethoven.
57) Dessin au trait pour la pochette d'un disque de Schubert et de Mozart dans une série de «chefs-d'œuvre».
58) Pochette d'un disque de chansons newyorkaises jouées par un orchestre de danse populaire.

52

53

55

56

51

ARTIST/KÜNSTLER/ARTISTE:

49) Saul Steinberg
50) Herb Lubalin/Ben Rose
51) Robert Osborn
52) Tom Woodward
53) Andy Warhol
54) Reid Miles/Esmond Edwards
55) Ed Renfro
56) Ivan Chermayeff
57) Leo Lionni
58) Charles Goslin

ART DIRECTOR/DIRECTEUR ARTISTIQUE:

50) Robert M. Jones
51) Acy R. Lehman
52) Ray Hayner
53) Reid Miles
55) Ed Renfro
57) S. Neil Fujita
58) Hal Buksbaum

PUBLISHER/VERLEGER/EDITEUR:

49) Odéon Disques, Paris
50) 51) 56) RCA/Victor, New York
52) Capitol Records, Hollywood
53) 54) Prestige Records, New York
55) Fantasy Records
57) Columbia Records, New York
58) Decca Records, New York

54

57

58

Stefan Böhle

The graphic designers who devote themselves primarily to record covers ought really to have square eyes and large round disc-like ears.

The unchanging format actually does little to hinder creativity, and may even encourage it. The limits of the square are known and accepted in advance, so that the artist can concentrate on essentials. There have, for that matter, been plenty of attempts to pack the round record in something other than a square, but most of them have been a cause of annoyance to manufacturers and dealers, who have their standard production processes and storage systems.

Classical music, even in its progressive forms, demands an aesthetically serious approach, an optical interpretation that should reflect the quality standards applied by the manufacturer to the musical reproduction. The somewhat conservative presentation also results from the higher average age of the listening public and their attitude to music. The dividing line is fading somewhat, however, as progressive pop music and avant-garde classical experimentation draw nearer to each other.

The aim, in the classical cover as elsewhere, is an accurate visual image of the acoustic emotions involved, in conjunction with the verbal title of the work. A triple accord must be achieved as between music, words and picture, accuracy of information being the point of primordial importance.

Classical music, untrammelled by hit parades, requires long-term planning to allow for the time-tables of orchestras and for production processes. The time that thus becomes available for careful treatment is a great boon to the cover designer.

Problems may of course arise from other sources. An identification mark such as the large yellow label of the Deutsche Grammophon Gesellschaft, which must always form part of a cover, prevents the use of many preconceived motifs, since they would not allow of the insertion of this label over the top quarter of the surface. The value of this standard feature may be considerable as a trade mark, but it stands in the way of the differentiation of individual records.

The record cover has its attractions for almost every designer. The dissemination of progressive music calls for a visual communication of equal quality on the cover. The result is often enough a cover with an optical impact in no way inferior to the acoustic impact of the record itself.

Eigentlich müssten Graphik-Designer, die sich mit dem Entwurf von Plattenhüllen beschäftigen, quadratische Augen und grosse runde Ohren haben.

Das immer wieder gleiche Format stört aber nicht die Kreativität, es kann sie sogar fördern. Denn durch die eingehende Betätigung mit dem Viereck sind die Grenzen bekannt und man kann sich auf das Wesentliche konzentrieren. Ausserdem gibt es ausreichende Versuche, die runde Schallplatte nicht quadratisch zu verpacken. Oft zum Ärger der Hersteller – bei einem eingefahrenen Produktionsablauf, und der Händler – bei genormten Lagersystemen.

Die Gruppe Klassische Musik erfordert auch bei den in ihr auftretenden progressiven Richtungen eine seriöse und ästhetische optische Interpretation des Inhalts, die an den vom Hersteller an die musikalische Reproduktion gelegten Massstab der höchsten Qualitätsstufe gebunden ist. Die insgesamt etwas konservative Aufmachung ergibt sich aus der im Durchschnitt etwas älteren Zielgruppe und ihrer Einstellung zur Musik, obwohl die musikalische Nähe von progressiver Popmusik und avantgardistischen Experimenten klassischer Natur diese Grenzen langsam verschwinden lässt.

Auch beim klassischen Quadrat geht es um eine möglichst nahe optische Darstellung der akustischen Emotionen in Verbindung mit dem verbalen Titel des Werkes. Es ist ein Dreiklang zu erzeugen aus Musik, Wort und Bild, wobei die Genauigkeit der Information an erster Stelle steht.

Die klassische Musik erfordert durch Einspieltermine und Produktionsprozesse eine lange Planungszeit. Dadurch ergibt sich auch eine nicht durch Termine gehetzte, ausgefeiltere Ausarbeitung, die der Verpackungsgestaltung sehr zugute kommt.

Probleme können sich natürlich auch ganz anders entwickeln. Eine Marke, wie die grosse gelbe Kartusche der Deutschen Grammophon Gesellschaft, die in den zu erstellenden Entwurf eingeplant werden muss, verhindert oft die Verwendung von vorproduzierten Motiven, die den Einbau dieser das ganze obere Bildviertel verdeckenden Fläche nicht ermöglichen. So entsteht eine nicht zu unterschätzende Ähnlichkeit in der Optik, als Marke gewünscht, zur Differenzierung der Einzelprodukte aber zu gleichwertig.

Die Gestaltung von Plattenhüllen lockt natürlich alle Designer an. Wie in keiner anderen Branche erfordert die Veröffentlichung progressiver Musik eine qualitativ ebenbürtige visuelle Kommunikation auf dem Cover. So kommt es immer wieder zu optisch sehr reizvollen Ergebnissen, die dem Inhalt an Qualität in nichts nachstehen.

Les artistes graphiques qui «font» surtout de la pochette de disque devraient finir par ressembler à des monstres martiens aux grands yeux rectangulaires et aux énormes oreilles circulaires, tant le rectangle de la pochette et la courbure du disque doivent hanter leurs nuits. Pourtant, ils s'accomodent fort bien de cette limitation de forme, à laquelle s'ajoute celle du format, et en tirent même profit. Les données matérielles étant acquises une fois pour toutes, ils peuvent d'autant plus facilement se concentrer sur l'essentiel, la créativité. Toutes les tentatives pour sortir du cadre courant de la pochette sont restées vaines, tant l'opposition des fabricants et disquaires était vive, dont les processus de fabrication et les systèmes de stockage imposent des exigences strictes.

La musique classique, même progressiste, réclame une approche esthétique sérieuse, la visualisation de l'effort de qualité du fabricant, et le respect d'une catégorie d'acheteurs sensiblement plus âgée et habituée au commerce de la musique. Admettons toutefois que l'expérimentation d'avant-garde rapproche insensiblement la musique classique du pop le plus avancé.

La pochette du disque classique doit, comme toute autre pochette, fournir un support visuel adéquat aux émotions acoustiques en cause et ne pas négliger le titre de l'œuvre. Le triple accord de la musique, des mots et de l'image doit surtout servir la précision de l'information.

La prise de son en musique classique se fait selon un planning à long terme en fonction des disponibilités des orchestres et des exigences de la production. On imagine tout l'avantage que peut retirer de ce délai important l'artiste soucieux d'élaborer une pochette de classe.

Les problèmes surgissent à propos d'autres exigences. C'est ainsi que la marque jaune grand format de la Deutsche Grammophon Gesellschaft, qui ne doit manquer sur aucune des couvertures de cette société, écarte nombre de maquettes de pochettes utilisant autrement le quart supérieur de la surface. Ce n'est pas le seul exemple où un repère d'identité bienvenu du point de vue commercial constitue un obstacle à l'individualisation des pochettes.

La pochette a jusqu'ici toujours attiré les designers. La large diffusion des recherches musicales modernes exige une communication visuelle de qualité similaire par le biais de la pochette dont l'impact optique soutient parfaitement la comparaison avec l'impact acoustique du disque qu'elle habille et ouvre voie à la musique sur le plan pictural.

Classical Music
Klassische Musik
Musique classique

Classical Music / Klassische Musik / Musique classique

59)

59) Record cover, chiefly in green and brown shades, for harpsichord works by Handel. The artwork relates to a piece entitled *The Nightingale*.
60) Colourful graphic interpretation of music for two harpsichords.
61) Cover for a recording of two symphonies by Haydn.
62) 62a) Complete cover and detail for Tchaikovsky's *Swan Lake*. Blue ground.
63) Cover for Rossini's *William Tell* overture and other pieces. Green apple.
64) Combination of graphic and photographic elements on the cover of a Mahler symphony conducted by Bruno Walter.

59) Plattenhülle – vorwiegend in Senfgelb und Braun – für Cembalo-Werke von Händel. Die Umschlagillustration bezieht sich auf eines der Stücke mit dem Titel *Die Nachtigall*.
60) Graphische Interpretation als Hülle einer Platte mit Aufnahmen für zwei Cembalos. Farbig.
61) Schallplattenhülle für zwei Symphonien von Haydn.
62) 62a) Vollständige Hülle und Aufnahme für Tschaikowskys *Schwanensee*-Ballett. Blauer Grund.
63) Tells Apfelschuss als typische Umschlagillustration zum Titelstück der Platte, Rossinis *Tell*-Ouvertüre. Grüner Apfel.
64) Kombination von graphischen und photographischen Elementen für eine Wiedergabe von Gustav Mahlers 9. Symphonie, dirigiert von Bruno Walter.

59) Pochette aux tons verts et bruns prédominants pour un disque d'études de Haendel pour clavecin. Le sujet est emprunté au morceau intitulé *Le Rossignol*.
60) Interprétation graphique pittoresque de musique pour deux clavecins.
61) Pochette pour un enregistrement de deux symphonies de Haydn.
62) 62a) Pochette complète et détail. *Le Lac des Cygnes*, de Tchaïkovski. Fond bleu.
63) Pochette pour l'ouverture de *Guillaume Tell* et d'autres morceaux de Rossini. Pomme verte.
64) Combinaison d'éléments graphiques et photographiques sur la pochette d'une symphonie de Mahler dirigée par Bruno Walter.

62a

62

ARTIST/KÜNSTLER/ARTISTE:

59) Etienne Delessert
60) Milton Glaser
61) Henrietta Condak
62) 62a) Don Hunstein (Photo)
63) Roy Carruthers
64) James Cook

DESIGNER/GESTALTER/MAQUETTISTE:

59) Tony Lane
61) Henrietta Condak
62) 62a) 63) John Berg
64) James Cook

ART DIRECTOR/DIRECTEUR ARTISTIQUE:

59) John Berg/Tony Lane
60)–63) John Berg
64) John Berg/Richard Mantel

PUBLISHER/VERLEGER/EDITEUR:

59)–64) Columbia Records, New York/Hollywood

60

61

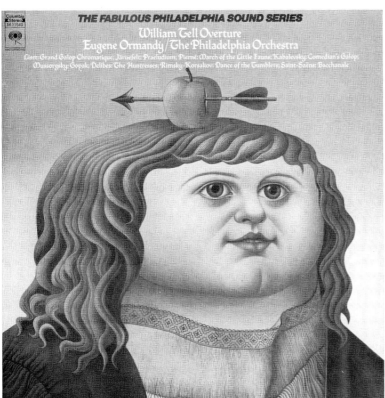

63

64

65

66

67

65) Record cover for interpretations of works by Bach on the Hammond organ. Three-dimensional head in sombre shades, brightly coloured neckerchief.
66) From a series of Bach records. The powdered ''wig'' is composed of silver-grey cherubs.
67) A Russian Orthodox church sets the mood on this cover for Tchaikovsky's Fifth Symphony. Colour photograph.
68) 69) Typographic treatment of record covers for renderings by the Symphony Orchestra of the Austrian radio. Dark blue lettering on silver-grey, red emblem.
70) Large decorative illustrations of solo instruments are used on the covers of this *Universo* series.
71) Black-and-white cover for organ concerts by Bach, incorporating a stylized organ.
72) 73) Complete cover and detail of the assemblage for piano compositions by Debussy.

65) Plattenhülle für Interpretationen von Bach-Werken auf der Hammondorgel. Dunkle Töne, Halsbinde als Farbakzent in Gelb, Rosa, Lila und Blau.
66) Aus einer Serie von Bach-Platten. Das ausdrucksvolle Portrait Bachs wird nicht von einer gepuderten Perücke, sondern von silbergrauen Putten umgeben.
67) Russisch-orthodoxe Kirche als Aufnahme zu Tschaikowskys 5. Symphonie.
68) 69) Typographische. Gestaltung von Plattenhüllen für Aufnahmen des Symphonieorchesters des Österreichischen Rundfunks. Dunkelblaue Schrift auf silbergrauem Grund, rotes Emblem.
70) Grosszügige dekorative Illustrationen der Soloinstrumente kennzeichnen diese *Universo*-Serie.
71) Schwarzweisse Hülle für Orgelkonzerte von Bach, mit stilisierter Orgel als Umschlagillustration.
72) 73) Vollständige Hülle und Assemblage für Klavierkonzerte von Claude Debussy.

65) Pochette pour un disque d'interprétation de Bach à l'orgue de Hammond. Tête tridimensionnelle aux tons sombres, foulard aux couleurs vives.
66) Pochette figurant dans une série de disques de Bach. Perruque poudrée composée de chérubins gris argenté.
67) Eglise orthodoxe russe évocatrice pour une pochette de la 5e Symphonie de Tchaikovski. Photo couleur.
68) 69) Maquettes typo de pochettes de concerts de l'Orchestre Symphonique de la Radio autrichienne. Lettres bleu foncé sur gris argenté, emblème rouge.
70) Illustrations décoratives au grand format d'instruments solos pour les pochettes de la série *Universo*.
71) Pochette noir-blanc pour des concerts d'orgue de Bach, avec représentation stylisée d'un orgue.
72) 73) Pochette complète et détail de l'assemblage pour des études pour piano de Debussy.

68

69

70

71

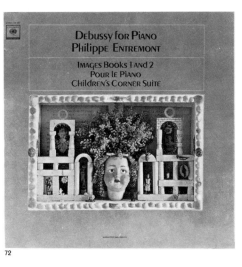

72

ARTIST/KÜNSTLER/ARTISTE:

65) Alain Marouani (Photo)
66) Roger Hane
67) John Lewis Stage (Photo)
68) 69) Georg Schmid
70) Ben Griepink
71) Roland Young
72) 73) Robert Sullivan

DESIGNER/GESTALTER/MAQUETTISTE:

65) Claude Caudron
66) John Berg
67) 72) 73) Edwin Lee
68) 69) Georg Schmid
70) Ben Griepink
71) Rod Dyer

ART DIRECTOR/DIRECTEUR ARTISTIQUE:

65) Alain Marouani
66) John Berg
67) Edwin Lee/John Berg
68) 69) Georg Schmid

70) Gaston Richter
71) George Osaki/Marvin Schwartz
72) 73) John Berg/Bob Cato

PUBLISHER/VERLEGER/EDITEUR:

65) Barclay Disques, Paris
66) 72) 73) Columbia Records, New York
67) Odyssey/Columbia Records, New York
68) 69) Österreichischer Rundfunk, Wien
70) Phonogram, Baarn
71) Angel Records, Hollywood

73

74

ARTIST/KÜNSTLER/ARTISTE:

74) 75) Horn/Griner (Photo)
76) Gilbert Stone
77) Don Hunstein (Photo)
78) Richard Mantel
79) Henrietta Condak
80) Paul Davis
81) Milton Glaser

DESIGNER/GESTALTER/MAQUETTISTE:

74) 75) Alan Weinberg
76) 78)–81) John Berg
77) Virginia Team

ART DIRECTOR/DIRECTEUR ARTISTIQUE:

74) 75) 77) 78) John Berg
76) Richard Mantel/John Berg
79) 80) John Berg/Bob Cato

PUBLISHER/VERLEGER/EDITEUR:

74)–81) Columbia Records, New York

75

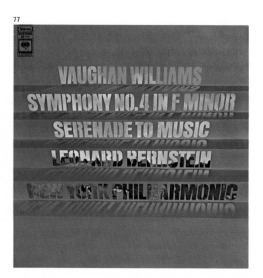

77

78

79

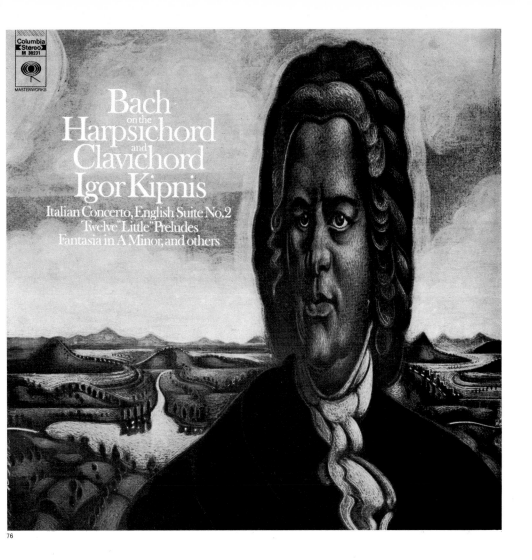

76

74) 75) Complete cover and detail for a recording of two operas by Stravinsky.
76) Record cover for works by Bach played on harpsichord and clavichord. Dull green, brown and blue shades.
77) Covers for works by an English and an American composer. A landscape is reflected in the lettering; the letters themselves are mirrored in the horizontal bands.
78) Cover for two suites by Stravinsky. The small figures are in colour, black lettering.
79) Cover for violin solos, playful variations on the lines of musical notation. Lettering puce and brown.
80) Polychrome cover for choral music.
81) A fantastic motif on a Berlioz cover.

74) 75) Vollständige Hülle und Detail der Aufnahme für *Mawra* und *Die Bauernhochzeit* von Stravinsky.
76) Hülle für Bach-Werke. Dumpfe Grün-, Braun- und Blautöne.
77) In den aus Spiegeln geschnittenen Buchstaben reflektiert sich eine Landschaft. Die Buchstaben wiederum spiegeln sich in den Querbalken wider. Hülle für zwei moderne Stücke.
78) Hülle für Werke von Stravinsky. Die kleinen farbigen Figuren stammen aus der *Histoire du Soldat*. Schwarze Schrift.
79) Verspielte Illustration mit Notenlinien für Werke von Schubert. Schwarzweiss, Schrift in Braun und Weinrot.
80) Mehrfarbige Plattenhülle für Chormusik.
81) Fantastische Illustration (mehrfarbig) für Werke von Berlioz.

74) 75) Pochette complète et détail. Enregistrement de deux opéras de Stravinski.
76) Pochette d'un disque de musique de Bach interprétée au clavecin et au clavichorde. Tons vert mat, bruns, bleus.
77) Pochettes pour des disques d'un compositeur anglais et d'un compositeur américain. Un paysage se reflète dans les lettres reflétées dans les bandes horizontales.
78) Pochette pour deux suites de Stravinski. Les petites figures sont en couleur, les lettres noires.
79) Pochette pour des solos de violon, variations gracieuses sur les lignes de musique. Lettres puce et brun.
80) Pochette polychrome pour un disque de chorals.
81) Motif fantastique pour un disque de Berlioz.

80

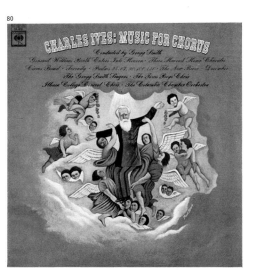

81

E. POWER BIGGS
The Magnificent Mr. Handel
Concertos,
Curtain Tunes,
Marches, Ayres and Divers Pieces
The Royal Philharmonic Orchestra
Charles Groves, Conductor

82

FIRST RECORDINGS
ELLIOTT CARTER/CONCERTO FOR ORCHESTRA
WILLIAM SCHUMAN/IN PRAISE OF SHAHN
(CANTICLE FOR ORCHESTRA)
LEONARD BERNSTEIN
NEW YORK PHILHARMONIC

83

TCHAIKOVSKY/SYMPHONY NO.2 "LITTLE RUSSIAN"
BERNSTEIN/NEW YORK PHILHARMONIC

85

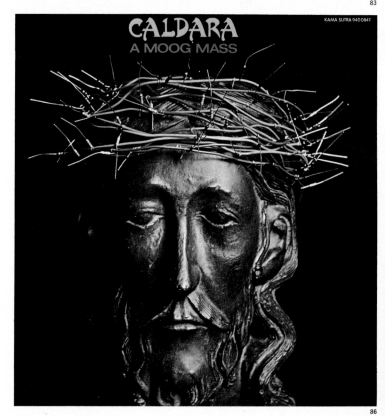

CALDARA
A MOOG MASS

KAMA SUTRA 940 084T

86

84

87

82) Polychrome record cover for a selection of works by Handel.
83) The record *In Praise of Shahn* was made after the death of Ben Shahn. William Schuman, commissioned to compose a work about the artist, drew on Jewish and Eastern European folk-songs which Morris Bressler had often sung for Shahn.
84) Polychrome record cover for a modern composition. The artwork was inspired by the title and shows scenes from the Colonial era in America.
85) Reproduction of a tapestry on the cover of a recording of a Tchaikovsky symphony.
86) Cover for an interpretation of religious music on a Moog Synthesizer. Carved wooden head with the crown of thorns in the form of coloured wires with small aerials.
87) Cover for works by an American composer. Blue legs, red sun, dark green ground.

82) Mehrfarbige Schallplattenhülle für verschiedene Werke von Händel.
83) Das Werk *In Praise of Shahn* (zu Ehren von Shahn) entstand kurz nach Ben Shahns Tod. W. Schuman erhielt den Auftrag, in Erinnerung an Shahn ein Werk zu komponieren, welchem er osteuropäische und jüdische Volkslieder zugrunde legte, die der Sänger Morris Bressler Shahn regelmässig vorsang.
84) Mehrfarbige Plattenhülle für Werke von zwei Komponisten. Die Illustration, inspiriert durch das Titelstück «Das rote Pony», zeigt Szenen aus der amerikanischen Kolonialzeit.
85) Tapisserie als Umschlagillustration zu Tschaikowskys 2. oder Russischer Symphonie.
86) Für eine Interpretation sakraler Musik auf einem Moog Synthesizer. Schwarzer Grund, geschnitzter Kopf, «Dornenkrone» aus farbigen Drähten und kleinen Antennen.
87) Für Werke eines amerikanischen Komponisten. Dunkelgrüner Grund, rote Sonne.

82) Pochette polychrome pour une sélection des œuvres de Hændel.
83) Le disque *In Praise of Shahn* (En l'honneur de Shahn) a été réalisé après la mort de Ben Shahn. L'artiste William Schuman s'est inspiré de chansons populaires juives et est-européennes que Morris Bressler avait souvent chantées pour Shahn.
84) Pochette polychrome pour une composition musicale moderne. Le motif s'inspire du titre et retrace des scènes américaines de l'époque coloniale.
85) Reproduction d'une tapisserie sur la pochette d'une symphonie de Tchaikovski.
86) Pochette pour une interprétation de musique religieuse sur un Synthétiseur Moog. Tête de bois sculpté, couronne d'épines faite de fils de couleur et de micro-antennes.
87) Disque d'un compositeur américain. Jambes bleues, soleil rouge, fond vert foncé.

ARTIST/KÜNSTLER/ARTISTE:

82) John Alcorn
83) Ben Shahn
84) Richard Hess
85) Manik Pirian Condak
86) Alain Marouani (Photo)
87) Don Ivan Punchatz

DESIGNER/GESTALTER/MAQUETTISTE:

82) 84) 85) John Berg
83) Nereus Bell
86) Claude Caudron
87) George Estes/Acy R. Lehman

ART DIRECTOR/DIRECTEUR ARTISTIQUE:

82) 84) 85) John Berg
83) Richard Mantel/John Berg
86) Alain Marouani
87) Acy R. Lehman

PUBLISHER/VERLEGER/EDITEUR:

82) 83) 85) Columbia Records, New York
84) Odyssey/Columbia Records, New York
86) Barclay Disques, Paris
87) RCA Records, New York

88) Record cover from an educational series.
89) Polychrome cover for a one-act English opera.
90) Record cover in muted colours for two concertos by Carl Philipp Emanuel Bach.
91) Cover for a Berlioz symphony. Title on yellowish ground, drawing in brown and orange shades.
92) Cover for Stravinsky's *Histoire du Soldat*. The two figures in the foreground symbolize the soldier with the violin and the devil who tempts him.
93) For pieces in the style of various well-known composers played on the Hammond organ. Colour photograph on a pale grey ground.
94) 95) Detail of the artwork and complete cover for a recording of *Carnival of the Animals* by Saint-Saëns. Voted album of the year 1964 by the National Academy of Recording Arts and Sciences.

88) Plattenhülle aus einer Serie zu Unterrichtszwecken.
89) Mehrfarbige Hülle für eine englische Oper in einem Akt.
90) Plattenhülle in matten Farben für zwei Konzerte von Carl Philipp Emanuel Bach.
91) Zu Berlioz' *Symphonie Fantastique*. Titel auf gelblichem Grund, Illustration auf mattem Orange-Rosa.
92) Hülle zu Stravinskys *Histoire du Soldat*. Die beiden Figuren im Vordergrund symbolisieren den Soldaten (mit der Geige) und den verführerischen Teufel.
93) Für Hammondorgel-Interpretationen im Stil bekannter Komponisten. Die brennenden Notenblätter sollen zeigen, dass ältere Werke heute nicht mehr gefragt sind.
94) 95) Detail der Illustration und vollständige Hülle zu einer Wiedergabe von Saint-Saëns' *Carnaval des Animaux*. 1964 von der National Academy of Recording Arts and Sciences als Hülle des Jahres ausgezeichnet.

88) Pochette d'un disque éducatif.
89) Pochette polychrome pour un opéra anglais en 1 acte.
90) Pochette aux couleurs mates pour deux concertos de Carl Philipp Emanuel Bach.
91) Pochette pour une symphonie de Berlioz. Titre sur fond jaunâtre, dessin aux tons bruns et orange.
92) Pochette pour l'*Histoire du Soldat* de Stravinski. Les deux figures au premier plan symbolisent le soldat au violon et le diable tentateur.
93) Pour des morceaux joués à l'orgue de Hammond à la manière de divers compositeurs connus. Photo couleur sur fond gris pâle.
94) 95) Détail de la composition et pochette complète pour un enregistrement du *Carnaval des Animaux*, par Saint-Saëns. Couronné en 1964 Album de l'année par la National Academy of Recording Arts and Sciences.

ARTIST/KÜNSTLER/ARTISTE:

88) Winter + Bischoff
89) Marvin Schwartz
90) Virginia Team
91) Clifford Condak
92) Shmuel Bak
93) Ontañon (Photo)
94) 95) Jan Balet

88)

89)

90)

91)

92)

93)

94

95

DESIGNER/GESTALTER/MAQUETTISTE:

88) Winter + Bischoff
90) 91) John Berg
92) Leon Lopata/United Artists Ltd.
93) Armando Tomas
94) 95) Robert M. Jones

ART DIRECTOR/DIRECTEUR ARTISTIQUE:

89) Marvin Schwartz
90) John Berg
91) John Berg/Bob Cato
92) Zeev Lewin
93) Armando Tomas
94) 95) Robert M. Jones

PUBLISHER/VERLEGER/EDITEUR:

88) Harmonia Mundi Schallplattengesellschaft, Freiburg i. B.
89) Angel Records, Hollywood
90) 91) Columbia Records, New York
92) Hed Arzi, Ramat-Gan/ISR
93) Hispavox, Madrid
94) 95) RCA Records, New York

Classical Music
Klassische Musik
Musique classique

Classical Music
Klassische Musik
Musique classique

ARTIST/KÜNSTLER/ARTISTE:

96) Hans Hurter (Photo)
97)–99) Milton Glaser
100) Richard Hess
101) Eugene Karlin
102) Gary Winogrand (Photo)
103) Nick Fasciano
104) Hans Uster
105) Charles E. Murphy

DESIGNER/GESTALTER/MAQUETTISTE:

96) Hans Hurter
97) Milton Glaser
98) 99) John Berg
100) Henrietta Condak
101) Robert M. Jones
102) Alan Weinberg
103) Virginia Team
104) Hans Uster
105) Charles E. Murphy

ART DIRECTOR/DIRECTEUR ARTISTIQUE:

96) Hans Hurter
97) Jules Helfant
98)–100) 103) John Berg
101) Robert M. Jones
102) Bob Cato/John Berg
104) Oswald Dubacher
105) Charles E. Murphy

PUBLISHER/VERLEGER/EDITEUR:

96) Hedy Salquin, Kriens/SWI
97) Vanguard Record Corp., New York
98)–100) 102) 103) Columbia Records, New York
101) RCA Records, New York
104) Ex Libris, Zürich
105) Command Records, New York

HEDY SALQUIN SPIELT

96

97

98

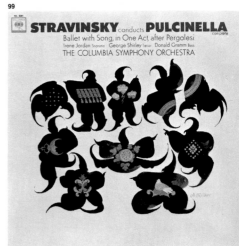

99

100

101

102

103

104

105

96) Abstract cover for a piano recital to collect funds for the renovation of Schauensee Castle near Lucerne.
97) Cover for Italian baroque music.
98) Watercolour figures in green, yellow and red used on a recording of *Don Quixote* by Richard Strauss.
99) Cover for the ballet *Pulcinella*, conducted by Stravinsky, using the familiar figure of the heroine as she appears in the *Commedia dell'Arte* performances.
100) From a series of records of the piano sonatas of Mozart. Colour photograph.
101) For a recording of Tchaikovsky's *Pathétique*. Pale grey and blue-green shades on white.
102) A Scottish ruin as a cover motif for a recording of Mendelssohn's *Scotch Symphony*.
103) Cover of an album containing three records, with photographic elements in the lettering.
104) Cover in three colours for a Brahms symphony.
105) Polychrome cover for guitar music with a stylized rendering of the Colosseum.

96) Diese Platte der Pianistin Hedy Salquin wurde für die Renovation des Schlosses Schauensee herausgegeben.
97) Umschlag einer Platte für italienische Barockmusik.
98) Für eine Aufnahme von Richard Strauss' *Don Quichote*. Don Quichote und Sancho Pansa in Wasserfarbe.
99) Hülle für Stravinskys Ballett *Pulcinella*. Die typische Figur der Pulcinella mit Pluderhosen aus der *Commedia dell'Arte* dient hier als Umschlagillustration.
100) Aus einer Serie von Schallplattenhüllen für Klaviersonaten von Mozart. Dunkelbrauner Grund.
101) Für eine Wiedergabe von Tschaikowskys *Pathétique*. Feine Grau- und Blautöne auf weissem Grund.
102) Photo einer schottischen Burgruine als Umschlagillustration zu Mendelssohns *Schottischer Symphonie*.
103) Hülle eines Albums für drei Platten. Aus Farbphotos ausgeschnittene Buchstaben auf weissem Grund.
104) Dreifarbige Hülle für eine Symphonie von Brahms.
105) Mehrfarbige Hülle für Gitarrenmusik. Stilisiertes Kolosseum in Rom als Umschlagsujet.

96) Pochette abstraite pour un récital de piano en faveur de la réfection du château de Schauensee/Lucerne.
97) Pochette pour un disque de musique baroque italienne
98) Personnages à l'aquarelle en vert, jaune et rouge sur une pochette pour le *Don Quichotte* de Richard Strauss.
99) Pochette pour le ballet *Pulcinella* dirigé par Stravinski. L'artiste a repris la figure traditionnelle du personnage dans la *Commedia dell'Arte*.
100) Exemple d'une série de pochettes pour les sonates pour piano de Mozart. Photo couleur.
101) Pour un enregistrement de la *Pathétique* de Tchaïkovski. Tons gris pâle et bleu-vert sur blanc.
102) Ruine écossaise comme motif de pochette pour la *Symphonie écossaise* de Mendelssohn.
103) Couverture d'un album de trois disques. Lettres composées d'éléments photographiques.
104) Pochette trichrome pour une symphonie de Brahms.
105) Pochette polychrome pour un disque de guitariste. Représentation stylisée du Colisée.

106

107

108

109

110

111

106)–111) Examples from a series of record covers for classical works issued by Nonesuch Records. Compared with the older covers in this series (figs. 107 and 110), the later ones are more generously illustrated, often in bright colours, with the titles integrated in the artwork.

112) Cover for a Shostakovich symphony. Figure modelled in plastic on a background of sacking which had first been soaked in polymer emulsion and then covered with sand. The painting itself is done in watercolours, acrylics and oils.

113) Polychrome case for the recording of a performance in the Czech National Theatre, Prague.

114) Record cover for a guitar concerto. Green leaf, pale blue droplet and polychrome bird.

115) Cover for a recording by Stockhausen of "transformed" themes from Beethoven. Lettering in graduated shades of blue, red, green and magenta.

106)–111) Beispiele aus einer Serie von Plattenhüllen von Nonesuch Records für klassische Werke. Verglichen mit den älteren Hüllen dieser Serie (Abb. 107, 110) werden die modernen durch grosszügige Illustrationen, oft in bunten Farben, gekennzeichnet. Auch die Titel werden frei in die Illustration integriert.

112) Aus Kunststoff modellierte Totenfigur mit grober Jute als Hintergrund, die mit einer Polymer-Emulsion getränkt und teilweise mit Sand beklebt wurde. Das Bild ist in Wasser-, Acryl- und Ölfarben ausgeführt.

113) Mehrfarbige Kassette für die Aufnahme einer Aufführung am Tschechischen Nationaltheater in Prag.

114) Hülle für Gitarrenkonzerte. Giftgrünes Blatt in Form einer Gitarre, hellblauer Tropfen, bunter Vogel.

115) Für eine Aufnahme Beethovenscher Themen nach Stockhausen, die von vier Musikern nach einem bestimmten Regelsystem interpretiert werden. Schrift (blau, rot, grün und magenta) in helle Töne auslaufend.

106)–111) Exemples d'une série de pochettes de disques classiques de Nonesuch Records. Comparées aux pochettes plus anciennes de la série (fig. 107, 110), les plus récentes ont une illustration plus abondante, souvent des couleurs vives, des titres intégrés dans la composition.

112) Pochette pour une symphonie de Chostakovitch. Figure moulée en plastique sur fond de toile à sacs trempée dans une émulsion polymérisée et recouverte de sable. Peinture à l'aquarelle, aux couleurs acryliques et à l'huile.

113) Etui polychrome pour le disque d'une représentation au Théâtre national tchèque de Prague.

114) Pochette pour un concerto de guitare. Feuille verte, gouttelette bleu pâle, oiseau polychrome.

115) Pochette d'un disque de Stockhausen «transformant» des thèmes de Beethoven. Lettres en tons dégradés de bleu, rouge, vert et magenta.

112

ARTIST/KÜNSTLER/ARTISTE:

106) Peter Schauman
107) 110) Edward Sorel
108) Laliberté
109) Bob Pepper
111) Frank Bozzo
112) Ted Coconis
113) Manfred Vormstein
114) Don Ivan Punchatz
115) Holger Matthies

DESIGNER/GESTALTER/MAQUETTISTE:

106)–111) Robert L. Heimall
114) Acy R. Lehman/George Estes

ART DIRECTOR/DIRECTEUR ARTISTIQUE:

106)–111) William S. Harvey
113) Manfred Vormstein
114) Acy R. Lehman
115) Pali Meller-Marcovicz

PUBLISHER/VERLEGER/EDITEUR:

106)–111) Elektra Records, New York
112) 114) RCA Records, New York
113) Ariola-Eurodisc, München
115) Deutsche Grammophon Gesellschaft, Hamburg

113

114

115

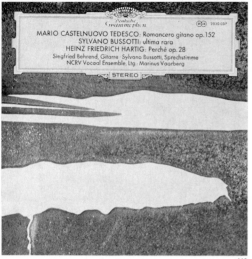

MARIO CASTELNUOVO TEDESCO: Romancero gitano op.152
SYLVANO BUSSOTTI: ultima rara
HEINZ FRIEDRICH HARTIG: Perché op. 28
Siegfried Behrend, Gitarre · Sylvano Bussotti, Sprechstimme
NCRV Vocaal Ensemble, Ltg. Marinus Voorberg

116

Richard Strauss: Also sprach Zarathustra
Boston Symphony Orchestra · William Steinberg

117

HANS WERNER HENZE
2. Konzert für Klavier und Orchester
2nd Concert for Piano and Orchestra
CHRISTOPH ESCHENBACH, PIANO
LONDON PHILHARMONIC ORCHESTRA · HANS WERNER HENZE

118

CARL ORFF · CARMINA BURANA
Gundula Janowitz · Gerhard Stolze · Dietrich Fischer-Dieskau
CHOR UND ORCHESTER DER DEUTSCHEN OPER BERLIN
Dirigent: Eugen Jochum

119

HAYDN: »SONNENQUARTETTE« OP. 20, 1-3
"SUN QUARTETS", OP. 20, 1-3 · QUATUORS DU SOLEIL· OP. 20, 1-3
Koeckert-Quartett

120

JOHANN SEBASTIAN BACH
Goldberg-Variationen BWV 988 (Clavierübung IV)
WILHELM KEMPFF, PIANO

121

116)–122) Complete record covers and one detail from a classical series issued by the Deutsche Grammophon Gesellschaft. The yellow panel appears on all the covers and contains basic information on the record. It also distinguishes this series from others issued by the same company. Otherwise the full-colour covers vary in their treatment, using, for instance, photographs with an atmosphere attuned to the spirit of the music (fig. 116); graphics or paintings relating to the title (figs. 117, 119, 120 and 122); illustrations of the music resulting from contacts between composer and artist (fig. 118); or even abstract designs (fig. 121, a vibration figure obtained by the late Hans Jenny).

116)–122) Vollständige Hüllen und Detail einer Illustration aus der «klassischen» Serie der Deutschen Grammophon-Gesellschaft. Das charakteristische gelbe Panel ist für Kurzinformation bestimmt und soll diese Stammmarke gegenüber andern DGG-Reihen unterscheiden (in Qualität und Preis). Innerhalb der «klassischen» Serie wird in bezug auf die Illustration auf weitere Unterscheidungsmerkmale geachtet: Stimmungsphotos, die den Gefühlsgehalt der Musik visualisieren sollen (Abb. 116); freie Graphik zur Illustration von Musiktiteln (Abb. 117, 120, 122); Illustration von Musikinhalten in Abstimmung zwischen Komponist und Gestalter (Abb. 118); angewandte Graphik im malerischen Duktus (Abb. 119); oder auch abstrakte Gestaltungen (Abb. 121, experimentell sichtbar gemachte Schwingungen, aufgenommen vom verstorbenen Hans Jenny).

116)–122) Pochettes complètes et élément de détail d'une série classique de la Deutsche Grammophon-Gesellschaft. Le panneau jaune, qui figure sur toutes les pochettes, contient des renseignements sur le disque tout en différenciant la série des autres du même éditeur. Le style varie de pochette à pochette: photos d'atmosphère accordées à la musique du disque (116); interprétation graphique ou picturale du titre (117, 119, 120, 122); interprétation musicale née d'une rencontre entre le musicien et l'artiste (118); et même des compositions abstraites (121: figure vibratoire obtenue par feu Hans Jenny).

ARTIST/KÜNSTLER/ARTISTE:

116) Harro Wolter (Photo)
117) 122) Peter Wandrey
118) Maria Antonietta Gambaro
119) Johann Georg Geyger
120) Horst Breitkreuz
121) Hans Jenny (Photo)

ART DIRECTOR/DIRECTEUR ARTISTIQUE:

116) 117) 121) 122) Franz Neuss
119) 120) Willi Mailand

PUBLISHER/VERLEGER/EDITEUR:

116)–122) Deutsche Grammophon Gesellschaft, Hamburg

Classical Music / Klassische Musik Musique classique

Classical Music / Klassische Musik
Musique classique

123) 124) From a series of covers for recordings of music for the Japanese puppet theatre.
125) Cover for music and songs from Japanese puppet plays. Grey lettering on white ground, with a colour illustration showing a scene from a performance.
126) For classical Japanese music interpreted by vocalists. Dark shapes torn from coloured paper on silver.
127) 128) Complete record albums for instrumental music from the Japanese Imperial Household.
129) 130) Inside panel and front of a record cover. The blue and gold Buddha figures in white ovals on black are an allusion to the subject of the record, viz. Zen meditation. Front of cover in colour, with a combination of graphics and photography, Buddhas in gold.

123) 124) Aus einer Serie von Schallplatten mit Musik für das japanische Puppentheater.
125) Musik und Gesang für das japanische Puppentheater. Weisser Grund, graue Schriftzeichen; die farbige Illustration zeigt eine Szene aus einer Aufführung.
126) Für klassische japanische Musik, von Sängern interpretiert. Ausgerissene Papierformen in dunklen Farbtönen auf Silber, weisser Grund.
127) 128) Geöffnete Hüllen für japanische Hofmusik.
129) 130) Innen- und Vorderseite einer Plattenhülle. Die blauen und goldenen Buddha-Figuren in weissem Oval auf Schwarz deuten auf das Thema der Platte hin – Zen-Meditationen. Vorderseite in Farbe, kombinierte Graphik und Photographie, goldene Buddha-Figuren.

123) 124) Exemples d'une série de pochettes pour la musique du théâtre de marionnettes japonais.
125) Pochette pour un enregistrement de musique et de chansons du même théâtre. Lettres grises sur blanc, avec l'illustration couleur d'une scène de théâtre.
126) Pour un disque de musique vocale japonaise classique. Formes sombres (papier couleur déchiré) sur argent.
127) 128) Albums de disques complets pour de la musique instrumentale jouée à la cour impériale du Japon.
129) 130) Intérieur et recto d'une pochette de disque. Les bouddhas en différentes positions dans un ovale blanc sur fond noir se réfèrent au sujet du disque – Méditations Zen. Recto en couleur, éléments graphiques et photographiques combinés, bouddhas en or.

124

123

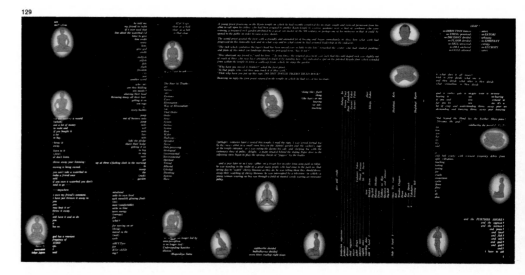

129

58

125

126

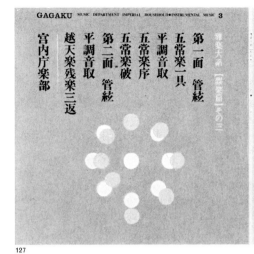

127

128

130

ARTIST/KÜNSTLER/ARTISTE:

123) 124) Yasuo Shigehara
125) Ukiyoe
126) Yoshiaki Kohyama
127) 128) Ikuo Sakuray
129) 130) Tadanori Yokoo

DESIGNER/GESTALTER/MAQUETTISTE:

123) 124) Yasuo Shigehara
125) 126) Yoshiaki Kohyama
129) 130) Tadanori Yokoo

ART DIRECTOR/DIRECTEUR ARTISTIQUE:

123) 124) Yasuo Shigehara
125) 126) Yoshiaki Kohyama
129) 130) Tadanori Yokoo

PUBLISHER/VERLEGER/EDITEUR:

123) 124) King Record Co., Tokyo
125) 126) CBS/Sony Records, Tokyo
127) 128) Music Dept. Imperial Household, Tokyo
129) 130) Philips Japan Co. Ltd., Tokyo

Colman Andrews

Jazz, the native American art form, has never been an extremely popular music in the United States. Even among the urban blacks who were its principal creators, it has gained surprisingly little real support. Jazz record companies, like jazz audiences, have traditionally been small but dedicated, and record-company individualism among these companies has persisted longer than it has in most other areas. Easily recognizable, though graphically limited, styles of album design became strongly identified with particular labels (Francis Woolf's high-contrast photographs and linear constructions for his Blue Note label; the widely imitated back-cover liner-note arrangements worked out by the first owners of Prestige; the single-image photographic statements encouraged by Dick Bock at World-Pacific and Pacific Jazz, etc.).

In the late sixties and early seventies, though, a newly awakened (yet still small-scale) consumer interest in jazz music—brought about largely by the popularity of jazz-influenced rock groups like Blood Sweat & Tears, Chicago, the Mahavishnu Orchestra, etc.—had several important effects on jazz album design. First, smaller jazz labels were bought up by larger general record companies (Blue Note by United Artists, Prestige and Riverside and Milestone by the newly revivified Fantasy label, etc.). Second, many other large companies began to build up their own rosters of jazz artists (Columbia, for example, seemed to spend the early seventies signing every unattached avant-garde performer they could find). Both these phenomena had the effect of allowing top graphic designers, like Bob Cato or Norman Seeff, working with top contemporary artists and photographers, to apply their own highly sophisticated concepts to a kind of music with a very different kind of dynamic energy from rock or other popular musics.

A chance to capture a new record-buying public has also led fledgling jazz record companies, like CTI and Kudu, to be especially conscious of the visual image they project. (Large, high-quality reproductions of CTI covers are available to record-buyers for decorative purposes.)

Some record marketing experts question the wisdom of bringing jazz album design into the same context as other music packaging, claiming that jazz sales have depended for many years on a limited but regular audience which has become accustomed to a certain predictable look to their albums, and which will probably be confused by the visual pyrotechnics of a Pete Turner or a John van Hamersveld. Others reply that quality design will help to build the new, knowledgeable audience jazz needs if it is to survive.

Jazz, diese eigenständige amerikanische Kunstform, ist in den Vereinigten Staaten nie übermässig populär gewesen. Selbst unter den Schwarzen in den Städten, die seine eigentlichen Schöpfer waren, hat er überraschend wenig Unterstützung gefunden. Jazz-Plattenfirmen sind, wie das Publikum von Jazzkonzerten, von jeher klein aber hingebungsvoll gewesen. Der Individualismus der Plattenfirmen hat sich in diesem Bereich länger gehalten als in den meisten anderen Bereichen. Leicht erkennbare, aber im Stil begrenzte Graphik wurde stark mit bestimmten Plattenmarken identifiziert. (Francis Woolfs scharf kontrastierende Photos und Linearkonstruktionen mit seiner Marke Blue Note, die oft imitierten Textanordnungen der ersten Besitzer von Prestige usw.)

Gegen Ende der sechziger und Anfang der siebziger Jahre hatte jedoch ein neuerwachtes (aber noch relativ bescheidenes) Konsumenteninteresse an Jazzmusik – hauptsächlich hervorgerufen von populären, vom Jazz beeinflussten Rock-Gruppen wie Blood Sweat & Tears, Chicago, dem Mahavishnu Orchestra usw. – mehrere wichtige Auswirkungen auf das Design von Jazzalben. Zunächst wurden kleinere Jazzmarken von grösseren Plattenfirmen aufgekauft (Blue Note von United Artists, Prestige, Riverside und Milestone von Fantasy usw.). Sodann begannen grosse Firmen, ihren Stamm von Jazzmusikern aufzubauen. (Columbia schien seit anfangs 1970 jeden firmenungebundenen Avantgarde-Musiker unter Vertrag zu nehmen.) Diese beiden Phänomene hatten zur Folge, dass Spitzengraphiker wie Bob Cato oder Norman Seeff in Zusammenarbeit mit Spitzenkünstlern und -photographen ihre eigenen, raffinierten Vorstellungen auf eine Art von Musik anwenden konnten, deren Dynamismus sich stark von Rock oder anderen populären Musikarten unterscheidet.

Die Chance, das neue Publikum zu gewinnen, hat auch junge Jazz-Plattenfirmen wie CTI und Kudu besonderen Wert auf ihr visuelles Image legen lassen. (Grosse Reproduktionen von CTI Plattenhüllen sind für Plattenkäufer in Form von Postern erhältlich.)

Experten für Plattenmarketing bezweifeln, dass es klug ist, das Design von Jazzalben anderen Musikverpackungen anzugleichen. Jazzverkäufe seien jahrelang von einer Käuferschicht getätigt worden, die an ein bestimmtes Aussehen ihrer Alben gewöhnt ist und wahrscheinlich vom visuellen Feuerwerkszauber eines Pete Turner oder John van Hamersveld verwirrt wird. Darauf erwidern andere, dass qualifiziertes Design helfen wird, ein sachverständiges Publikum anzusprechen, das der Jazz zum Überleben braucht.

Jazz

Le jazz, la forme d'art musicale du peuple noir des Etats-Unis, n'a jamais été très populaire dans son pays d'origine. Même parmi les Noirs des villes, où il est né, il n'a pu s'assurer une audience importante, aussi surprenant que cela puisse paraître. De tout temps, les sociétés de production de disques de jazz, à l'instar du public, ont été de petites entreprises dévouées à la cause, mais défendant leurs droits avec un individualisme farouche périmé ailleurs. C'est ainsi que les styles des pochettes de jazz, aisément identifiables, quoique assez sommaires du point de vue graphique, en sont venus à caractériser certains producteurs. Citons à titre d'exemple les photos fortement contrastées et les constructions linéaires de Francis Woolf pour la marque Blue Note.

A la fin des années 60 et au début des années 70, un intérêt nouveau – quoique toujours limité – s'est manifesté pour le jazz, en particulier sous l'influence de groupes populaires de rock fortement marqués par le jazz, tels Blood Sweat & Tears, Chicago, le Mahavishnu Orchestra, etc. Ce regain de faveur a eu certaines incidences importantes sur la présentation des pochettes de disques. D'une part, il y a eu un phénomène de concentration commerciale, un certain nombre de petits producteurs étant absorbés par les grandes sociétés produisant des disques en tous genres (Blue Note par United Artists, Prestige, Riverside, Milestone par Fantasy à l'occasion du retour en force de cette marque, etc.). D'autre part, un grand nombre de producteurs de disques de premier plan se sont attaché une écurie de musiciens de jazz. Columbia, par exemple, semble avoir recruté depuis 1970 tous les musiciens d'avant-garde qui n'étaient pas encore sous contrat ailleurs. Grâce à cette double évolution, des artistes graphiques de renom, tels Bob Cato ou Norman Seeff, aidés d'artistes et de photographes réputés, ont pu appliquer leurs conceptions très sophistiquées à un genre de musique bien différente du rock ou d'autres formes de musique populaire par l'énergie dynamique qui s'y investit.

Les nouveaux venus sur le marché, CTI et Kudu par exemple, se sont par ailleurs évertués à captiver l'attention d'un nouveau public par une image visuelle élaborée. C'est ainsi que CTI met à la disposition de ses clients d'excellentes reproductions grand format de ses pochettes pouvant être utilisées comme posters hautement décoratifs. Les traditionnalistes regrettent évidemment cet élargissement du public spécialisé par le biais des feux d'artifice graphiques d'un Pete Turner ou d'un John van Hamersveld, alors que les novateurs y voient une chance unique pour la survie et la promotion du jazz.

Jazz

131) Polychrome cover for recordings by a jazz trio.
132) Black-and-white cover for a blues record.
133) Blues record by a big band. Dark blue apple, green leaf, silver-grey background.
134) Polychrome cover for a live blues concert. Blue ground.
135) Cover for a blues record. Blue shades.
136) Cover for a blues record. Trunk with relief effects.
137) Cover for blues sung by J. B. Lenoir. Black ground.
138) Cover for a recording by a jazz pianist. Protrait painted on wood, blue background.
139) Cover for the blues singer Yusef Lateef. Green and purple shadows on face, blue ground.
140) Record cover for blues. Blue title on grey.
141) Cover for a concert by two jazz musicians.

131) Mehrfarbige Hülle für Aufnahmen eines Jazz-Trios.
132) Schwarzweisser Umschlag für eine Blues-Platte.
133) Blues-Platte einer Big Band. Dunkelblauer Apfel, grünes Blatt auf silbergrauem Hintergrund.
134) Mehrfarbige Plattenhülle für ein Blues-Konzert.
135) Umschlag einer Blues-Platte. Blau, rot-weisse Schrift.
136) Für Blues-Stücke von Ike Turner. Helle Schrift, helle Lichtreflexe in Eisenbeschlägen, schwarzer Grund.
137) Schwarzweisse Hülle für den Blues-Sänger J. B. Lenoir.
138) Auf Holz gemaltes Portrait auf blauem Grund. Plattenhülle für Aufnahmen eines Jazz-Pianisten.
139) Plattenhülle für den Blues-Sänger Yusef Lateef. Grauer Kopf, Schatten in dunklem Violett, auf blauem Grund.
140) Hülle in düsterem Grau für Aufnahmen Jimmy Rushings.
141) Für ein Konzert der beiden Jazz-Musiker Mulligan und Monk.

131) Pochette polychrome. Enregistrement d'un trio de jazz.
132) Pochette noir-blanc pour un disque de blues.
133) Disque de blues enregistré par un grand orchestre. Pomme bleu foncé, feuille verte, fond gris argenté.
134) Pochette polychrome pour un concert de blues. Fond bleu.
135) Pochette d'un disque de blues. Tons bleus.
136) Pochette d'un disque de blues. Malle avec effet de relief.
137) Disque de blues du chanteur J. B. Lenoir. Fond noir.
138) Pochette pour l'enregistrement d'un pianiste de jazz Portrait peint sur bois, fond bleu.
139) Pochette d'un disque du chanteur de blues Yusef Lateef. Ombres vertes et pourpres sur le visage, fond bleu.
140) Pochette d'un disque de blues. Titre bleu sur gris.
141) Pochette d'un concert donné par deux musiciens de jazz.

ARTIST/KÜNSTLER/ARTISTE:

131) Bill Binzen (Photo)
132) Gabriele Matthies (Photo)
133) Heinz Bähr (Photo)
134) Holger Matthies (Photo)
135) J. H. Löffler (Photo)
136) Frédéric Valentine (Photo)
137) Günther Kieser
138) Stanislav Zagorski
139) Roland Scherman (Photo)
140) William Duevell/Mel Cheren (Photo)
141) Leopoldo Pomes (Photo)

DESIGNER/GESTALTER/MAQUETTISTE:

131) 139) John Berg
132) 134) Holger Matthies
133) Heinz Bähr
135) J. H. Löffler
136) John Echevarrieta
138) Stanislav Zagorski
140) William Duevell
141) Juan C. Friart

131

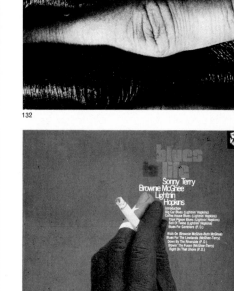

132

133

134

138

139

135

136

137

140

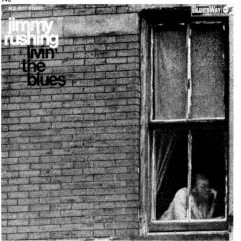

141

ART DIRECTOR/DIRECTEUR ARTISTIQUE:

131) 139) John Berg
132) 134) Jochen Hinze
133) Heinz Bähr
135) J. H. Löffler
136) Norman Seeff
137) H. R. Müller
138) Nesuhi Ertegun
140) Henry Epstein
141) Juan C. Friart

PUBLISHER/VERLEGER/EDITEUR:

131) 139) Columbia Records, New York
132) Deutsche Grammophon Ges., Hamburg
133) MPS Records, Villingen/GER
134) Karussell/Deutsche Grammophon Ges., Hamburg
135) Metronome Records, Hamburg
136) United Artists Records, Los Angeles
137) Lippmann + Rau/CBS Schallplatten,
    Frankfurt/M
138) Atlantic Recording Corp., New York
140) ABC Records, New York
141) Scherzo Discos, Barcelona

142

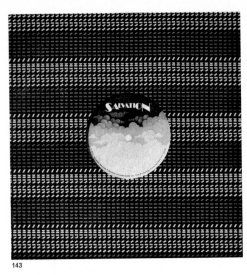

143

144

145

146

147

148

149

ART DIRECTOR/DIRECTEUR ARTISTIQUE:

142) 143) Bob Ciano
144) Michael Malatak
145) John Berg
147) Stefan Böhle
148) Wilfried Mannes
149) Marvin Schwartz

PUBLISHER/VERLEGER/EDITEUR:

142) 143) Salvation/Creed Taylor, New York
144) Verve Records, New York
145) Columbia Records, New York
146) 148) Mercury/Phonogram, Hamburg
147) Buddah/Deutsche Grammophon Ges., Hamburg
149) Capitol Records, Hollywood

142) Record cover for gospel music sung by a choir. Sombre colours with brown hands, grey bird.
143) Inside sleeve and label for a series devoted to gospel music. Pale and bright blue type on black.
144) Cover for recordings by a jazz trumpeter.
145) Cover for a Duke Ellington record employing collage and photographs.
146) Black-and-white cover for modern jazz by a quartet.
147) Album containing two gospel records by a group of negro singers. Orange sleeves, yellow ground.
148) Cover for negro spirituals sung by a choir.
149) Polychrome cover for jazz recordings at a film festival in Cannes.

142) 143) Aussen- und Innenhülle mit Plattenlabel für die Serie *Salvation*, die ausschliesslich Gospelmusik gewidmet ist. Abb. 142: braune Hände, weisse Taube auf dunklem Grund; Abb. 143: hell- und dunkelblau auf Schwarz; Label in verschiedenen Blautönen.
144) Für Aufnahmen des Jazz-Trompeters Johnny Hodges.
145) Plattenhülle für Aufnahmen der Duke Ellington-Band. Kombination von Photographie und Collage.
146) Schwarzweisse Hülle für modernen Jazz.
147) Kassette mit zwei Platten einer Gruppe schwarzer Sänger und Sängerinnen. Orange Ärmel, gelber Grund.
148) Hülle für Negro Spirituals, gesungen von den Lee Patterson Singers. Schwarze Hände auf hellem Grund.
149) Mehrfarbige Hülle für Jazz-Aufnahmen, die am Filmfestival in Cannes gemacht wurden.

142) Pochette d'un disque de gospel music chantée par une chorale. Couleurs sombres, mains brunes, oiseau gris.
143) Chemise intérieure et étiquette d'une série de gospel music. Typographie bleu pâle et vif sur fond noir.
144) Pochette pour l'enregistrement d'un trompette de jazz.
145) Pochette pour un disque de Duke Ellington. Technique mixte collage-photo.
146) Pochette noir-blanc pour un disque de jazz enregistré par un quartette.
147) Album groupant deux disques de gospel par un groupe de chanteurs noirs. Chemises orange, fond jaune.
148) Pochette pour les negro spirituals d'une chorale.
149) Pochette polychrome pour des enregistrements de jazz lors d'un festival du cinéma à Cannes.

Jazz

65

150

151

Jazz

ARTIST/KÜNSTLER/ARTISTE:

150) 154) Peter Wandrey
151) Heinz Bähr (Photo)
152) Roland Young (Photo)
153) Wolfgang Baumann
155) Ernst Jünger
156)–158) Peter Turner

DESIGNER/GESTALTER:

150) 154) Peter Wandrey
151) Heinz Bähr
152) Roland Young
153) Wolfgang Baumann
156) 157) Sam Antupit
158) Bob Ciano

ART DIRECTOR/DIRECTEUR ARTISTIQUE:

150) 154) Peter Wandrey
151) 153) H. B. Pfitzer
152) George Osaki
155) Hans Schweiss
156) 157) Sam Antupit
158) Bob Ciano

PUBLISHER/VERLEGER/EDITEUR:

150) 154) Verve, Hamburg
151) 153) MPS Records, Villingen/GER
152) Capitol Records, Hollywood
155) Werkkunstschule, Offenbach
156) 157) A&M/Creed Taylor, New York
158) Creed Taylor, New York

152

153

150) Cover for recordings by Charlie Parker. Red, blue, black.
151) Superimposed shots of London, with a mannequin and waste paper in Soho, on a record cover for the Dave Pike Set.
152) Cover for a recording by a quintet. Scraps of paper with copy on a packing paper ground.
153) Cover for a jazz trio. Brightly coloured "lashes".
154) Cover for recordings by a famous trumpeter.
155) Project for a record cover.
156) 157) Complete cover and detail of photography.

150) Für Aufnahmen von Charlie Parker. Rot, blau, schwarz.
151) Übereinanderkopierte Londoner Schnappschüsse – Schaufensterpuppe auf gelbem Grund und Papierabfälle in Soho – als Umschlagaufnahme für das Dave Pike Set.
152) Zerknülltes Packpapier mit ausgerissenen Papierstreifen als Hülle einer Platte von Cannonball Adderley.
153) Für ein Jazz-Trio. Augenwimpern aus farbigen Blättern.
154) Hülle für Aufnahmen eines bekannten Jazz-Trompeters.
155) Entwurf zu einer Plattenhülle für Aufnahmen von Kid Ory.
156) 157) Plattenhülle zu Wes Montgomerys *Road Songs*.

150) Pochette d'un disque de Charlie Parker. Rouge, bleu, noir.
151) Photos surimprimées de Londres, avec un mannequin et des papiers sales à Soho, pour un disque du Dave Pike Set.
152) Pochette de l'enregistrement d'un quintette. Bouts de papier imprimé sur fond de papier d'emballage.
153) Disque d'un trio de jazz. «Cils» aux couleurs vives.
154) Pochette pour les enregistrements d'un célèbre trompette.
155) Projet de pochette de disque.
156) 157) Pochette complète et détail photographique.

Following spread / Nächste Doppelseite / Double page suivante:

158) Photograph used on a cover for African jazz.
158) Photo einer Hülle zu Hubert Laws «Afro-classic Songs».
158) Photo pour une pochette de disque de jazz «africain».

154

155

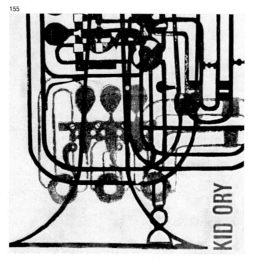

159

160

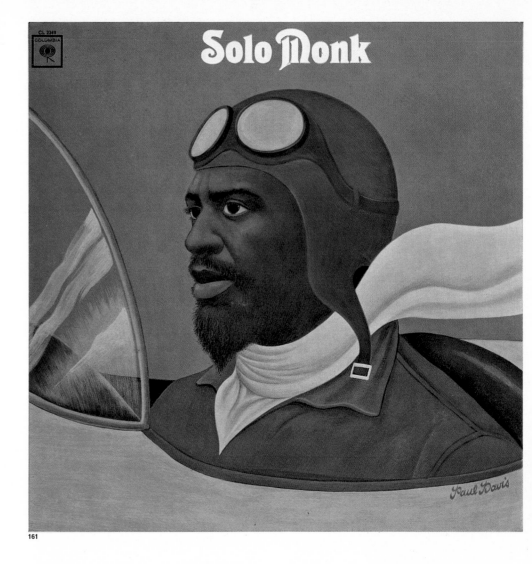

161

162

163

164

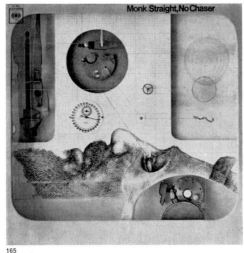

165

166

167

168

169

159) Cover for a blues record.
160) 161) 165) Three covers for recordings by the jazz pianist Thelonious Monk. Each one incorporates a portrait of the musician.
162) 163) Front and back of a double album containing records by Sam Hopkins.
164) Cover for recordings by a black singer.
166) Photographic interpretation of the title of a jazz record. Green sky, brown clouds.
167) Cover of a record featuring the winners of a jazz poll. Orange box with yellow label.
168) Cover for a selection of pieces by the jazz pianist Herbie Hancock.
169) Cover for the evergreen *Stormy Weather*, here symbolized by muddy shoes in full colour.

159) Umschlag für eine Blues-Platte.
160) 161) 165) Schallplattenhülle für Aufnahmen des Jazz-Pianisten Thelonious Monk. Auf allen drei Hüllen erscheint Monk mit seinem charakteristischen Spitzbart.
162) 163) Vorder- und Rückseite eines Doppelalbums für Aufnahmen des Jazz-Musikers Sam Hopkins.
164) Schallplattenhülle für eine schwarze Sängerin.
166) Photographische Interpretation des Plattentitels einer

Jazz-Band — Time & Space (Raum und Zeit). Hintergrund: grünlicher Himmel, braune Erde.
167) Unter Mithilfe der Lufthansa herausgegebene Platte mit den Gewinnern aus der Umfrage einer Jazzzeitschrift. Orange Schachtel, gelbes Etikett.
168) Für eine Auswahl von Stücken des Jazz-Pianisten Hancock. Dunkelbrauner Hintergrund.
169) Für die Jazz-Platte *Stormy Weather*. Die schmutzigen Schuhe sollen den Titel illustrieren.

159) Pochette d'un disque de blues.
160) 161) 165) Pochettes de trois disques du pianiste de jazz Thelonious Monk, chacune avec un portrait de l'artiste.
162) 163) Recto et verso d'un album double contenant des disques de Sam Hopkins.
164) Pochette pour le disque d'une chanteuse noire.
166) Interprétation photographique du titre d'un disque de jazz. Ciel vert, nuages bruns.
167) Disque enregistré par les gagnants d'un test de popularité (jazz). Boîte orange, étiquette jaune.
168) Pochette pour une sélection des œuvres du pianiste de jazz Herbie Hancock.
169) Pochette pour l'evergreen *Stormy Weather*, symbolisé ici par des souliers pleins de boue. En polychromie.

ART DIRECTOR/DIRECTEUR ARTISTIQUE:

159) Holger Matthies
160) John Berg
161) 165) John Berg/Bob Cato
162) 163) Kevin Eggers
164) George Osaki
166) Anne Garner
167) Heinz Bähr
168) Ronald Wolin
169) Peter Sibley

PUBLISHER/VERLEGER/EDITEUR:

159) Karussell/Deutsche Grammophon Ges., Hamburg
160) 161) 165) Columbia Records, New York
162) 163) Poppy Records, New York
164) Capitol Records, Hollywood
166) Epic/Columbia Records, New York
167) MPS Records, Villingen/GER
168) Blue Note/United Artists Records, Los Angeles
169) Polydor/Deutsche Grammophon Ges., Hamburg

170

171

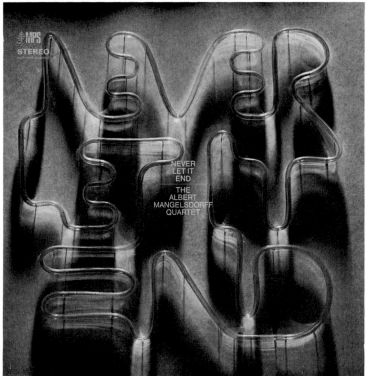

173

174

172

Jazz

170) Cover for a recording by a blues singer. The illustration refers to his very first records, which were made in a hotel room in San Antonio fitted up as a studio.
171) Cover for songs by Junior Parker. Mask and face reflect the two moods of his songs. Blue and red shirt, black ground.
172) Polychrome cover for blues, with portraits of the band members in the windscreen.
173) A polychrome transparent tube is used on this cover to interpret the title.
174) Cover giving the impression of a torn package for recordings by prize-winning bands at European jazz festivals. Yellow and red label.
175) Record cover for a well-known jazz singer. Sombre colours on a grey ground.
176) From a series of record covers for songs by Billie Holiday.

170) Hülle für die Platte eines Blues-Sängers. Die Illustration spielt auf seine erste Aufnahme an, die in einem Hotelzimmer in San Antonio gemacht wurde.
171) Für den Blues-Sänger Parker: «Ich erzähle traurige und wahre Geschichten, ich singe den Blues und spiele Harmonika, es ist sehr traurig.» Dunkler Grund, blaues Hemd, rotes Muster.
172) Farbige Hülle für eine Jazz-Band, mit Abbildung der Mitglieder in der Windschutzscheibe.
173) Hülle für Mangelsdorffs «Never let it end». Eine mehrfarbige Röhre auf blauem Hintergrund zeichnet den Titel nach.
174) Angerissene Versandhülle als Plattenumschlag für Aufnahmen mit preisgekrönten Bands von drei europäischen Jazz-Festivals. Gelb-rot-gelbe Etikette.
175) Schallplattenhülle in dunklen Farben auf grauem Grund für Aufnahmen einer Jazz-Sängerin.
176) Aus einer Serie von Plattenhüllen mit Aufnahmen von Billie Holiday.

170) Pochette du disque d'un chanteur de blues. L'illustration évoque ses tout premiers enregistrements faits dans une chambre d'hôtel de San Antonio transformée en studio.
171) Pochette pour un disque de chansons de Junior Parker. Le masque et le visage reflètent les deux veines principales de ses chansons. Chemise bleue et rouge, fond noir.
172) Pochette pour un disque de blues. Les interprètes sont visibles dans le pare-brise.
173) Un tube polychrome transparent interprète le titre sur cette pochette.
174) Pochette évoquant un emballage déchiré pour des enregistrements d'orchestres primés lors de festivals du jazz en Europe. Etiquette jaune et rouge.
175) Pochette de disque pour une chanteuse de jazz réputée. Couleurs sombres sur fond gris.
176) Exemple d'une série de pochettes pour des enregistrements des chansons de Billie Holiday.

175

ARTIST/KÜNSTLER/ARTISTE:

170) Tom Wilson
171) Cliff McReynolds
172) Don Weller
173) Volker Hartmann (Photo)
174) Heinz Bähr (Photo)
175) Stanislav Zagorski
176) Philip Hays

DESIGNER/GESTALTER/MAQUETTISTE:

170) Nick Fasciano
171) Joan Marker
173) Günther Kieser
174) Heinz Bähr
175) Stanislav Zagorski
176) Henrietta Condak

ART DIRECTOR/DIRECTEUR ARTISTIQUE:

170) John Berg
171) Norman Seeff
172) John LePrevost
174) H. B. Pfitzer
175) Nesuhi Ertegun
176) John Berg/Bob Cato

PUBLISHER/VERLEGER/EDITEUR:

170) 176) Columbia Records, New York
171) United Artists Records, Los Angeles
172) Universal City Records, Los Angeles
173) MPS Records, Villingen/GER
174) MPS/BASF, Villingen/Hamburg
175) Atlantic Recording Corp., New York

176

177) Cover in muted colours for a soul symphony.
178) Cover for a record by a jazz saxophonist. Brown shades, with green and red neon signs.
179) Cover of a double album containing the most popular hits of Louis Armstrong. Photograph taken in evening light, with yellow title.
180) Cover for a recording of soul music. Blue-black background, carmine lips.
181) Black-and-white cover for music by a sextet, led by the German jazz musician Joki Freund, whose name may have suggested the title and thus the witty graphic interpretation of it.
182) Cover for a jazz record. Brown face with green eyes and red lips on a blue-and-white wave pattern.
183) 184) Artwork and complete record cover for a concert by Cannonball Adderley recorded in Japan. The illustration attempts to give an impression of the visit of a Western jazz band to Japan.

177) Schallplattenhülle in gedämpften Farben für eine «Soul-Symphonie».
178) Hülle für den Jazz-Saxophonisten Lou Donaldson. Brauntöne, rote und grüne Leuchtschrift.
179) Umschlag eines Doppelalbums mit den bekanntesten Hits von Louis Armstrong. Abendstimmung.
180) Umschlag einer Platte mit Soul-Musik der Beefeaters. Blauschwarzer Grund, rote Lippen.
181) Schwarzweiss-Hülle für Aufnahmen des Joki Freund-Sextetts. Photographische Interpretation des Namens mit kopfstehendem Brustbild Joki Freunds. Die Haare bilden den Bart um das richtigstehende Gesicht.
182) Hülle für eine Jazz-Platte. Blau-weisse Wellenlinien, braunes Gesicht, grüne Augen.
183) 184) Illustration und vollständige Hülle für ein Konzert von Adderley in Japan. Es wurde versucht, den Besuch einer Jazz-Band illustrativ so zu interpretieren, wie er aus japanischer Sicht gesehen wird.

177) Pochette pour une symphonie de soul. Couleurs mates.
178) Pochette du disque enregistré par un saxophoniste de jazz. Tons bruns, signes néon verts et rouges.
179) Pochette d'un album double contenant les plus grands succès de Louis Armstrong. Photo prise à la lumière du soir, titre jaune.
180) Pochette d'un disque de soul. Fond bleu-noir, lèvres carminées.
181) Pochette noir-blanc pour un sextette de jazz avec, en vedette, l'Allemand Joki Freund, dont le nom Joki est peut-être à l'origine du titre et de l'interprétation spirituelle que le graphiste en a fait.
182) Pochette d'un disque de jazz. Visage brun, yeux verts, lèvres rouges sur dessin d'ondes bleu et blanc.
183) 184) Composition et pochette complète pour un concert de Cannonball Adderley donné au Japon. L'illustration cherche à traduire les impressions d'un orchestre de jazz occidental en visite au Japon.

183

ARTIST/KÜNSTLER/ARTISTE:

177) Sharleen Pedersen
178) Mike Salisbury
179) Art Kane (Photo)
180) Holger Matthies (Photo)
181) Hans Michel/
     Günther Kieser (Photo)
182) John Van Hammersveld
183) 184) Tom Daly

DESIGNER/GESTALTER:

177) Ronald Wolin
178) Mike Salisbury
179) Job Schönigh
180) Holger Matthies
181) Hans Michel/G. Kieser
182) John Van Hammersveld
183) 184) Tom Daly

ART DIRECTOR:

177) Ronald Wolin
178) Mike Salisbury
180) Jochen Hinze
181) Hans Michel/G. Kieser
182) Norman Seeff
183) 184) Kenneth R. Deardoff

184

PUBLISHER/VERLEGER/EDITEUR:

177) 182) Blue Note/United Artists Records, Los Angeles
178) United Artists Records, Los Angeles
179) TELDEC «Telefunken-Decca» Schallplatten, Hamburg
180) Karussell/Deutsche Grammophon Gesellschaft, Hamburg
181) Lippmann + Rau/CBS Schallplatten, Frankfurt/M
183) 184) Riverside Records, New York

185

186

DESIGNER/GESTALTER/MAQUETTISTE:

187) Heinz Bähr
188) Eberhard Henschel
189)–191) Holger Matthies

ART DIRECTOR/DIRECTEUR ARTISTIQUE:

185) Arnold Meyers
187) Heinz Bähr
188) Eberhard Henschel
189)–191) Peter Sibley

PUBLISHER/VERLEGER/EDITEUR:

185) Roulette Records, New York
186) Brunswick Records, New York
187) MPS Records, Villingen/GER
188) Deutscher Bücherbund/Intercord, Stuttgart
189)–191) Metro/Deutsche Grammophon
　　　　　　Gesellschaft, Hamburg

185) Record cover for a Latin American orchestra.
186) For a recording by Duke Ellington and his band.
187) Cover for a recording of the Grand Prix of Monaco with a superimposed jazz composition.
188) Cover design suggested by a song title.
189)–191) From a series of recordings of music by famous jazz musicians, with abstract colour patterns.

185) Schallplattenhülle für ein lateinamerikanisches Orchester.
186) Für die Ellington-Band. Rosa, hellviolett, rot, schwarz.
187) Saxophonist und Auto-Fan Barney Wilen nahm 1967 den Grand-Prix de Monaco auf, der mit dem Tod Bandinis endete, und schuf um den Soundtrack seine Free-Jazz-Komposition.
188) Photographisch interpretierter Titel (Land der Puppen).
189)–191) Aus einer Serie mit Aufnahmen grosser Jazz-Musiker.

185) Pochette pour le disque d'un orchestre latino-américain.
186) Pochette pour un disque de l'orchestre Duke Ellington.
187) Pochette pour un enregistrement du Grand Prix de Monaco, avec une composition de jazz en surimpression.
188) Design de pochette suggéré par le titre (Pays des poupons).
189)–191) Exemples d'une série d'enregistrements par des musiciens de jazz célèbres. Structures polychromes abstraites.

187

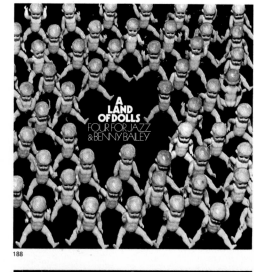

188

ARTIST/KÜNSTLER/ARTISTE:

185) Robert Brownjohn
186) Coordt von Mannstein (Photo)
187) François de Ménil (Photo)
188) Wilm Sehr (Photo)
189)–191) Holger Matthies (Photo)

Jazz

189

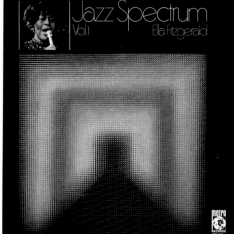

190

THE COUNT BASIE BAND WITH JOE WILLIAMS AND THE DIZZY GILLESPIE BAND AT NEWPORT

V-8560

193

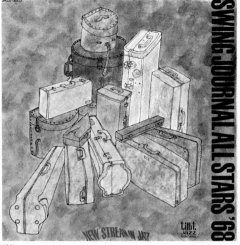

194

195

196

197

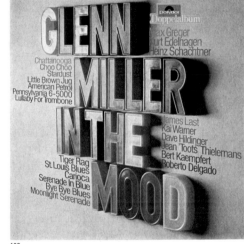

198

ARTIST/KÜNSTLER/ARTISTE:

192) 193) John Murello
194) Makoto Wada
195) Stanislav Zagorski
196) Tomi Ungerer
197) Chas B. Slackman
198) Holger Matthies (Photo)

DESIGNER/ART DIRECTOR:

192) 193) John Murello
194) Ryohei Kojima/Makoto Wada
195) Stanislav Zagorski/Nesuhi Ertegun
196) John Berg/Bob Cato
197) Kenneth R. Deardoff
198) Holger Matthies/Jochen Hinze

PUBLISHER/VERLEGER/EDITEUR:

192) 193) Verve Records/MGM, New York
194) Takt Records, Tokyo
195) Atlantic Recording Corp., New York
196) Columbia Records, New York
197) Riverside Records, New York
198) Polydor/Deutsche Grammophon Ges., Hamburg

192) 193) Two covers using "flags" of lettering from a series of recordings of famous jazz musicians at the Newport Jazz Festival. Fig. 193 with lettering in purple, green, blue and orange on white.
194) From a series of jazz covers. Baggage and instrument cases in pastel shades on a grey ground.
195) Cover for a recording by a jazz quartet. Yellow and red plastic shapes on a blue ground.
196) Graphic treatment of the instrument and title suggesting the life of Broadway and Hollywood stars.
197) For a record made by two English jazz musicians.
198) Double album for evergreens by Glen Miller. Lettering in polychrome plastic.

192) 193) Aus einer Serie mit Aufnahmen berühmter Jazz-Musiker vom Newport Jazz-Festival. Abb. 193: weiss, Schrift in Violett, Grün, Türkis und Orange.
194) Aus einer Serie von Jazz-Platten. Grauer Hintergrund, Gepäck und Instrumentenkoffer in verschiedenen gedämpften Farben, schwarze Schrift.
195) Hülle für Aufnahmen des Modern Jazz Quartet. Formen aus Plastik in Gelb und Himbeerrot auf blauem Grund.
196) Graphische Interpretation von Instrument und Titel: Starleben am Broadway und in Hollywood.
197) Hülle für zwei englische Jazz-Musiker. Beiger Grund.
198) Doppelalbum für Miller-Evergreens. Buchstaben aus farbigem Plastik.

192) 193) Deux pochettes utilisant des assemblages de caractères en drapeaux. Série d'enregistrements de musiciens de jazz célèbres au Festival de Newport. 193) Lettres pourpres, vertes, bleues, orange sur blanc.
194) Exemple d'une série de pochettes pour disques de jazz. Valises et étuis à instruments pastels sur gris.
195) Pochette de disque pour un quartette de jazz. Formes plastiques jaunes et rouges sur fond bleu.
196) Interprétation de l'instrument et titre suggérant la vie des vedettes du Broadway et de Hollywood.
197) Pour le disque de deux musiciens de jazz anglais.
198) Album double groupant des evergreens de Glen Miller. Caractères en plastique polychrome.

199

200

203

204

205

201

202

PUBLISHER/VERLEGER/EDITEUR:

199) United Artists Records, Los Angeles
200) Polydor/Deutsche Grammophon Ges., Hamburg
201) Epic/Columbia Records, New York
202)–204) Columbia Records, New York
205) Creed Taylor, New York
206) Atlantic Recording Corp., New York

199) Front and back of a cover for recordings by a famous jazz pianist. Modelled figures in bright colours.
200) Black-and-white cover for a Dutch jazz pianist.
201) Cover for a record telling the musical story of 52nd Street in New York.
202) Cover for the live recording of a quartet's concert at Carnegie Hall in 1963.
203) Complete cover of a record with Miles Davis.
204) Record for film music by the trumpeter Miles Davis. Yellow car on a silver ground.
205) Photograph of surf used on the front and back of a cover as an interpretation of the title.
206) Record cover for flute solos by a jazz musician. Green figure on orange ground.

199) Geöffnetes Album für Aufnahmen eines Jazz-Pianisten. Himbeerroter Flügel, Fats in hellblauem Anzug.
200) Schwarzweiss-Hülle für Aufnahmen des Jazz-Musikers Bley. Blutstropfen als Symbol des Titels.
201) Mehrfarbige Plattenhülle mit Aufnahmen aus der Musikgeschichte der 52. Strasse in New York.
202) Schwarzweisse Hülle mit Farbaufnahme des Quartetts für ein Live-Konzert aus der Carnegie Hall.
203) Geöffnete Hülle für eine Miles Davis Platte.
204) Plattenhülle für Filmmusik des Jazz-Trompeters Miles Davis. Gelber Wagen, silberner Grund.
205) Aufnahme der Brandung als photographisch interpretierter Titel. Geöffnete Schallplattenhülle für Turrentine.
206) Hülle für Flötenstücke des Jazz-Musikers Herbie Mann. Grüne Gestalt auf orangem Grund.

199) Recto et verso de la pochette du disque d'un célèbre pianiste de jazz. Figures modelées. couleurs vives.
200) Pochette noir-blanc pour le disque d'un pianiste de jazz hollandais.
201) Pochette pour un disque contant l'histoire musicale de la 52e rue, à New York.
202) Pochette pour l'enregistrement du concert d'un quatuor au Carnegie Hall, en 1963.
203) Pochette complète d'un disque de Miles Davis.
204) Pochette pour la musique d'un film exécutée par le trompette Miles Davis. Auto jaune sur fond argenté.
205) Photo des brisants utilisée au recto et verso d'une pochette en interprétation du titre.
206) Pochette d'un disque de soli de flûte par un musicien de jazz. Figure verte sur fond orange.

206

Jazz

Jazz

207

207) Record cover for piano music by Thelonious Monk.
208) Cover of a three-record album from a series of "vintage" recordings, here of a solo singer and pianist.
209) Record for music by a jazz band, the members of which are reflected in the glasses. The same photograph was printed as a negative on the back of the cover.
210) Black-and-white cover, with the name "Sade" in magenta, for jazz compositions.
211) Cover for a recording by a jazz group. Assemblage combined with a bust of the main performer. Colour photograph.
212) Polychrome cover for music by a dance orchestra.

207) Hülle in Blau-, Lila- und Grautönen für Aufnahmen des Jazz-Pianisten Monk. Graphische Interpretation: Hand des Pianisten mit Monks Profil und typischem Spitzbart als Handrücken.
208) Vorderseite einer Kassette für drei Platten des Jazz-Sänger-Komponisten John Lee Hooker.
209) Hülle für eine Platte von Bobby Womack. Die Mitglieder der Band spiegeln sich in den Brillengläsern. Die gleiche Aufnahme, jedoch negativ, wurde für die Rückseite verwendet.
210) Schwarzweiss-Hülle für Jazz-Kompositionen von Schifrin. «Sade» in Himbeerrot.
211) Umschlag für die Platte einer Jazz-Band. Verschiedene Gegenstände und Griffin-Büste mit Portraitphoto auf dunklem Grund.
212) Mehrfarbige Plattenhülle für Aufnahmen des Tanzorchesters von Peter Dean.

207) Pochette pour un disque de piano enregistré par Thelonious Monk.
208) Couverture d'un album de trois disques figurant dans une série de «grands moments musicaux» et mettant ici en vedette un chanteur et un pianiste.
209) Pochette du disque d'un orchestre de jazz, dont les membres apparaissent dans les lunettes. Au verso, on a utilisé une version négative de la même photo.
210) Pochette noir et blanc, le nom de Sade étant imprimé en magenta. Enregistrement d'une composition de jazz
211) Pochette pour un groupe de jazz. Assemblage combiné avec le buste de la vedette du groupe Photo couleur.
212) Pochette polychrome pour un orchestre de musique de danse.

210

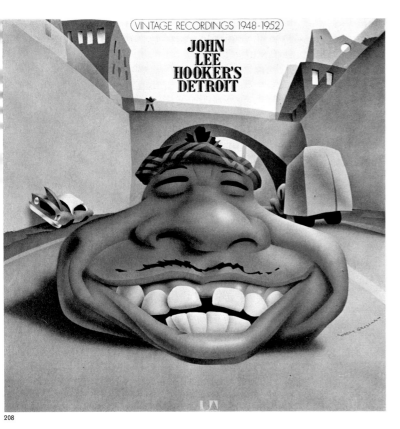

208

209

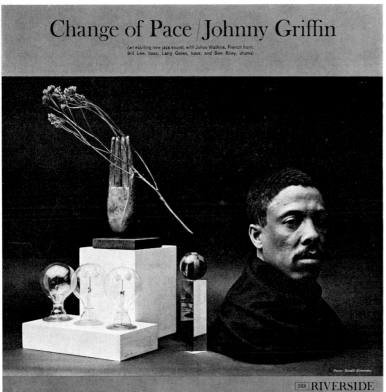

211

212

83

Colman Andrews

Some light music forms, like dance music, and the so-called "easy listening" and "middle-of-the-road" idioms, are sold primarily as background music, as a kind of "musical furniture" (to borrow Satie's term) which simply exists in a room, for the purpose of enhancing a particular mood or perhaps creating one. A slick, romantic photographic style has seemed appropriate as cover illustration for many of these albums—a photographic style characterized by soft focus and diffused lighthing, and by the employment of a kind of romantic heraldry in which subjects like wine bottles, half-filled glasses, beautiful women and pastoral settings are used as symbolic objects to typify the sort of musical feeling presumably expressed within. (The most obvious exception to this school of middle-of-the-road lp illustration is the style developed a decade or more ago under the aegis of Randy Wood of Dot Records: no illustrations of any kind were used, and album after album appeared bearing nothing but the name of the artist and the names of several popular hit songs which he was performing, in repetitious but apparently successful profusion.)

Other types of light music—folk, country and Western, gospel songs, topical protest songs, motion picture sound-tracks, etc.—have each generated their own design styles or variations. In general, it is important to remember that most light music styles are directed at a more general, less sophisticated audience than are, for instance, jazz and classical music.

It is also interesting to consider that, particularly in the fields of gospel and country and Western music, there has been virtually no graphic innovation on the part of record companies who produce these kinds of music exclusively; newcomers to the field may feel free to apply contemporary design concepts to albums in these idioms, but the true best-sellers in the field seldom venture beyond conventional photographic portraiture or embarrassingly sentimental set pieces which would pass for outrageous second degree humour in most circles.

It is worth noting, too, that the independent design of motion-picture and stage-play sound-track album jackets is a relatively recent phenomenon. The overwhelming majority of pre-1966 sound-track album art was simply adapted from promotional art which had originally been designed for the film or play itself. This is still largely the case, but the artist today at least occasionally has the possibility of creating new imagery appropriate to the music, though not necessarily to the music's source.

Einige Formen der leichten Musik, wie Tanzmusik, die sogenannte «Musik zum Träumen» und «leichte Unterhaltungsmusik», werden primär als Hintergrundmusik verkauft, als eine Art «musikalisches Mobiliar» (um Saties Wort anzuwenden), das ganz einfach in einem Raum existiert, um eine bestimmte Stimmung zu fördern oder gar zu schaffen. Für viele dieser Alben schien romantischer Photostil angebracht – ein Photostil, der durch unscharfe Einstellung und diffuses Licht eine sentimentale Stimmung versinnbildlichen soll und mit Weinflaschen, halbvollen Gläsern, schönen Frauen und einem idyllischen Rahmen symbolhaft das von der Platte zu erwartende musikalische Gefühl typisiert. (Die bemerkenswerteste Ausnahme von Albenillustrationen für Unterhaltungsmusik bildet der vor über einem Jahrzehnt unter Randy Wood von Dot Records entwickelte Stil: Es wurde keinerlei Illustration benützt. Auf den Alben erschien nur der Name des Künstlers und die Titel einiger von ihm gesungener Schlager in sich ewig wiederholender, aber offensichtlich erfolgreicher Anordnung.)

Andere Arten leichter Musik – Folk, Country und Western, Gospelsongs, aktuelle Protestsongs, Original-Filmmusik usw. – haben ihren eigenen Designstil oder Variationen hervorgebracht. Es ist im allgemeinen wichtig, im Auge zu behalten, dass leichte Musik meistens auf ein breiteres, weniger kritisches Publikum ausgerichtet ist als zum Beispiel Jazz und klassische Musik. Interessant ist die Tatsache, dass besonders im Bereich von Gospel, Country und Western Musik von seiten der Plattenfirmen, die ausschliesslich diese Art Musik produzieren, so gut wie keine graphische Erneuerung erfolgt ist. Ein Neuling auf diesem Gebiet mag sich nicht gehindert sehen, bei Alben dieses Genres moderne Designvorstellungen anzuwenden, aber die echten Bestseller dieser Kategorie gehen selten über konventionelle Porträtphotos oder peinlich sentimentale Bildarrangements hinaus, die in den meisten Kreisen als ausgesprochen zweitklassiger Humor gelten würden.

Bemerkenswert ist, dass das unabhängige Design von Plattenhüllen für Film- und Bühnen-Originalaufnahmen eine relativ neue Erscheinung ist. Die überwältigende Mehrheit der Graphik aller Original-ton-Alben wurde in der Zeit vor 1966 einfach aus der Werbung übernommen, die ursprünglich für den Film oder das Bühnenstück entworfen worden war. Grösstenteils ist es dabei auch geblieben, aber heute hat der Künstler wenigstens gelegentlich die Möglichkeit, eine neue Bildersprache zu schaffen, die sich auf die Musik bezieht und ihr entspricht.

Certaines formes de musique légère telles que la musique de danse et ce que l'on pourrait qualifier d'«écoute-bête» par analogie avec «pense-bête», ou de «musique du juste milieu», sont diffusées principalement comme musique d'ambiance, comme «ameublement musical» (pour parler comme Erik Satie), comme sonorisation d'une pièce contribuant au confort spatial des occupants. D'où le style photographique romantique employé avec discernement pour les pochettes des disques du genre et combinant les contours flous avec un éclairage diffus et une symbolique de vague-à-l'âme appropriée: bouteilles de vin, verres à demi remplis, belles femmes, décors champêtres – le tout censé exprimer parfaitement la radiation sentimentale se dégageant de cette musique. Toute règle comportant son exception, il faut mentionner ici une approche toute différente: le style développé il y a un peu plus d'une décennie sous l'égide de Randy Wood, pour Dot Records: aucune illustration, juste le nom du musicien et les titres des tubes qu'il interprète employés à profusion de façon répétitive, avec un succès confirmé.

Les autres genres de musique légère – populaire, country, western, gospel, chansons de contestation, bandes sonores de films, etc. – ont produit des styles ou variations graphiques spécifiques pour chaque catégorie. Il faut bien se représenter que la musique légère s'adresse en général à un public bien plus vaste et moins différencié, moins cultivé aussi que, mettons, le jazz ou la musique classique. Il est aussi instructif d'observer que les producteurs spécialisés dans la musique de gospel, country et western ou analogues n'ont risqué aucune innovation graphique de taille. Les nouveaux venus dans ce domaine ont toute liberté d'appliquer les concepts graphiques modernes à leurs pochettes, mais les best-sellers du genre, eux, restent fidèles à un style photographique conventionnel platement descriptif ou à des mises en scènes d'un sentimentalisme outré qu'un public évolué prendrait sans hésiter pour de l'humour larvé.

Autre trait intéressant à noter: le design des pochettes de bandes sonores (cinéma et théâtre) n'a acquis que très récemment son indépendance. La grande majorité des pochettes de ce genre réalisées avant 1966 se contentaient de reprendre les éléments publicitaires ayant servi à la promotion du film ou du spectacle. La tradition pèse encore lourdement dans ce domaine, mais le créateur graphique des années 70 a tout de même les coudées un peu plus franches et peut à l'occasion se permettre le luxe d'une visualisation nouvelle de la musique sans rapport avec son décor d'origine.

Light Music
Unterhaltungsmusik
Musique légère

Dance Music
Hits/Chansons
Spirituals
Folk Songs
Protest Songs
Film Music

Tanzmusik
Hits/Chansons
Spirituals
Volkslieder
Protestlieder
Filmmusik

Musique de danse
Hits/Chansons
Spirituals
Musique populaire
Chansons contestataires
Bandes sonores

213

214

215

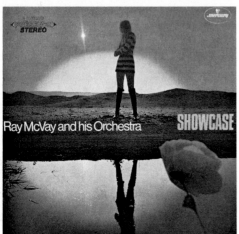

216

217

218

ARTIST/KÜNSTLER/ARTISTE:

213) Don S. Bronstein (Photo)
214) 215) Roland Young (Photo)
216) Helmut Schiefer (Photo)
217) Kai Brune (Photo)
218) Jeff Niki (Photo)
219) 220) Cliff McReynolds

DESIGNER/ART DIRECTOR:

213) James J. Griffith
214) 215) Roland Young/George Osaki
216) Helmut Schiefer/Hans Leyssius
217) Dieter Schwarz/Jochen Hinze
218) Yoshio Nakanishi/Eiko Ishioka
219) 220) Dave Bhang/Ed Thrasher

PUBLISHER/VERLEGER/ÉDITEUR:

213) Cadet Records, Chicago
214) 215) Capitol Records, Hollywood
216) Mercury/Phonogram, Baarn
217) Polydor/Deutsche Grammophon Ges., Hamburg
218) CBS/Sony Records, Tokyo
219) 220) Reprise/Warner Bros. Records, Burbank, Ca.

213) Photographic record cover for string arrangements of popular tunes.
214) Full-colour cover for music by a famous dance band.
215) For dance music by a well-known pianist.
216) Cover for music by a dance orchestra using a specially made colour photograph.
217) Polychrome cover for orchestral arrangements of dance tunes on the subject of holidays.
218) From a series of record covers for popular hits. Front in shades of green with the same photograph reversed in blue shades on the back.
219) 220) Complete cover and detail of artwork for recordings by a rock group.

213) Schallplattenhülle für bekannte Schlager.
214) Mehrfarbige Hülle für eine Tanzplatte einer Band.
215) Plattenhülle für Stücke eines bekannten Pianisten, der zum Tanz aufspielt.
216) Grosszügige Photographie für die Plattenhülle eines Tanzorchesters. Roter Himmel, graugrüner Sand.
217) Mehrfarbige Plattenhülle für Schlager, die an die Ferien erinnern, von Kai Warner und seinem Orchester.
218) Aus einer Serie von Plattenhüllen für Aufnahmen bekannter Hits mit Ray Coniff. Vorderseite in hellen Grüntönen, Rückseite mit gegengleicher Photo in Blau.
219) 220) Illustration und vollständige Hülle für Aufnahmen der Rockgruppe Savage Grace.

213) Pochette photographique pour des arrangements de musique populaire pour instruments à cordes.
214) Pochette pour un orchestre de danse réputé.
215) Pour de la musique de danse par un pianiste renommé.
216) Pochette pour l'enregistrement d'un orchestre de danse. Photo couleur spéciale.
217) Couverture polychrome pour des arrangements de musique de danse estivale pour orchestre.
218) Exemple d'une série de pochettes pour des enregistrements de tubes. Recto aux tons verts; au verso, même photo, mais inversée et imprimée en divers tons bleus.
219) 220) Pochette complète et détail de la composition pour un disque enregistré par un groupe de rock.

Dance Music
Tanzmusik
Musique de danse

221

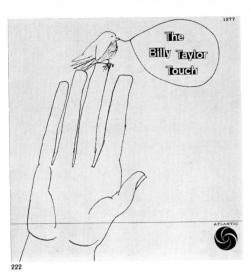

222

223

ARTIST/KÜNSTLER/ARTISTE:

221) Heinrich Weippert
222) Marvin Israel
223) John McEuen
224) Rod Dyer (Photo)
225) Milton Glaser
226) Malcolm Hart/Fred Eng (Photo)
227) Giancarlo Buonfino
228) Peter Wandrey
229) 230) Heinz Huke

DESIGNER/GESTALTER/MAQUETTISTE:

222) Margaret Ponce-Israel
223) Paul Bruhwiler, Inc.
224) John Van Hammersveld
225) John Crocker
226) Matsuo Yasumura
227) Giancarlo Buonfino
228) Peter Wandrey
229) 230) Heinz Huke

ART DIRECTOR/DIRECTEUR ARTISTIQUE:

222) Marvin Israel
223) 224) Norman Seeff
225) John Berg/Bob Cato
226) Stephen O. Frankfurt
228) Peter Schmidt
229) 230) Tostmann Werbeagentur

224

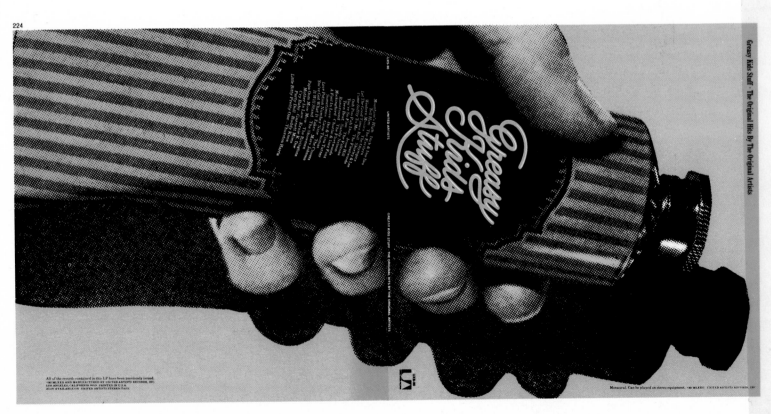

221) Cover for a recording of a selection of modern hits. Four colours, red ground.
222) Cover for renderings by a well-known jazz musician.
223) Cover of a double album recording the influence of Bob Wills on country music. Hand-coloured photograph of band.
224) Front and back of an album of evergreens played by the original artists.
225) Cover for a "recital" by a beat group.
226) Record cover for dance music.
227) Cover for a recording of modern dances.
228) Cover for songs to the guitar.
229) Record cover for a musical journey. Brightly coloured waves on a black ground, white lettering.
230) For a recording of the hits of 1970. Orange, pink and mauve record, green ground.

221) Mehrfarbige Illustration auf rotem Grund. Schallplattenhülle für bekannte Schlager.
222) Plattenhülle für Modern-Jazz-Stücke.
223) Hülle eines Doppelalbums mit handkolorierter Photo für Aufnahmen von Bob Wills, einem Begründer der amerikanischen Country-Musik.
224) Vorder- und Rückseite einer Plattenhülle für bekannte Evergreens. Alles sind Originalaufnahmen mit den ursprünglichen Musikern und Orchestern.
225) Schallplattenhülle für Schlagermusik.
226) Umschlag für eine Tanzmusikplatte, was durch die Aufnahme angedeutet wird.
227) Umschlag einer Platte mit Musik zu modernen Tänzen.
228) Umschlag einer Schlagerplatte.
229) Plattenhülle für «Eine Reise mit Musik». Wellen in popigen Farben auf schwarzem Grund, weisse Schrift.
230) Für eine Platte mit den besten Hits des Jahres 1970. Grün, halbe Schallplatte in Rot, Rosa und Lila gestreift.

221) Pochette pour une sélection de tubes modernes. Quatre couleurs, fond rouge.
222) Pochette pour le récital d'un musicien de jazz renommé.
223) Pochette d'un album double montrant ce que la country music doit à Bob Wills. Photo coloriée main de l'orchestre.
224) Recto et verso d'un album d'evergreens joués par les musiciens qui les ont créés.
225) Pochette pour le "récital" d'un groupe de beat.
226) Pochette d'un disque de musique de danse.
227) Pochette pour un disque de musique de danse moderne.
228) Pochette d'un disque de chansons pour guitare.
229) Pochette d'un disque présentant un voyage musical. Vagues aux couleurs vives sur fond noir, lettres blanches.
230) Pochette d'une sélection des tubes de 1970. Disque orange, rose et mauve sur fond vert.

PUBLISHER/VERLEGER/EDITEUR:
221) Fa. Saar, Milan
222) Atlantic Recording Corp., New York
223) 224) United Artists Records, Los Angeles
225) Columbia Records, New York
226) Young & Rubicam, New York
227) Bel Air, Milan
228) Tip Schallplattenproduktion, Hamburg
229) Karussell/Deutsche Grammophon Ges., Hamburg
230) Tip/Deutsche Grammophon Ges., Hamburg

**Dance Music / Tanzmusik
Musique de danse**

225

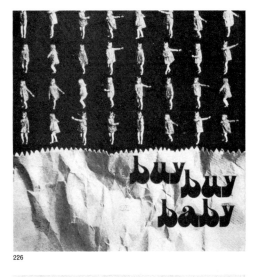

226

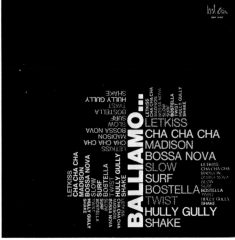

227

228

229

230

Dance Music
Tanzmusik
Musique de danse

PUBLISHER/VERLEGER/EDITEUR:

231) Tip/Deutsche Grammophon Gesellschaft, Hamburg
232) 242) Polydor/Deutsche Grammophon Ges., Hamburg
233) Reprise/Warner Bros. Records, Burbank, Ca.
234) Universal City Records, Los Angeles
235) 235a) 236) Kindler & Schiermeyer Verlag, München
237) Columbia Records, New York
238) Karussell/Deutsche Grammophon Ges., Hamburg
239) Fontana/Phonogram, London
240) Troubadour Records, London
241) Amadeo, Österr. Schallplatten AG, Wien
243) Command Records, New York

235

235a

231

232

236

237

ARTIST/KÜNSTLER/ARTISTE:

231) 232) 238) 242) Holger Matthies (Photo)
233) Al Medoro
234) Don Weller
235) Marino Averara (Photo)
235a) David Hamilton (Photo)
236) Guido Mangold
237) Ginger Tilly
239) Brian Pike
240) Bob Gill (Photo)
241) Erich Buchegger (Photo)
243) George Giusti

DESIGNER/GESTALTER/MAQUETTISTE:

231) 232) 238) 242) Holger Matthies
234) Tom Lazarus
240) Bob Gill
241) Erich Buchegger

ART DIRECTOR/DIRECTEUR ARTISTIQUE:

231) 232) 238) 242) Jochen Hinze
233) Merle Shore
234) John LePrevost
235) 235a) 236) Dieter Kaulmann
237) Dick O'Brian
239) Leo G. Schofield
243) Daniel Pezza

240

241

90

233

231) For a recording of popular tunes by a beat group. Colour photograph on grey ground.
232) From a series of record covers, with twenty-eight hits played by a well-known dance orchestra. Brightly coloured darts on a black ground.
233) Record cover for dance tunes. Polychrome title.
234) Record cover for music by a beat group. The artwork takes up the suggestion of the title.
235) 235a) 236) Two double spreads from a booklet and cover of the album for "Music for two" in which the booklet was inserted.
237) Record cover for a jazz quartet with the Hammond organ as a solo instrument.
238) For homage to Nat King Cole played by a trio. Dark blue ground with colour insert.
239) Polychrome cover for a selection of pop hits.
240) Cover for a selection of light music. Black and white with red label.
241) Record cover for a piano medley. Colour photograph. From a series.
242) The cover of this record refers to the prohibition of jazz music on the radio and in public in Germany in 1935. Black and white.
243) Record cover for music by a brass band, using a three-dimensional composition in brass.

234

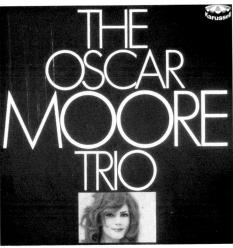

238

231) Hülle für eine Schlagerplatte. Hellblauer Grund.
232) Aus einer Serie von Plattenhüllen für 28 Hits des bekannten Tanzorchesters von Kai Warner. Schwarzer Grund, Pfeile in verschiedenen bunten Farben.
233) Tanzmusikplatte. Schwarze Linien, Titel mehrfarbig.
234) Plattenhülle für eine Liedersammlung. Graphische Interpretation des Titels (Die Welt in einer Muschel).
235) 235a) 236) Zwei Doppelseiten einer eingefügten Broschüre und Plattenumschlag für «Musik für zwei».
237) Titel und Soloinstrument (Hammondorgel) werden in der Illustration angedeutet. Für ein Jazzquartett.
238) Für Stücke eines Trios in Erinnerung an Nat King Cole. Dunkelblauer Grund, weisse Schrift, Farbphoto.
239) Mehrfarbige Hülle für eine Schlagerparade.
240) Schallplattenhülle für Unterhaltungsmusik. Schwarzweiss, rotes Plattenlabel.
241) Mehrfarbige Hülle für leichte Unterhaltung am Klavier.
242) Der Titel dieser Platte bezieht sich auf das in Deutschland 1935 verfügte Verbot, Jazz am Radio und in der Öffentlichkeit zu spielen. Weiter getanzt und gespielt wurde die gleiche Musik unter dem Decknamen «Swing». Schwarzweiss.
243) Hülle für Blechmusik. Komposition aus Blech als Umschlagillustration in Anlehnung an die Instrumente.

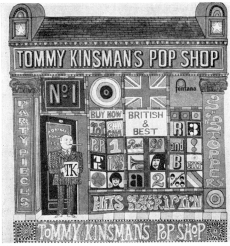

239

242

231) Pour un enregistrement de mélodies populaires par un groupe de beat. Photo couleur sur fond gris.
232) Exemple d'une série de pochettes, avec 28 tubes joués par un orchestre de danse réputé. Fléchettes aux couleurs vives sur fond noir.
233) Pochette pour de la musique de danse. Titre polychrome.
234) Pochette de disque pour un groupe de beat. La composition interprète la suggestion contenue dans le titre.
235) 235a) 236) Deux doubles pages d'un livret et la pochette de l'album contenant ce livret, intitulé «Music for two» (Musique pour deux).
237) Pochette pour le disque d'un quartette de jazz. Orgue Hammond solo.
238) Pour le disque d'un trio, offert en hommage à Nat King Cole. Fond bleu foncé, photo couleur.
239) Pochette polychrome pour une sélection de tubes.
240) Pochette pour une sélection de musique légère. Noir et blanc, étiquette rouge.
241) Pochette de série. Pot-pourri de piano. Photo couleur.
242) La pochette de ce disque fait allusion à l'interdiction du jazz à la radio et dans les spectacles publics en Allemagne, en 1935. Noir et blanc.
243) Pochette pour le disque d'une fanfare, comportant une composition tridimensionnelle en cuivre.

243

Dance Music / Tanzmusik

244) Photographic cover for a singer. Face in blue shades.
245) Complete cover for a recording by a beat group, whose portraits appear on the cigarette.
246) Complete drawn cover, incorporating a portrait of the musician, for pieces played by a string quartet.
247) Cover for a hit parade. Colour photography.
248) Polychrome cover for music from a Broadway hit.
249) 250) From a series of records of European music using colour photographs framed in standard typography.
251) Cover for light music making use of a painting by the Belgian artist René Magritte.
252) Polychrome cover for electronic interpretations of well-known compositions.

244) Schallplattenhülle für einen Sänger. Dunkle Blautöne.
245) Vorder- und Rückseite der Hülle einer Schlagerplatte. Die Mitglieder der Band sind auf der Zigarette abgebildet.
246) Geöffnete Hülle für Unterhaltungsmusik mit Burt Bacharach.
247) Schallplattenhülle für eine Schlagerhitparade. Wassermelone auf blaugrünem Grund.
248) Mehrfarbiger Umschlag mit Musik eines Broadway-Hits.
249) 250) Aus einer einheitlich gestalteten Serie mit runder Farbphoto und grosser Schrift als Identifikation der Reihe.
251) Plattenhülle für leichte Musik. Als Umschlagillustration wurde ein Bild Magrittes verwendet.
252) Mehrfarbige Plattenhülle für elektronische Interpretationen bekannter Stücke.

244) Pochette photo pour un chanteur. Visage aux tons bleus.
245) Pochette complète pour l'enregistrement d'un groupe de beat dont les portraits figurent sur la cigarette.
246) Pochette dessinée complète, avec le portrait du musicien, pour des œuvres jouées par un quatuor à cordes.
247) Pochette pour une hit parade. Photo couleur.
248) Pochette polychrome pour une pièce à succès du Broadway.
249) 250) Exemples d'une série de pochettes de musique européenne. Photos couleurs, encadrement de typo uniforme.
251) Pochette pour un disque de musique légère. Peinture du surréaliste René Magritte.
252) Pochette polychrome pour des interprétations électroniques de morceaux célèbres.

244

ARTIST/KÜNSTLER/ARTISTE:

244) John Rowlands (Photo)
245) Graphicteam (Photo)
246) Masamichi Soikawa
247) Michael Rosenfeld (Photo)
248) Lionel Kalish
249) 250) Bart Mulder (Photo)
251) René Magritte

DESIGNER/GESTALTER/MAQUETTISTE:

244) Anthony Battaglia/Vito Laudadio
245) Graphicteam
246) Masamichi Soikawa
247) Fact-Design
248) John Berg
249) 250) Cor Van Tol
251) Richard Mantel
252) Tostmann Werbeagentur

245

247

246

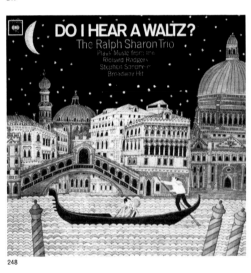

248

251

252

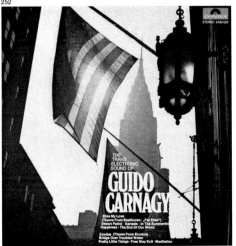

ART DIRECTOR/DIRECTEUR ARTISTIQUE:

244) Anthony Battaglia/Vito Laudadio
245) Graphicteam
246) Masamichi Soikawa
247) 252) Stefan Böhle
248) John Berg/Bob Cato
249) 250) Cor Van Tol

PUBLISHER/VERLEGER/EDITEUR:

244) GRT of Canada, Willowdale, Ont.
245) Cornet Music, Köln
246) Japan Philips Co., Tokyo
247) Karussell/Deutsche Grammophon Gesellschaft, Hamburg
248) 251) Columbia Records, New York
249) 250) Mercury/Phonogram, Baarn
252) Polydor/Deutsche Grammophon Gesellschaft, Hamburg

93

253) Record cover for 16 country and Western hits.
254) Cover for songs by a Western group.
255) For a recording by a singer of folk music.
256) Cover for negro spirituals by three black singers.
257) Cover for a concert recorded live in New York, incorporating the Manhattan skyline.
258) Cover for songs composed by a protest singer. Grey and yellow, with orange title.
259) Polychrome cover for songs by a black soloist.
260) Polychrome cover suggesting a Mississippi steamboat, for negro spirituals and blues.
261) 261a) Complete cover and back of an album of recordings by a black singer.
262) "Camp" cover for recordings by a number of popular singers and musicians.

253) Für amerikanische Volksmusik und Cowboy-Lieder.
254) Plattenhülle für Lieder aus dem amerikanischen Westen.
255) Für Aufnahmen des Volksliedersängers van Zandt.
256) Schallplattenhülle für Negro Spirituals, gesungen von drei schwarzen Sängerinnen.
257) Hülle eines Live-Konzerts aus New York, mit New-yorker Skyline im Anklang an den Titel.
258) Umschlag in Grau und Gelb, Titel in Orange, für Protestlieder eines Sängers und Komponisten.
259) Mehrfarbige Hülle für Songs von David Newman, mit Rettungsring als Anspielung auf den Titel.
260) Mehrfarbige Plattenhülle mit stilisiertem Mississippi-Dampfer als Umschlagillustration für Spirituals und Blues.
261) 261a) Geöffnete Hülle und Rückseite eines Albums mit Liedern von Tony Williams.
262) Mehrfarbige Plattenhülle für Schlagermusik.

253) Pochette pour 16 tubes de musique country et western.
254) Pochette pour les chansons d'un groupe de western.
255) Pour le disque d'un chanteur d'airs populaires.
256) Pour trois chanteurs noirs de negro spirituals.
257) Pochette d'un concert enregistré en direct à New York, avec la silhouette de Manhattan.
258) Pochette pour un chanteur contestataire. Gris et jaune, titre orange.
259) Pochette polychrome pour le disque d'un chanteur noir.
260) Pochette polychrome avec illustration évoquant un bateau sur le Mississippi, pour un disque de negro spirituals et de blues.
261) 261a) Pochette complète et verso d'un album contenant les enregistrements d'un chanteur noir.
262) Pochette pour un disque enregistré par plusieurs chanteurs et musiciens populaires.

253

254

258

259

261

261 a

262

255

256

257

260

ARTIST/KÜNSTLER/ARTISTE:

253) Mike Dempsey
254) Jerome Martin
255) 262) Milton Glaser
256) Don Weller
257) Mike Naiki
258) Tom Wilson
259) Stanislav Zagorski
260) Hanspeter Wyss
261) 261a) Michael Gross

DESIGNER/GESTALTER/MAQUETTISTE:

253) Mike Dempsey
255) Milton Glaser
256) Tom Lazarus
257) Ronald Wolin
258) John Berg
259) Stanislav Zagorski
260) Oswald Dubacher
261) 261a) Michael Gross
262) Rod Dyer

ART DIRECTOR/DIRECTEUR ARTISTIQUE:

253) John Hayes
254) Bob Cato
255) Kevin Eggers
256) John LePrevost
257) Ronald Wolin
258) John Berg
259) Mark Schulman
260) Oswald Dubacher
261) 261a) Michael Gross
262) George Osaki

PUBLISHER/VERLEGER/EDITEUR:

253) Columbia Records, London
254) Epic/Columbia Records, New York
255) Poppy Records, New York
256) Universal City Records, Los Angeles
257) United Artists Records, Los Angeles
258) Columbia Records, New York
259) Atlantic Recording Corp., New York
260) Ex Libris, Zürich
261) 261a) Polydor, New York
262) Capitol Records, Hollywood

Songs / Hits / Chansons

263

264

Songs / Hits / Chansons

265

266

267

268

263) Cover for a recording by a popular girl singer. Photograph in sandwich technique with cloth texture effect.
264) Cover of an album for a German singer.
265) From a series of ten records by a well-known French chansonnier. All the covers use photographs taken in the workshop of the guitar maker Favino in Paris.
266) *Trompe-l'oeil* cover for a recording of country music.
267) Cover for a record by a Dutch singer. Colour photograph "torn" to make room for the name.
268) Record cover for a popular singer.
269) 270) Complete cover and detail of the colour photograph for a recording by Ferrante and Teicher.

263) Aufnahme in Sandwich-Technik mit grober Stoffstruktur für eine Platte der Schlagersängerin Melanie. Brauntöne.
264) Album für den deutschen Schlagersänger Udo Jürgens.
265) Aus einer Serie von 10 Platten mit Aufnahmen des bekannten französischen Chansonniers Georges Brassens. Einheitliche Gestaltung der Serie mit Photographien aus dem Atelier des Lautenbauers Favoin in Paris.
266) Mehrfarbige Hülle für Country-Musik.
267) Hülle für einen holländischen Schlagersänger. Zerrissene Farbphoto mit eingestripptem Namen.
268) Plattenhülle für den französischen Sänger Johnny Hallyday.
269) 270) Vollständige Hülle und Detail der Photo für eine Platte mit Unterhaltungsmusik.

263) Pochette pour le disque d'une jeune chanteuse. Photo en sandwich avec effet de texture textile.
264) Pochette d'un album enregistré par un chanteur allemand.
265) Exemple d'une série de 10 pochettes pour le célèbre chansonnier français Brassens. Les photos ont été prises dans l'atelier parisien du luthier Favino, spécialiste des guitares.
266) Pochette en trompe-l'oeil pour un disque de country.
267) Pochette pour le disque d'un chanteur hollandais. Photo couleur déchirée pour faire place au nom.
268) Pochette de disque pour un chanteur populaire.
269) 270) Pochette complète et détail de la photo couleur pour un disque de Ferrante et Teicher.

PUBLISHER/VERLEGER/EDITEUR:

263) Barclay Disques, Paris
264) Ariola-Eurodisc, München
265) 268) Phonogram, Paris
266) Columbia Records, New York
267) Phonogram, Baarn
269) 270) United Artists Records, Los Angeles

PHOTOGRAPHER/PHOTOGRAPH:

263) Bernard Leloup
264) M. Bockelmann
265) Jacques Denimal
266) Don Hunstein/Sandy Speiser
267) Bart Mulder
268) Jean-Marie Perier/Bob Elia
269) 270) Frank Laffitte

DESIGNER:

263) Alain Marouani
264) M.+M. Vormstein
265) André Decamp
266) Richard Mantel
267) Martijn Hagoort
268) R. Laplace
269) 270) Paul Bruhwiler

ART DIRECTOR:

263) Alain Marouani
264) M.+M. Vormstein
265) A. Trouvé
266) John Berg
267) Chris Thiele
268) R. Laplace
269) 270) Norman Seeff

269

©MCMLXXII

271

271) 272) Detail of the photograph and complete cover of a record by two well-known singers from Israel.
273) Black-and-white cover for a record by a popular American singer.
274) Complete record cover for a collection of songs. Full colour.
275) Cover for a "pastorale" by a popular Dutch girl singer. Colour photograph chiefly in shades of green.
276) Polychrome cover for romantic tunes played by an orchestra.

271) 272) Detail der Aufnahme und vollständige Hülle eines Albums von Esther und Abi Ofarim, zwei israelischen Chansonniers.
273) Schwarzweisshülle für eine Platte der amerikanischen Sängerin Barbra Streisand.
274) Geöffnete Schallplattenhülle für Songs. Mehrfarbig.
275) Plattenhülle für Aufnahmen einer holländischen Sängerin. Die Farbphoto – vorwiegend in Grüntönen – soll die Stimmung der Musik wiedergeben.
276) Mehrfarbige Hülle für Schlager eines Unterhaltungsorchesters.

271) 272) Détail de la photo et pochette complète pour le disque de deux chanteurs israéliens célèbres, Esther et Abi Ofarim.
273) Pochette noir et blanc pour le disque d'une chanteuse américaine populaire.
274) Pochette complète pour un recueil de chansons. En polychromie.
275) Pochette pour une «pastorale» enregistrée par une chanteuse hollandaise populaire. Photo couleur avec prédominance de tons verts.
276) Pochette polychrome pour un concert d'orchestre romantique

PUBLISHER/VERLEGER/EDITEUR:

271) 272) Phonogram, London
273) Columbia Records, New York
274) Capitol Records, Hollywood
275) 276) Phonogram, Baarn

272

98

Je m'appelle Barbra

STEREO

What Now My Love
Autumn Leaves
Speak to Me of Love
Once Upon a Summertime
I Wish You Love
Free Again
Martina
Le Mur
I've Been Here
Love and Learn
Clopin Clopant
Ma Première Chanson

273

A Gift From Euphoria

274

liesbeth list pastorale

275

LOVE TOKEN

MYSTIC MOODS ORCHESTRA

276

PHOTOGRAPHER/PHOTOGRAPH/PHOTOGRAPHE:

271) 272) John Kelly
273) Richard Avedon
274) Ken Veeder
275) Eddy Posthuma De Boer
276) Helmut Schiefer

DESIGNER/GESTALTER/MAQUETTISTE:

271) 272) Alan Aldridge
273) John Berg
274) John Hoernle
275) Cor Van Tol
276) Helmut Schiefer

ART DIRECTOR/DIRECTEUR ARTISTIQUE:

271) 272) Alan Aldridge
273) Bob Cato/John Berg
274) George Osaki
275) Cor Van Tol/Chris Thiele
276) Hans Leyssius

Songs / Hits / Chansons

277

278

279

280

277) Polychrome cover for a recording of Russian folk songs.
278) 283) Two covers painted by the Austrian artist Erich Brauer for his own musical compositions. Brauer sings his songs to the lute and guitar.
279) 280) Covers of two double albums for live recordings of American folk blues festivals in Germany, 1965 and 1970. Both in full colour.
281) 282) From a series of small record covers in black and one colour with chansons by Bernese singers.

277) Mehrfarbige Plattenhülle für russische Volkslieder.
278) 283) Zwei von Arik (Erich) Brauer für seine Eigenkompositionen gemalte Plattenhüllen. Brauer ist Kunstmaler, daneben komponiert und singt er und begleitet sich dazu auf der Laute und Gitarre.
279) 280) Hüllen von zwei Doppelalben für Live-Aufnahmen von Folk-Blues-Festivals in Deutschland.
281) 282) Aus einer Serie zweifarbiger Plattenhüllen mit Chansons einze!ner Mitglieder der Berner Troubadours.

277) Pochette polychrome. Chansons populaires russes.
278) 283) Deux pochettes peintes par l'artiste, Erich Brauer, pour des enregistrements de ses propres chansons, qu'il interprète en s'accompagnant du luth et de la guitare.
279) 280) Pochettes en couleurs de deux albums doubles. Enregistrements directs de festivals populaires de blues en Allemagne, 1965 et 1970.
281) 282) Exemples d'une série de pochettes de petit format pour des disques de chansons bernoises. Noir et une couleur.

281   282

ARTIST/KÜNSTLER/ARTISTE:

277) Heinrich Weippert
278) 283) Erich (Arik) Brauer
279) Günther Kieser (Photo)
280) Volker Hartmann (Photo)
281) 282) Kurt Wirth

DESIGNER/GESTALTER/MAQUETTISTE:

279) 280) Günther Kieser
281) 282) Kurt Wirth

ART DIRECTOR/DIRECTEUR ARTISTIQUE:

280) Günther Kieser
281) 282) Kurt Wirth

PUBLISHER/VERLEGER/EDITEUR:

277) Fa. Saar, Milan
278) Polydor/ORF, Wien
279) Fontana/Phonogram/Lippmann+Rau
280) CBS Schallplatten/Lippmann+Rau, Frankfurt/M.
281) 282) Zytglogge Verlag, Bern
283) Galerie Sydow, Frankfurt/M.

Songs / Hits / Chansons

ARTIST/KÜNSTLER/ARTISTE:

284) 285) Heinz Edelmann
286) Nicole Claveloux
287) Roger Hane
288) Bill Basso
289) Ron Bradford
290) David Smee

DESIGNER/GESTALTER/MAQUETTISTE:

286) Alain Marouani
287) Ron Coro
288) Acy R. Lehman
289) Howard Blume

ART DIRECTOR/DIRECTEUR ARTISTIQUE:

284) 285) Günther Halden
286) Alain Marouani
287) John Berg/Edwin Lee
288) Acy R. Lehman
289) Howard Blume
290) Clare Osborn

PUBLISHER/VERLEGER/EDITEUR:

284) 285) Twen/Deutsche Grammophon
Gesellschaft, Hamburg
286) Vanguard/Barclay Disques, Paris
287) Columbia Records, New York
288) MGM Records, New York
289) Chess Records, Chicago
290) EMI/Music for Pleasure, London

285

286

287

288

284) 285) Artwork and complete cover of a double album of country and Western songs by the late Hank Williams.
286) Record cover for electric music by a group. The design alludes to the title ("for the mind and body").
287) Record cover for beat music. The artwork refers to one of the songs entitled *Magic Carpet Ride*. Orange and yellow carpet, green hands, dark blue ground.
288) Record cover for a selection of "jungle" songs from a series of fun classics.
289) Cover for new interpretations of evergreens.
290) Polychrome cover for a small record of humorous songs.

284) 285) Illustration und vollständige Vorderseite eines Doppelalbums mit Songs von Hank Williams.
286) Hülle für «elektrische» Country-Musik, mit Anspielung auf den Titel (für Geist und Körper). Gelber und blauer Grund.
287) Typisches Sujet als Illustration des Plattentitels «Gen Osten». Fliegender Teppich in Orange und Gelb, giftgrüne Hände auf dunkelblauem Grund.
288) Schallplattenhülle für «Dschungel»-Lieder.
289) Plattenhülle in matten Farben für Billy Stewarts Neuinterpretationen alter Songs.
290) Mehrfarbige Hülle einer kleinen Platte für Songs.

284) 285) Composition et pochette complète d'un album double de chansons country et western par feu Hank Williams.
286) Pochette pour le disque de musique électrique d'un groupe. Allusion au titre («pour le corps et l'esprit»).
287) Pochette pour un disque de beat. Le thème se rapporte à l'une des chansons, *Magic Carpet Ride*. Tapis volant orange, jaune, mains vertes, fond bleu foncé.
288) Pochette pour une sélection de chansons de la «jungle». Collection de classiques de l'humour.
289) Pochette pour des versions nouvelles d'evergreens.
290) Pochette polychrome pour un petit disque de chansons.

289

290

Songs / Hits / Chansons

ARTIST/KÜNSTLER/ARTISTE:

291) Verlinde
292) Alain Marouani (Photo)
293) Ron Schwerin (Photo)
294) Rick Mayerowitz
295) Georges Tourdjman (Photo)
296) Slick Lawson (Photo)

DESIGNER/GESTALTER/MAQUETTISTE:

291) 292) 295) Claude Caudron
293) Richard Mantel
294) Tony Lane
296) Bill Barnes

ART DIRECTOR/DIRECTEUR ARTISTIQUE:

291) 292) 295) Alain Marouani
293) Richard Mantel
294) John Berg
296) John Berg/Bill Barnes

PUBLISHER/VERLEGER/EDITEUR:

291) Riviera/Barclay Disques, Paris
292) 295) Barclay Disques, Paris
293) Epic/Columbia Records, New York
294) 296) Columbia Records, New York

291

291) Polychrome cover for a record by a French chansonnier, using a surrealist painting entitled *Le Métronome* by the artist Verlinde.
292) Cover for a selection of humorous songs by Henri Salvador. Superimposed photographs, predominantly in blue shades.
293) Colour photograph of hands as a record cover for a popular singer.
294) Cover for a recording of evergreens by two old-time favourites.
295) Enlargement of the actual record used as a cover for French chansons. Side two of the record is used as the back cover.
296) Double-exposure photography in blue shades for a song recording.

291) Mehrfarbige Hülle für die Platte «Métronomie» des französischen Chansonniers Nino Ferrer. Auf dem Umschlag wurde ein Bild von Verlinde mit dem Titel *Le Métronome* verwendet.
292) Plattenhülle für lustige Chansons von Henri Salvador. Übereinanderkopierte Photographien mit Anspielung auf den Titel. Vorwiegend Blautöne.
293) Hülle für eine Auswahl von Songs von Bobby Hebb.
294) Schallplattenhülle für Evergreens von zwei bekannten Stars von Gestern. Mehrfarbig. Mae West mit hellblauen Federn am Hut.
295) Vergrösserte Aufnahme der Schallplatte als Hülle für französische Chansons von Michel Delpech. Die 2. Seite der Schallplatte dient als Rückseite der Hülle.
296) Schallplattenhülle für Songs von Danny Epps. Doppelt belichtete Photo in verschiedenen Blautönen.

291) Pochette polychrome pour le disque d'un chansonnier français, d'après le tableau surréaliste de Verlinde *Le Métronome*.
292) Pochette pour une sélection de chansons satiriques de Henri Salvador. Photos en surimpression, prédominance de tons bleus.
293) Photo couleur de deux mains en guise de pochette pour le disque d'un chanteur populaire.
294) Pochette pour un disque d'evergreens interprétés par deux anciennes vedettes.
295) Cet agrandissement du disque sert de pochette (face 1 au recto, face 2 au verso). Enregistrement de chansons françaises.
296) Photo exposée deux fois illustrant la pochette d'un disque de chansons. Tons bleus.

294

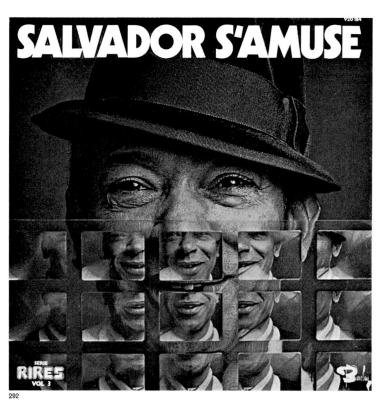

292

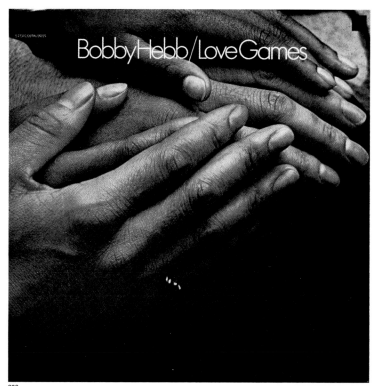

293

295

296

Folk Songs / Volkslieder / Musique populaire

297) Cover for a selection of folk music by a famous black performer.
298) Cover of a double album containing American country music. When the album is opened, the whole landscape appears between the giant's feet.
299) Record cover using an assemblage for songs by a South American singer.
300) Cover for "handmade" country music. The handwriting and collage technique of the cover are also meant to appear handmade.
301) Record cover for soul from Paris on a French record.
302) Polychrome cover for recordings by a popular folk singer.

297) Schallplattenhülle für Volksmusik. Die Platte enthält bereits legendär gewordene Stücke von Leadbelly, die bisher noch nie veröffentlicht wurden.
298) Hülle eines Doppelalbums mit amerikanischer Country-Musik. Bei geöffneter Hülle wird die ganze Landschaft, zwischen den Beinen des Giganten hindurch gesehen, sichtbar.
299) Schallplattenhülle mit Assemblage für Songs von Juarez.
300) Plattenhülle für «handgemachte» Volksmusik von Mason Williams und seiner Gruppe. «Handgemacht» scheint auch die Hülle, mit ausgerissenen Photos, Klebesternen, handschriftlichem Text (auch auf der Rückseite).
301) Schallplattenhülle mit bekannten Pariser Melodien.
302) Plattenhülle für Aufnahmen des Folk-Singers Townes Van Zandt.

297) Pochette pour une sélection de musique populaire interprétée par un célèbre musicien noir.
298) Pochette d'un album double de country music américaine. En ouvrant l'album, on fait apparaître le paysage entier entre les pieds du géant.
299) Pochette pour le disque d'un chanteur sud-américain, illustrée d'un assemblage.
300) Pochette pour de la country music «faite à la main» – d'où les éléments «faits main» de la composition: l'écriture manuscrite, le collage.
301) Pochette pour une interprétation de soul parisien sur un disque français.
302) Pochette polychrome pour les enregistrements d'un chanteur populaire en vogue.

297

300

ARTIST/KÜNSTLER/ARTISTE:

297) Paul Davis
298) Richard Hess
299) Arthur Korb (Photo)
300) Ed Thrasher (Photo)
301) Bonhomme
302) Sol Mednick (Photo)

DESIGNER/GESTALTER/MAQUETTISTE:

297) John Berg
298) Ron Coro
299) Virginia Clark
300) Dave Bhang
301) Jean Paul Théodul
302) Milton Glaser

ART DIRECTOR/DIRECTEUR ARTISTIQUE:

297) John Berg
298) John Berg/Edwin Lee
299) John LePrevost
300) Ed Thrasher
301) Alain Marouani
302) Milton Glaser

PUBLISHER/VERLEGER/EDITEUR:

297) 298) Columbia Records, New York
299) Decca Records, New York
300) Warner Bros. Records, Burbank, Ca.
301) Barclay Disques, Neuilly s/Seine
302) Poppy Records, New York

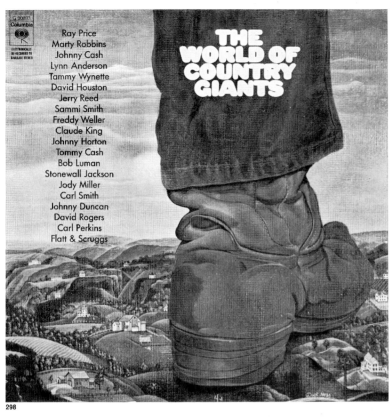

298

299

301

302

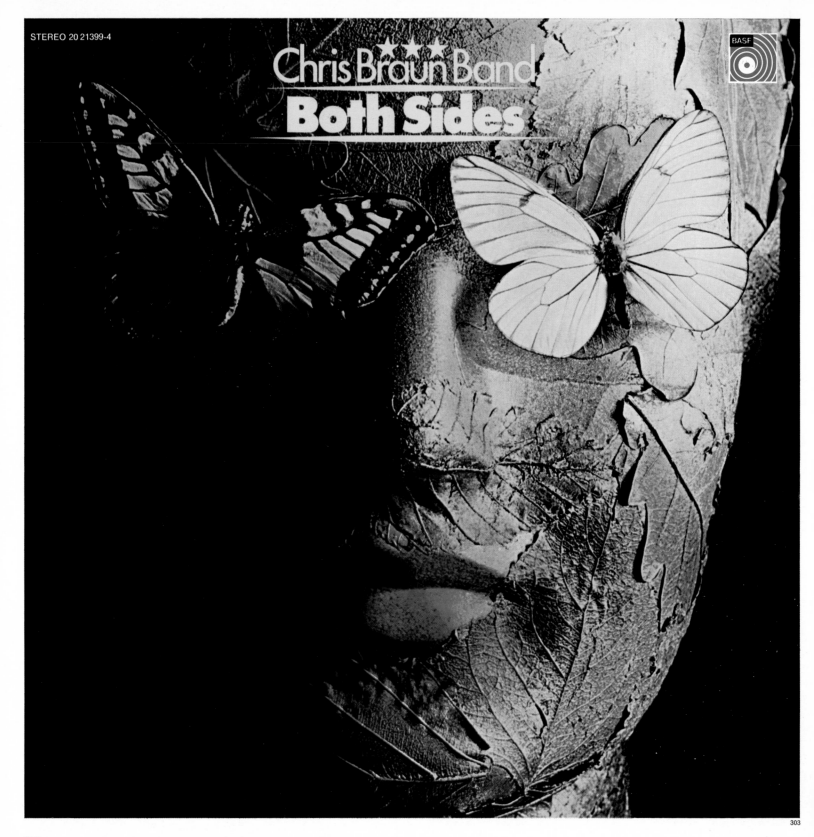

STEREO 20 21399-4

Chris Braun Band ★★★
Both Sides

BASF

304

305

306

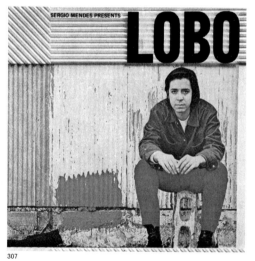

307

308

309

303) For a record of hard and soft rock by the Chris Braun Band.
304) Polychrome cover for a recording of a folklore festival of Brazilian music since the bossa nova.
305) Black-and-white cover for African songs. Yellow title.
306) Photographic cover for a collection of road songs by a country music singer.
307) For an album presenting the Brazilian singer and musician Edu Lobo. Grey corrugated iron, red clothing.
308) *Trompe-l'oeil* cover for an anthology of folk songs by well-known performers.
309) Cover for a selection of country duets, suggested by the double chair. Pale blue-grey shades.

303) Plattenhülle der Chris-Braun-Band für hard und soft Rock.
304) Farbige Hülle für das Album eines brasilianischen Orchesters, das den Bossa Nova mit Popelementen neu auflegt.
305) Schwarzweisshülle, Titel in Gelb, für afrikanische Songs.
306) Photographische Interpretation des Titels als Umschlagillustration einer Plattenhülle für Country-Musik.
307) Hülle eines Albums mit Liedern des Brasilianers Edu Lobo. Graues Wellblech, rote Farbakzente.
308) Mehrfarbige Hülle für Volkslieder verschiedener Interpreten.
309) Hülle für Country-Musik mit je zwei Interpreten, was durch den doppelsitzigen Stuhl angedeutet wird. Blaugrau.

303) Pochette pour un enregistrement de *hard and soft rock*.
304) Pochette polychrome pour l'enregistrement d'un festival de musique populaire brésilienne depuis la bossa nova.
305) Pochette noir-blanc. Chansons africaines. Titre jaune.
306) Pochette pour un recueil de chansons sur le thème de la route et du voyage, par un chanteur de country music.
307) Pour un album présentant le chanteur et musicien brésilien Edu Lobo. Tôle ondulée grise, vêtements rouges.
308) Pochette en trompe-l'œil pour une anthologie de chansons populaires enregistrées par des interprètes renommés.
309) Pochette pour une sélection de duos de country music (allusion de la chaise double). Tons bleu gris pâles.

ARTIST/KÜNSTLER/ARTISTE:
303) Holger Matthies (Photo)
304) Wolfgang Baumann
305) Oscar Zarate
306) Dave Coleman (Photo)
307) Guy Webster (Photo)
308) Three Lions (Photo)
309) Edwin Lee (Photo)

DESIGNER/GESTALTER/MAQUETTISTE:
303) Holger Matthies
304) Wolfgang Baumann
305) Oscar Zarate
306) Dave Coleman
307) Roland Young
308) Claude Arnaud
309) Edwin Lee

ART DIRECTOR/DIRECTEUR ARTISTIQUE:
303) Christoph Berg
304) H. B. Pfitzer
305) Oscar Zarate
306) George Osaki
307) Roland Young
308) Claude Arnaud
309) Edwin Lee/John Berg

PUBLISHER/VERLEGER/EDITEUR:
303) BASF Musikproduktion, Hamburg
304) MPS Records, Villingen/GER
305) Trova, Buenos Aires
306) Capitol Records, Hollywood
307) A&M Records, Hollywood
308) Disques CBS, Paris
309) Columbia Records, New York

Folk Songs / Volkslieder

Protest Songs

310) Cover for a collection of songs about birth control. The back cover shows women with slit bellies and—as a fata morgana on the horizon—the Pope with warning finger raised. The inside spread shows the digestive process of the child-devouring monster.
311) Polychrome cover of a satirical record about American politics with the performers imitating the voices of leading U.S. political figures.
312) Cover for live recordings by the German protest singer Degenhardt. The coloured strip is in black, red and yellow, the colours of the German flag.
313) Cover for a joint record by two protest singers from East and West Germany. The illustration symbolizes the division of the two halves of Germany.
314)–316) From a series of song recordings containing social and political criticism—here on the Italian resistance, anarchism and the simple soldier.
317) 318) Front cover and inside (also a poster) of a double album of live social protest recordings.

Protestlieder

310) Hülle für Songs über Geburtenkontrolle. Auf der Rückseite Frauen mit aufgeschlitzten Bäuchen und – als Fata Morgana am Horizont – der Papst mit aufgehobenem Drohfinger. Die Innenseite zeigt die Verdauungsmaschinerie des kinderfressenden Ungetüms.
311) Mehrfarbige Hülle einer satirischen Platte. Titel aus Sternenbanner. Abbildungen von Johnson, Agnew, Nixon, William Buckley, Humphrey und Rockefeller.
312) Hülle für eine Live-Aufnahme mit dem Protestsänger Degenhardt. Schwarz-Rot-Gelb.
313) Für einen Wechselgesang des schnauzbärtigen ostberliner Chansonniers Wolf Biermann mit dem scharfzüngigen Protestsänger Wolfgang Neuss aus der BRD. «Zerrissene» Illustration für die zwei Deutschland.
314)–316) Aus einer Serie politischer und sozialkritischer Lieder: aus der italienischen Widerstandsbewegung anarchistische Lieder und Soldatenlieder.
317) 318) Vorder- und Innenseite (auch als Plakat) eines Doppelalbums des Protestsängers Dick Gregory.

Chansons contestataires

310) Pochette pour un recueil de chansons sur le thème de la contraception. Le verso montre des femmes au ventre ouvert et, tel un mirage à l'horizon, le Pape levant le doigt d'un air menaçant. A l'intérieur, double page avec un monstre dévorant les enfants.
311) Pochette polychrome d'un disque satirique où des imitateurs doués singent les vedettes de la scène politique américaine.
312) Pochette pour des enregistrements en direct du chanteur contestataire allemand Degenhardt. La bande présente les couleurs nationales, le noir, le rouge, le jaune.
313) Pochette d'un disque enregistré par deux chanteurs contestataires allemands, de la RFA et de la RDA. Illustration «déchirée» symbolisant les deux Allemagnes.
314)–316) Exemples d'une série de pochettes pour des chansons de critique sociale et politique, portant ici sur la résistance italienne, l'anarchisme et le rôle du troufion.
317) 318) Recto et intérieur d'une pochette (avec poster). Album double contestataire, enregistrements directs.

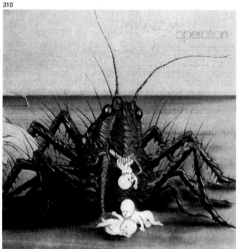

310

311

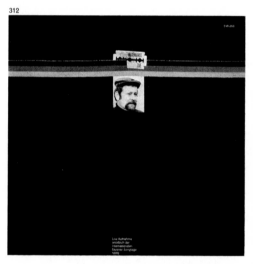

312

314

315

316

ARTIST/KÜNSTLER/ARTISTE:

310) Heinz Dorfflein
311) Edward Sorel
312) Gisela Groenewold/Günter Zint (Photo)
313) Heinz Edelmann
314)–316) Giancarlo Iliprandi
317) 318) Milton Glaser

DESIGNER/ART DIRECTOR:

310) Clemens Krauss
311) William S. Harvey
312) Holger Matthies
313) Willy Fleckhaus
314)–316) Giancarlo Iliprandi
317) 318) Milton Glaser

PUBLISHER/VERLEGER/EDITEUR:

310) Metronome Records/Ohr, Hamburg
311) Elektra Records, New York
312) Deutsche Grammophon Gesellschaft, Hamburg
313) Phonogram/Twen, Hamburg
314)–316) Dischi Del Sole/Edizioni Del Gallo, Milan
317) 318) Poppy Records, New York

313

317

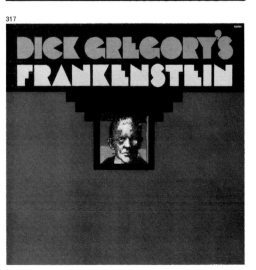

318

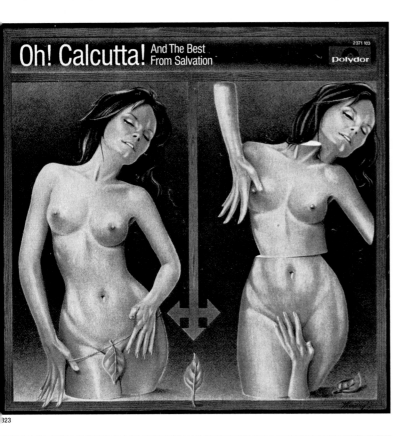

323

Protest Songs
Protestlieder
Chansons contestataires

ARTIST/KÜNSTLER/ARTISTE:

319)–322) Horst Janssen
323) Peter Wandrey
324) Robert Grossman

DESIGNER/GESTALTER/MAQUETTISTE:

319)–322) Tostmann Werbeagentur
323) Peter Wandrey
324) Virginia Team

ART DIRECTOR/DIRECTEUR ARTISTIQUE:

319) 321)–323) Stefan Böhle
320) Jochen Hinze
324) John Berg/Virginia Team

PUBLISHER/VERLEGER/EDITEUR:

319) 320) 322) 323) Polydor/Deutsche Grammophon Gesellschaft, Hamburg
321) Polydor/Twen/Deutsche Grammophon Gesellschaft, Hamburg
324) Columbia Records, New York

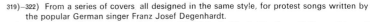

324

319)–322) From a series of covers all designed in the same style, for protest songs written by the popular German singer Franz Josef Degenhardt.
323) Record cover for music from the shows *Oh! Calcutta!* (called by Kenneth Tynan "elegant pornography for the thinking voyeur") and *Salvation*.
324) Polychrome cover for a recording of two comedies by The Firesign Theatre. Orange ground.

319)–322) Beispiele aus einer Serie von einheitlich gestalteten Plattenhüllen (Abb. 321 Kassette für zwei Platten) für Chansons von und mit Franz Josef Degenhardt, dem bekannten deutschen Protestsänger.
323) Mehrfarbige Schallplattenhülle für Aufnahmen aus der Broadway-Show *Oh! Calcutta!* (eine Revue, die von Kenneth Tynan als «elegante Pornographie für den denkenden Voyeur» bezeichnet wurde) und *Salvation*.
324) Hülle für zwei Komödien des Firesign Theatre (Zermalmt diesen Zwerg nicht; Gib mir die Zange). Hintergrund in Orange.

319)–322) Exemples d'une série de pochettes de style identique pour des chansons contestataires écrites et interprétées par le chanteur allemand populaire Franz Josef Degenhardt. Fig. 321 pour une cassette à deux disques.
323) Pochette pour des mélodies des revues *Oh! Calcutta!* (d'après Kenneth Tynan «de la pornographie élégante pour le voyeur intellectuel») et *Salvation*.
324) Pochette polychrome pour un enregistrement de deux comédies jouées par le Firesign Theatre. Fond orange.

325) Cover for a record by a popular Japanese singer.
326) Cover for a musical interpretation of ten chapters from Colin Wilson's *Encyclopaedia of Murder*.
327) Record cover for a song accompanied by classical Japanese instruments. Grey shades with only hair, eyes and target in colour.
328)–330) From a series of record covers in a traditional style for popular Japanese melodies.
331) 332) 334) From a series of covers of standard design for a selection of Japanese popular music.
333) 335) Cover and inside spread of an album of hits sung by Ruri Asaoka.

325) Für Lieder eines populären japanischen Sängers.
326) Hülle für eine musikalische Interpretation von 10 Kapiteln aus Colin Wilsons «Enzyklopädie des Mordes».
327) «Die Geschichte der Blume», gesungen von Ari Ei mit Begleitung auf klassischen japanischen Instrumenten.
328)–330) Aus einer Serie von Schallplattenhüllen für bekannte japanische Melodien.
331) 332) Einheitlich gestaltete Serie von Schallplattenhüllen für japanische Volksmusik.
333) 335) Vorderseite und geöffnete Innenseite einer Hülle für Aufnahmen der Schlagersängerin Ruri Asaoka.
334) Schallplattenhülle für japanische Schlager.

325) Pour le disque d'un chanteur japonais populaire.
326) Pochette pour une interprétation musicale de 10 chapitres de l'*Encyclopédie du Meurtre* de Colin Wilson.
327) Pochette de disque pour une chanson accompagnée d'instruments japonais traditionnels. Tons gris, seuls les cheveux, les yeux et la cible sont en couleur.
328)–330) Exemples d'une série de pochettes de style traditionnel pour des mélodies populaires japonaises.
331) 332) 334) Exemples d'une série de pochettes standards pour une sélection de musique populaire japonaise.
333) 335) Pochette et double page intérieure d'un album de tubes chantés par Ruri Asaoka.

ARTIST/KÜNSTLER/ARTISTE:

325) Tadanori Yokoo
326) Uabo Yoshinori (Photo)
327) Ado Maeda
328)–330) Tsunao Harada
331) 332) 334) Masaaki Nishimiya (Photo)
333) 335) Sigeru Izumi

DESIGNER/GESTALTER/MAQUETTISTE:

325) 333) 335) Tadanori Yokoo
326) Toshio Sakai
327) Yoshiaki Kohyama
331) 332) 334) Hiroshi Kusaka

ART DIRECTOR/DIRECTEUR ARTISTIQUE:

325) 333) 335) Tadanori Yokoo
326) Toshio Sakai
327) Yoshiaki Kohyama
331) 332) 334) Hiroshi Kusaka

PUBLISHER/VERLEGER/EDITEUR:

325) King Record Co., Tokyo
326) 327) CBS/Sony Records, Tokyo
331) 332) 334) Nippon Columbia Co., Tokyo
333) 335) Teichiku Records, Tokyo

Japanese Folk-Music
Japanische Volksmusik
Musique populaire japonais

325

328

326

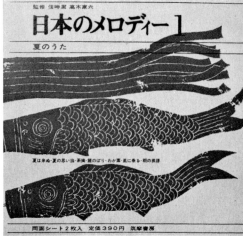

329

327

330

331

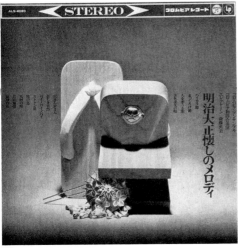

332

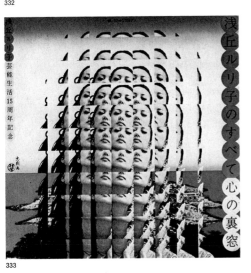

333

334

335

Film Music / Filmmusik
Bandes sonores

ARTIST/KÜNSTLER/ARTISTE:

336) Jacques Schumacher/Fred Dostal (Photo)
337) Lanning Stern
338) Richard Hess
339) Edward Sorel
340) Ken Veeder (Photo)
341) Hatami (Photo)
342) Edward Simpson (Photo)
343) Bill Imhoff/Norman Seeff (Photo)
344) Jochen Hinze (Photo)
345) Bob Wortham (Photo)

DESIGNER/GESTALTER/MAQUETTISTE:

336) Stefan Böhle/R. Pfingsten
338) 339) John Berg
340) 342) 345) John Hoernle
341) Hans Schleger
343) Dave Bhang
344) Jochen Hinze

ART DIRECTOR/DIRECTEUR ARTISTIQUE:

336) Stefan Böhle
337) 343) Norman Seeff
338) John Berg
339) John Berg/Bob Cato
340) 342) 345) George Osaki
341) Hans Schleger

PUBLISHER/VERLEGER/EDITEUR:

336) Deutsche Grammophon Gesellschaft, Hamburg
337) 343) United Artists Records, Los Angeles
338) 339) Columbia Records, New York
340) 342) 345) Capitol Records, Hollywood
341) Universal Pictures, London
344) Polydor/Deutsche Grammophon Ges., Hamburg

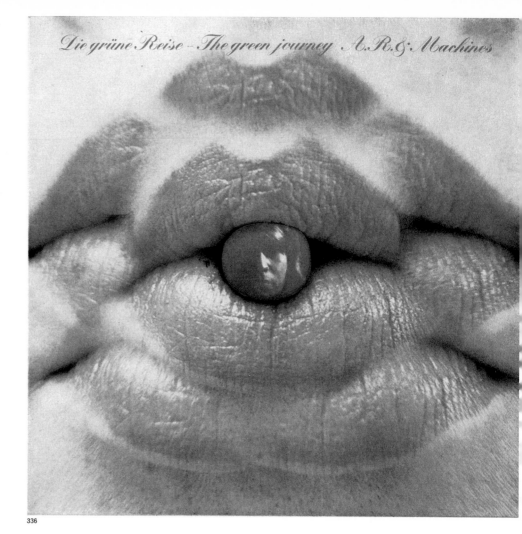

336

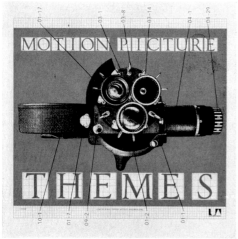

337

338

339

340

341

342

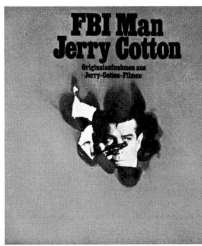

343

344

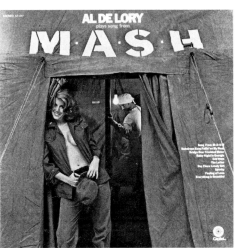

345

336) Record cover for the sound track of a film entitled *The Green Journey*. Red lips, green globe.
337) Cover for a selection of film melodies.
338) Cover for readings by the Russian poet Yevtushenko in New York and San Francisco.
339) Polychrome cover for a recording of a musical.
340) Cover for a recording of music from the film *Hair*.
341) Record cover for music from a Chaplin film.
342) For a record of music from the film *Bonnie and Clyde*. Printed in sepia to suggest an old photograph.
343) For a political satire spoken by Orson Welles. Clothing in the American colours.
344) Cover for original recordings from various detective films with Jerry Cotton.
345) Cover for a recording of the most popular songs from the film *Mash*.

336) Plattenhülle für den Sound-Track zum beabsichtigten Film *Die grüne Reise*. Rote Lippen, grüne Kugel mit Widerspiegelung eines Kopfes.
337) Plattenhülle für bekannte Filmmelodien.
338) Plattenhülle für musikalisch untermalte Dichterlesungen des russischen Schriftstellers Jewtuschenko.
339) Mehrfarbige Plattenhülle für ein Musical.
340) Schallplattenhülle für Aufnahmen aus dem Film *Hair*.
341) Für eine Platte mit Themen aus einem Chaplin-Film.
342) Für eine Platte mit Filmmelodien aus *Bonnie and Clyde*. Aufnahme in Sepia, um eine alte Photo vorzutäuschen.
343) Hülle vorwiegend in Blau, Hose und Zylinder rot-weiss, für eine politische Satire, erzählt von Orson Welles.
344) Schallplattenhülle für Originalaufnahmen aus verschiedenen Kriminalfilmen von Jerry Cotton.
345) Für eine Platte mit bekannten Songs aus dem Film *Mash*.

336) Pochette pour la bande sonore d'un film intituleé *Le Voyage vert*. Lèvres rouges, globe terrestre vert.
337) Pochette pour une sélection de musiques de films.
338) Pochette pour le poète russe Yevtuchenko lisant ses poèmes à New York et à San Francisco.
339) Pochette polychrome. Enregistrement d'un musical.
340) Pochette pour la musique du film *Hair*.
341) Pochette pour la musique d'un film de Charlie Chaplin.
342) Pour la musique du film *Bonnie and Clyde*. Imprimé sur papier bistre pour évoquer une vieille photographie.
343) Pochette pour l'enregistrement d'une satire politique par Orson Welles. Habits aux couleurs américaines.
344) Pochette pour des enregistrements originaux tirés de divers films policiers avec Jerry Cotton.
345) Pochette pour un disque regroupant les chansons les plus connues qui figurent dans le film *Mash*.

Colman Andrews

Contemporary popular music—"pop", "beat music", "rock", or whatever one chooses to call it—is a tremendously important social and cultural force in many countries of the world today; it is also the kind of music that has encouraged the most exciting, unusual and original contemporary graphic contributions to record-jacket design—and has in fact encouraged the acceptance of a new set of graphic priorities, which has influenced contiguous media as well.

Rock music is probably the most intensively competitive entertainment form in the world today, both in its commercial aspects and in the personal and artistic temperaments of its performers. A great quantity of record albums is released each week (in the United States, there are sometimes literally hundreds appearing in a single seven-day span); it makes good commercial sense for each album to look different, to look appealing to its segment of the market, and to convey some philosophical or emotional sense of the kind of music it masks. The personal egoism and/or promotional acumen of the performer usually causes him to seek the same goals. Good design and exciting artwork satisfy both the music-maker and the music-seller.

As Tony Cohan once pointed out in an issue of GRAPHIS, the graphic artist who wishes to survive in the rock-record design field must be "fast, eclectic, flexible and original", and must possess "a broad vocabulary of popular forms, both past and present". It is important to add that the graphic artist working in the rock music field today must also, in many cases, be able to communicate with the performer whose work he is illustrating, and even, sometimes, be able to reproduce visually the ideas or self-images of the musicians themselves. The artists who designed the Beatles' "white album", the Rolling Stones' "tongue", the "Chicago" script logo, etc., were not working only for themselves or for record company art directors: they were working for, and striving to satisfy, groups of highly talented musical personalities.

A new infusion of strength, a new fire of imagination, a new current of energy seem to have entered the world of record-jacket design; these qualities seem to have come not only from the music itself (which is usually, as Tony Cohan said about the artists who create for it, "eclectic, flexible and original"), but from the people who make the music and from the life-styles they have stimulated.

Die moderne Schlagermusik – «Pop», «Beat Musik», «Rock» oder wie immer man sie nennen will – ist heutzutage in vielen Ländern eine überaus wichtige soziale und kulturelle Kraft. Sie ist auch diejenige Musik, welche die aufregendsten, ungewöhnlichsten und originellsten zeitgenössischen graphischen Beiträge zum Design von Schallplattenhüllen hervorgebracht hat.

Rock-Musik ist heute sowohl im kommerziellen Bereich als auch bei den persönlichen und künstlerischen Temperamenten ihrer Musiker die wettbewerbsintensivste Unterhaltungsform der Welt. Jede Woche erscheint eine grosse Menge neuer Plattenalben (in den Vereinigten Staaten sind es manchmal Hunderte in einer einzigen Woche). Um seinen Marktbereich anzusprechen und den geistigen oder emotionellen Sinn der so umhüllten Musik zu vermitteln, ist es sinnvoll, dass jedes Album sein besonderes Gesicht hat. Der persönliche Egoismus und/oder das Werbeverständnis des Musikers veranlasst ihn gewöhnlich, dasselbe Ziel anzustreben. Gutes Design und anregende Graphik befriedigen den Musikmacher wie den Musikverkäufer.

Wie Tony Cohan in einer früheren Nummer von GRAPHIS gezeigt hat, muss der Graphiker, der im Bereich des Rock-Platten-Designs bestehen will, «schnell, eklektisch, flexibel und originell» sein und er muss «einen grossen Wortschatz populärer Ausdrucksmittel aus Vergangenheit und Gegenwart» haben. Es ist zudem wichtig, dass der Graphiker, der heute im Bereich der Rock-Musik arbeitet, oft fähig sein muss, die Ideen und Selbstbilder der Musiker visuell zu reproduzieren. Die Künstler, die das «weisse Album» der Beatles, die «Zunge» der Rolling Stones, den «Chicago»-Schriftzug usw. entwarfen, haben nicht für sich selbst oder für die Art Direktoren der Plattenfirmen gearbeitet, sondern für Gruppen äusserst talentierter musikalischer Persönlichkeiten, die zufriedenzustellen sie bemüht waren.

Neue Kraft, neues Feuer der Phantasie, ein neuer Energiestrom sind in die Welt des Schallplattenhüllen-Designs eingeflossen. Diese Qualitäten scheinen nicht nur aus der Musik selbst gekommen zu sein (die gewöhnlich – wie Tony Cohan es auf die für sie schaffenden Graphiker gemünzt hat – «eklektisch, flexibel und originell» sind), sondern auch aus den Menschen, die diese Musik machen, und aus dem Lebensstil, den sie stimuliert haben.

La musique populaire contemporaine – qu'on la baptise pop ou beat ou rock ou d'un autre terme en vogue – représente une force socio-culturelle irrésistible dans un grand nombre de pays. C'est aussi le genre de musique qui nous a valu les créations graphiques les plus fascinantes, les plus insolites et originales dans le domaine de la pochette de disque et a contribué à établir une nouvelle échelle des valeurs graphiques qui en est venue à influencer les médias voisins.

Le rock est probablement aujourd'hui le divertissement le plus engagé dans une âpre lutte concurrentielle, tant par ses aspects commerciaux que par le tempérament personnel et artistique de ses interprètes. Une masse énorme de disques est lancée périodiquement sur le marché (rien qu'aux Etats-Unis, on compte des centaines de nouveautés d'une semaine à l'autre); l'intérêt commercial recommande d'en varier la présentation et d'en renforcer l'attrait tout en explicitant les idées ou sentiments traduits dans la musique de chaque disque. L'égocentrisme ou la perspicacité de l'interprète agit dans le même sens, le design de qualité et la composition graphique accrochante satisfaisant à la fois le musicien et le disquaire.

Comme le disait Tony Cohan dans un numéro de GRAPHIS, l'artiste qui souhaite s'imposer dans la pochette de rock doit être «rapide, éclectique, souple et original» et posséder «un grand vocabulaire de formes populaires traditionnelles et contemporaines». Ajoutons une caractéristique essentielle à nos yeux: il doit souvent être capable de communiquer avec l'interprète et même parfois savoir reproduire sous une forme visuelle les idées que les musiciens se font de leur musique ou d'eux-mêmes. Les artistes qui ont créé l'«album blanc» des Beatles, la «langue» des Rolling Stones, le logo en écriture script «Chicago», etc. n'avaient pas simplement en vue les désirs du directeur artistique, du producteur ou leur propre déontologie artistique: ils œuvraient dans l'intérêt de groupes de musiciens de grand talent, dont ils cherchaient à satisfaire les aspirations.

Le monde de la pochette de disque semble avoir bénéficié d'une véritable injection de vigueur d'expression, d'imagination enthousiaste, d'énergie survoltée. Il doit ce bain de jouvence non seulement à la musique même (qui est, tout comme les designers travaillant pour elle, d'après la définition de Tony Cohan, «électrique, souple et originale»), mais aussi et surtout aux hommes et aux femmes qui font cette musique et aux styles de vie qu'ils ont inspirés.

Pop
Rock
Beat

346

347

348

349

350

351

ARTIST/KÜNSTLER/ARTISTE:

346) Alain Josset
347) Alain Marouani (Photo)
348) Brian Ward
349) Rosemarie Juhle
350) Mati Klarwein
351) John Wilkinson/Hamlet Photographics
352) M+M Vormstein (Photo)

DESIGNER/ART DIRECTOR:

346) Alain Josset/Alain Marouani
347) Jean-Paul Théodul/Alain Marouani
348) Jan Anderson/Roy Eldrige
349) Juligan Studio/Stefan Böhle
350) Desmond Strobel
351) Keef Hartley
352) M+M Vormstein

PUBLISHER/VERLEGER/EDITEUR:

346) Riviera/Barclay Disques, Neuilly s/Seine
347) Barclay Disques, Neuilly s/Seine
348) Reprise/Warner Bros. Records, Burbank, Ca.
349) Karussell/Deutsche Grammophon Ges., Hamburg
350) Mercury Record Production, Chicago
351) TELDEC «Telefunken-Decca» Schallplatten, Hamburg
352) Ariola-Eurodisc, München

346) Cover for music by a beat group. Clouds in shades of dark blue, red title.
347) For a recording of pop music. Blue ground.
348) Twelve-page newspaper as a record cover for pop music by Jethro Tull. The whole of the newspaper was specially written.
349) Cover for a record by a pop group. Blue tube, blue ground, yellow contents.
350) Double album for live recordings of concerts by Buddy Miles. The rock setting is intended to suggest the solidity and power of the music, while the flaming heart symbolizes its vitality.
351) Record cover for a band. Relief in blue shades incorporating a photograph of the band.
352) Double album for recordings by various pop groups qualified to make the listener "think".

346) Hülle für Beatmusik von J. Daydé. Wolken in verschiedenen dunklen Blautönen, rote Schrift.
347) Für die Gruppe Popcorn. Blau, rosa Schrift auf Rot.
348) 12 Seiten umfassende Zeitung, mit herunterklappbarem Teil, als Plattenhülle für den Popmusiker Jethro Tull.
349) Senfgelber Tubeninhalt mit Mitgliedern der Gruppe The Cream auf blauem Grund.
350) Doppelalbum für Live-Aufnahmen von Buddy-Miles-Konzerten. Die Darstellung Buddys als Felskopf entstand auf seinen Wunsch, um so die Kraft seiner Musik auszudrücken. Das flammende Herz soll die Lebenskraft symbolisieren.
351) Hülle für Aufnahmen der Keef-Hartley-Band. Relief in Blau mit einkopierter Photographie des Orchesters, farbige Rosette aus Glasperlen.
352) Doppelalbum für die besten Pop-Hits des Jahres 1971.

346) Pochette du disque d'un groupe de beat. Nuages aux tons bleu foncé, titre rouge.
347) Pour un enregistrement de musique pop. Fond bleu.
348) Journal de 12 pages (confectionné tout spécialement) en guise de pochette pour un disque de pop.
349) Pochette du disque d'un groupe pop. Tube bleu, fond bleu, contenu jaune.
350) Album double pour l'enregistrement en direct de concerts de Buddy Miles. Le décor rocheux symbolise la puissance et la solidité de la musique, le cœur enflammé sa vitalité.
351) Pochette de disque des enregistrements de l'orchestre de Keef Hartley. Relief aux teintes bleues comportant une photo des musiciens.
352) Album double pour la musique de différents groupes pop censés donner «à réfléchir» à l'auditeur.

think!

POP PROGRESS '71

Procol Harum
T. Rex
Elton John
Humble Pie
Gary Wright
Black Pearl
The Move
Supertramp
Paul Brett Sage
Fair Weather
Man
The Falcons
Titus Groan
Status Quo
Lee Michaels
Strawbs
and
Jimi Hendrix

353

354

357

353) 354) Front and inside of a record cover for a psychedelic trip to the underground.
355) Cover for a recording of music by a beat group.
356) Cover for a record made by a singer in collaboration with two other musicians.
357) Cover for recordings by various beat groups.
358) Cover for a Beatles record, with a photographic allusion to the title.
359) Cover for a record by a pop group.
360) For a recording by a group of teenagers.

353) 354) Vorder- und Innenseite einer Hülle für «einen psychedelischen Trip in den Untergrund». Photographische Interpretation des Titels.
355) Schallplattenhülle für Aufnahmen der Sauterelles.
356) Plattenalbum für Shawn Phillips, der mit zwei anderen Musikern zusammenarbeitet.
357) Hülle für Aufnahmen verschiedener Beatgruppen.
358) Umschlag für die Platte *Rubber Soul* der Beatles.
359) Mehrfarbige Hülle für eine Popgruppe.
360) Plattenhülle für Aufnahmen einer jungen Beatgruppe.

353) 354) Recto et intérieur d'une pochette invitant à un voyage psychédélique dans l'underground.
355) Pochette pour le disque d'un groupe de beat.
356) Pochette pour le disque d'un chanteur accompagné de deux musiciens.
357) Pochette pour la musique de divers groupes de beat.
358) Pochette pour un disque des Beatles, avec une allusion photographique au titre.
359) Pochette du disque d'un groupe pop.
360) Pour l'enregistrement d'un groupe d'adolescents.

PUBLISHER/VERLEGER/EDITEUR:

353) 354) Mercury/Phonogram, Hamburg
355) CBS/EMI Records (Switzerland), Zürich
356) A & M Records, London
357) 359) Capitol Records, Hollywood
358) EMI Records, London
360) MGM Records, New York

355

les sauterelles

356

ARTIST/KÜNSTLER/ARTISTE:

353) 354) Bernd Cardinal (Photo)
355) Ernst Wirz (Photo)
356) Ruan O'Lochlainn (Photo)
357) John Van Hammersveld
358) Robert Freeman (Photo)
359) Dick Brown (Photo)
360) De Wayne Dalrymple (Photo)

DESIGNER/ART DIRECTOR:

353) 354) Klaus Witt/Wilfried Mannes
355) Franklin Willi/Ernst Wirz
356) Michael Doud
357) George Osaki
358) Christian/Front/Robert Freeman
359) Roland Young/George Osaki
360) Acy R. Lehman/Dave Krieger

358

359

360

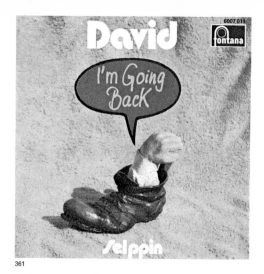

361

362

Pop / Rock / Beat

367a

ARTIST/KÜNSTLER:

361) Klaus Witt (Photo)
362) Michael Trevithick
363) Josse Goffin
364) Robert Lockart
365) Dave Bhang
366) Bloomsbury Group
367) 367a) Dino Danelli/
     Russell Beal (Photo)

DESIGNER/ART DIRECTOR:

361) Klaus Witt/Wilfried Mannes
362) Michael Trevithick
363) René Van Rossom
364) Norman Seeff/John Berg
365) Dave Bhang/Ed Thrasher
366) Bloomsbury Group/Michael Stanford
367) 367a) Dino Danelli

PUBLISHER/VERLEGER/EDITEUR:

361) Fontana/Phonogram, Hamburg
362) A & M Records, New York
363) Sovedi, Bruxelles
364) Columbia Records, New York
365) Warner Bros. Records, Burbank, Ca.
366) Vertigo/Phonogram, London
367) 367a) Atlantic Recording Corp., New York

363

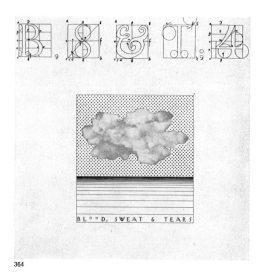

364

361) Cover for a recording of beat music. Three-dimensional artefact on yellow ground.
362) Cover for a beat recording including *Tobacco Road*.
363) Cover for a recording of works by the leader of a pop orchestra with allusion to the title.
364) Cover for the fourth recording by a beat group. Black and white, blue cloud.
365) Black-and-white cover for recordings by fourteen male performers.
366) Album cover for songs by a group in a philosophical vein. Purple and black, embossed lettering.
367) 367a) Cover for a recording by a beat group, with an assemblage of sculptures representing a dream environment.

361) Papierhülle einer kleinen Platte mit Beatmusik.
362) Umschlag der Beatplatte *Tobacco Road*, mit Illustration als Anspielung auf den Titel.
363) Stilisiertes Metronome als illustratorische Interpretation des Titels von Raymond Vincents Pop-Platte.
364) Umschlag einer Platte der Popgruppe Blood, Sweat & Tears. Schwarzweiss, blaue Wolke.
365) Schwarzweisshülle einer Pop-Platte mit Karikaturen aller auf dieser Platte vertretenen Musiker.
366) Schwarze Kassette für die Platte *Master of Reality* (blindgeprägt) der Gruppe Black Sabbath (violett).
367) 367a) Assemblage, die nach dem Künstler Danelli unsere Träume widerspiegeln soll. Für eine Beatgruppe.

365

366

361) Pochette pour un enregistrement de beat. Artefact tridimensionnel sur fond jaune.
362) Pochette d'un disque de beat comprenant *Tobacco Road*.
363) Pochette pour l'enregistrement des œuvres d'un chef d'orchestre pop avec allusion au titre.
364) Pochette du disque d'un groupe de beat dont le nom provient d'un discours de Churchill. Noir et blanc, nuage bleu.
365) Pochette en noir et blanc pour la musique des 14 interprètes masculins caricaturés.
366) Couverture d'un album de chansons de caractère philosophique. Noir et pourpre, lettres gaufrées.
367) 367a) Pochette pour l'enregistrement d'un groupe de beat. Assemblage de sculptures recréant une ambiance de rêve.

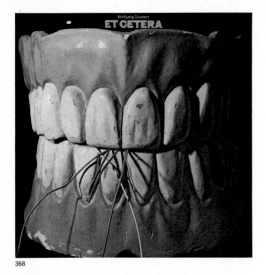

368

369

370

371

372

373

Pop / Rock / Beat

ARTIST/KÜNSTLER/ARTISTE:

368) Frieder Grindler
369) Eric Bach (Photo)
370) Jürgen Gesang
371) Joel Brodsky (Photo)
372) Willy Sehr (Photo)
373) Ray Rathbone (Photo)
374) Klaus Peter Weber (Photo)

DESIGNER/ART DIRECTOR:

368) Frieder Grindler
369) Tostmann Werbeagentur/Stefan Böhle
370) Jürgen Gesang
371) Larry Shaw/Dave Krieger
372) Eberhard Henschel/Stefan Böhle
373) Nigel Holmes/Douglas Maxwell
374) Ulfert Dirichs/Stefan Böhle

PUBLISHER/VERLEGER/EDITEUR:

368) MPS Records, Villingen/GER
369) 372) 374) Polydor/Deutsche Grammophon, Hamburg
370) Karussell/Deutsche Grammophon Ges., Hamburg
371) Stax/Deutsche Grammophon Ges., Hamburg
373) Island Records, London

368) Back cover for a recording by a German pop group. Pink gums, coloured wires.
369) Cover for an orchestra's renderings of a new dance from Jamaica. Colour photograph, red title.
370) Cover for pop and country music by an ''in'' group. Red title, US flag on guitar.
371) Cover for a recording by Albert King. On the back is a picture of the village of Lovejoy, Illinois.
372) Colour cover for a pop record. Real earthworms.
373) Cover for recordings by various pop singers and groups.
374) Cover for a record by a pop group.

368) Hülle für die Popgruppe Et Cetera. Gebiss aus rosa Gips, farbige Drähte, die zwischen den Zähnen heraushängen.
369) Hülle für den von den westindischen Inseln stammenden Tanz Reggae. Heller Grund, roter Titel.
370) Hülle für Gitarrenmusik im Pop-und-Country-Stil. Mann mit Gitarre mit weisser Gaze umwickelt, rote Schrift.
371) Hülle für die Gruppe von Albert King, dessen Name als Endstation des Busses angegeben wird.
372) Für die Platte «Drosselbart». Globus, aus welchem Regenwürmer und Heu quellen.
373) Hülle für Stücke verschiedener Popsänger und -gruppen.
374) Für die Platte «Nur eine Tagreise entfernt» von Abacus.

368) Verso de la pochette du disque d'un groupe pop allemand. Gencives roses, fils colorés.
369) Pochette pour l'interprétation d'une nouvelle danse jamaïquaine par un orchestre. Photo couleur, titre rouge.
370) Pochette pour de la musique pop et country par un groupe. Titre rouge, drapeau américain sur la guitare.
371) Pochette pour un disque d'Albert King. Au verso, le village de Lovejoy (Illinois).
372) Pochette couleur d'un disque pop. Vers de terre véritables.
373) Pochette d'un disque de divers chanteurs et groupes pop.
374) Pochette pour le disque d'un groupe pop.

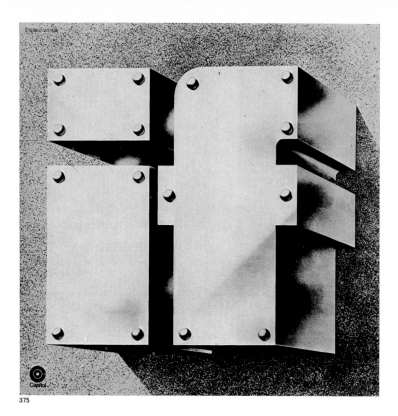

375

376

380

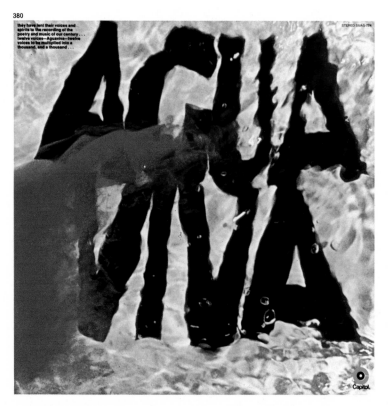

381

377

378

379

ARTIST/KÜNSTLER/ARTISTE:

375) CCS Advertising Assoc.
376) Alain Marouani (Photo)
377) 378) Nick Fasciano
379) Natalie Williams
381) Etienne Robial
382) M. C. Escher

DESIGNER/GESTALTER/MAQUETTISTE:

375) CCS Advertising Assoc.
375) 381) Claude Caudron
377)–379) John Berg/Nick Fasciano
380) Paul Bruhwiler
382) Guy Stevens

ART DIRECTOR/DIRECTEUR ARTISTIQUE:

376) 381) Alain Marouani
377)–379) John Berg
380) George Osaki
382) Mark Schulman

PUBLISHER/VERLEGER/EDITEUR:

375) 380) Capitol Records, Hollywood
376) Riviera/Barclay Disques, Neuilly s/Seine
377)–379) Columbia Records, New York
381) Barclay Disques, Neuilly s/Seine
382) Atlantic Recording Corp., New York

382

375) Cover for recordings by the beat group If.
376) Cover for a record by the Greek pop group Axis.
377)–379) From a series of covers for the pop group Chicago. Fig. 377 in silver-grey shades, fig. 378 with orange lettering on yellow plaque, fig. 379 with red name on worn blue cloth.
380) Cover for protest songs based on Spanish folk music. Photographic interpretation of the title (Living Water).
381) Cover for a recording of songs by a beat group.
382) Cover for recordings by a beat group. The design develops a famous drawing by M. C. Escher, from which lizards emerge at one point, to return to the pattern at another.

375) Schallplattenhülle für Aufnahmen der Beatgruppe If.
376) Umschlag für eine Schallplatte der griechischen Popgruppe Axis.
377)–379) Aus einer Serie von Plattenhüllen der Popgruppe Chicago. Abb. 377 in hellen Grautönen, Abb. 378 gelbe Tafel, orange Schrift, Abb. 379 abgeschossener Jeansstoff, rote Schrift.
380) Für Protestlieder mit Popmusikbegleitung, die auf spanischer Volksmusik basiert. Photographische Interpretation des Titels «Aguaviva» (bewegtes Wasser) als Umschlagillustration.
381) Schallplattenhülle für Aufnahmen bekannter Hits einer Beatgruppe.
382) Schallplattenhülle für Musik einer Beatgruppe mit einer bekannten Zeichnung von M. C. Escher, auf welcher Eidechsen aus der Zeichnung heraus- und wieder hineinkriechen.

375) Pochette pour des enregistrements du groupe de beat If.
376) Pochette pour le disque d'un groupe pop grec.
377)–379) Exemples d'une série de pochettes pour le groupe pop Chicago. 377) Tons gris argenté, 378) lettres orange sur plaque jaune, 379) nom rouge sur tissu bleu élimé.
380) Pochette pour des chansons contestataires inspirées de la musique populaire espagnole. Interprétation photographique du titre (Eau vive).
381) Pochette d'un disque de chansons par un groupe de beat.
382) Pochette pour les enregistrements d'un groupe de beat avec un célèbre dessin de M. C. Escher où des lézards bidimensionnels traversent les trois dimensions.

Pop / Rock / Beat

383) Cover with a graphic motif illustrating the title.
384) Cover for a recording of songs by a beat group, who are portrayed on it in full colour.
385) Cover for a record by a pop singer who is presented as a "wizard". The same design appears in reverse on the back of the cover. Full colour.
386) Polychrome cover for a pop group, who are shown on the clown's shoulders, while he holds the producer, photographer and art director in his hand.
387) Full-colour cover for a blend of country music and rock.
388) 389) Full-colour cover—not for a recording of the *Beggar's Opera*, but for a pop group of that name—and complete poster which it contained.

383) Mehrfarbige Hülle, deren Illustration auf den Plattentitel *Die Arche* anspielt.
384) Mehrfarbige Hülle für Aufnahmen einer Popgruppe mit Poster der Umschlagillustration. Die Texte der Songs wurden auf Packpapier gedruckt und in die Hülle eingeheftet.
385) Schallplattenhülle für den Popsänger Todd Rundgren. Die magischen Objekte sollen das Titelstück, «Ein Zauberer», symbolisieren.
386) Mehrfarbige Hülle für eine Popgruppe. Auf der Achsel des Clowns die 5 Mitglieder der Gruppe, rechts unten der Art Director, der Aufnahmeleiter und der Photograph.
387) Vom Plattentitel *Grass Roots* beeinflusste Umschlagillustration für Folk-Rock-Musik, gespielt von zwei verschiedenen Gruppen. Farbige Grasstiefel auf weissem Grund.
388) 389) Vorderseite und auseinandergeklappte Hülle für Stücke der Popgruppe Beggars Opera.

383) Pochette ornée d'un motif graphique illustrant le titre.
384) Pochette du disque de chansons d'un groupe de beat représenté en couleurs.
385) Pochette du disque d'un chanteur pop présenté comme sorcier. Le même dessin, inversé, se retrouve au verso. En polychromie.
386) Pochette polychrome pour un groupe pop installé sur les épaules d'un clown qui tient le producteur, le photographe et le directeur artistique dans ses mains.
387) Pochette polychrome pour de la musique intégrant le country et le rock.
388) 389) Pochette polychrome et poster complet qu'elle contient. *Beggar's Opera* ne se réfère pas à l'opéra, mais au nom du groupe pop.

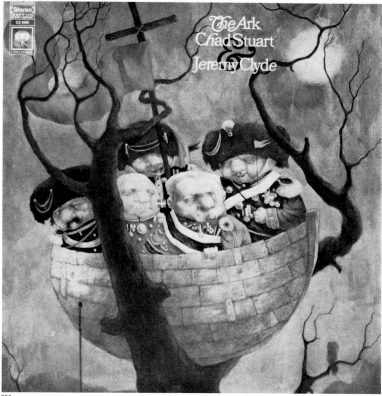

383

386

387

384

385

388

389

ARTIST/KÜNSTLER/ARTISTE:

383) Charlie Bragg
384) Michael Mathias Prechtl
385) Janson Eding Clapper
386) Etienne Delessert
387) Pauline Ellison
388) 389) Peter Goodfellow

DESIGNER/GESTALTER:

383) Ron Coro
384) Michael Mathias Prechtl
385) Janson Eding Clapper
386) William S. Harvey
387) John McConnell
388) 389) Bloomsbury Group

ART DIRECTOR:

383) John Berg
384) Manfred Schneider
385) Janson Eding Clapper
386) William S. Harvey
387) Michael Doud
388) 389) Blommsbury Group

PUBLISHER/VERLEGER:

383) Columbia Records,
New York
384) Liberty/United Artists,
München
385) Warner Bros. Records,
Burbank, Ca.
386) Elektra Records,
New York
387) A & M Records, London
388) 389) Vertigo/
Phonogram, London

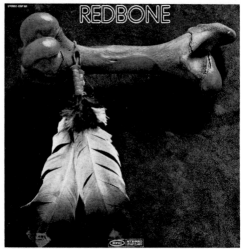

390

391

JEFFERSON AIRPLANE

BARK

392

394

ARTIST/KÜNSTLER/ARTISTE:

391) Holger Matthies (Photo)
392) Acy R. Lehman (Photo)
393) Ed Simpson (Photo)
394) Joel Brodsky (Photo)
395) Heinz Huke
396) Jim Marshall (Photo)

DESIGNER/GESTALTER/MAQUETTISTE:

390) Richard Mantel
391) Holger Matthies
392) Acy R. Lehman
393) Roland Young
394) William S. Harvey
395) Heinz Huke
396) Thomas Staller

ART DIRECTOR/DIRECTEUR ARTISTIQUE:

390) John Berg/Richard Mantel
391) Stefan Böhle
392) G. Blackman
393) George Osaki
394) William S. Harvey
395) Dieter Schwarz
396) Thomas Staller

132

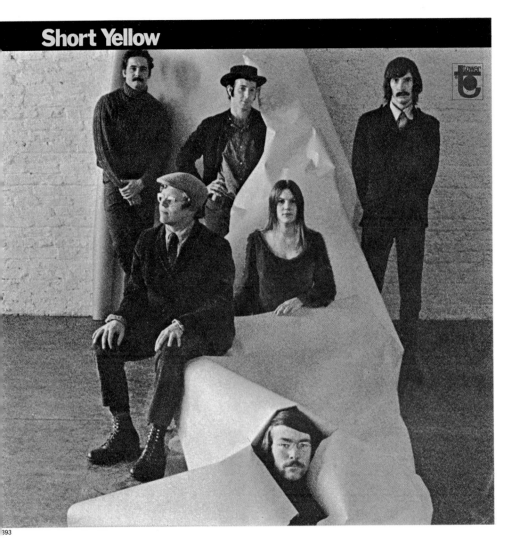

Short Yellow

PUBLISHER / VERLEGER / EDITEUR:

390) Epic/Columbia Records, New York
391) Karussell/Deutsche Grammophon Ges., Hamburg
392) TELDEC«Telefunken-Decca»/Decca,Hamburg/NewYork
393) Tower/Capitol Records, Hollywood
394) Elektra Records, New York
395) Tip/Deutsche Grammophon Gesellschaft, Hamburg
396) CBS Schallplatten, Frankfurt/M.

390) Cover for a record by a beat group, with Red Indian overtones. Red bone.
391) Cover for a double album with records by a group and a popular American singer.
392) Cover in the form of a parcel for a pop group.
393) Cover for recordings by the beat group shown on it.
394) Complete cover for a record by a well-known group.
395) Cover for a collection of beat hits.
396) Cover and part of the coloured record of underground music by various American beat groups.

390) Umschlag einer Platte für die Gruppe Redbone (roter Knochen), was durch die Photo illustriert wird.
391) Doppelalbum mit je einer Platte für The Who und Hendrix.
392) Als Paket aufgemachte Plattenhülle für eine Popgruppe.
393) Schallplattenhülle für Aufnahmen einer Beatband.
394) Vorder- und Rückseite einer Hülle für die Beatgruppe The Doors. Die aussergewöhnliche Szene auf der Strasse spielt auf den Plattentitel *Strange Days* an.
395) Schallplattenhülle für bekannte Hits.
396) Plattenhülle und Platte für verschiedene Gruppen.

390) Pochette du disque d'un groupe de beat, avec des reflets d'images de Peaux-Rouges. Os rouge.
391) Pochette d'un album double contenant la musique d'un groupe et d'un chanteur américain en vogue.
392) Pochette en forme de paquet pour les enregistrements d'un groupe pop.
393) Pochette de disque avec la photo d'un groupe de beat.
394) Pochette complète du disque d'un groupe bien connu.
395) Pochette pour une série de tubes de beat.
396) Pochette et partie du disque coloré enregistré par divers groupes de beat de l'underground américain.

393

395

396

398

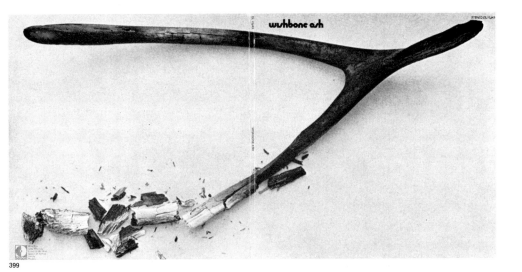

399

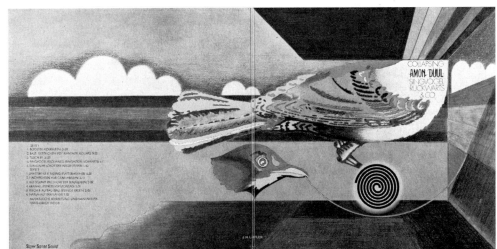

400

PUBLISHER/VERLEGER/EDITEUR:

397) Capitol Records, Inc., Hollywood
398) Kapp Records, New York
399) Decca Records, Los Angeles
400) Metronom Records, Hamburg

397) Design for a record cover for the group The Band.
398) Unfolded record cover with a photographic illustration of the name of the group.
399) Complete record cover with a photographic interpretation of the title. The inside spread shows the burning wishbone.
400) Brightly coloured inside spread of a German record, with an allusion to "songbirds" in the title.

397) Illustration der Plattenhülle für *Cahoots* der Popgruppe The Band.
398) Ratte mit Heiligenschein zur Illustration des Namens der Gruppe The Good Rats (Die guten Ratten).
399) Geöffnete Hülle für Wishbone Ash. Aussenseite mit angekohltem, Innenseite mit brennendem Brustbein.
400) Geöffnete Innenseite eines Albums in bunten Farben für Amon Düüls *Singvögel Rückwärts & Co.*, was durch die Umschlagillustration angedeutet wird.

397) Maquette d'une pochette pour le groupe intitulé The Band.
398) Pochette de disque ouverte, avec une illustration photographique du nom du groupe (les bons rats).
399) Pochette complète avec une interprétation photographique du titre. La double page intérieure montre une lunette fourchue d'oiseau enflammée (rappel du nom du groupe).
400) Double page intérieure de la pochette d'un disque allemand avec une allusion aux «oiseaux chanteurs» du titre. Couleurs vives; extérieure en noir avec titre en blanc.

ARTIST/KÜNSTLER/ARTISTE:

397) Gilbert Stone
398) Charles Keddy (Photo)
399) Gene Brownell (Photo)
400) J. H. Löffler

DESIGNER/GESTALTER/MAQUETTISTE:

397) Bob Cato
398) Bob Venosa
399) John LePrevost
400) J. H. Löffler

ART DIRECTOR/DIRECTEUR ARTISTIQUE:

397) Bob Cato
398) Bob Venosa
399) John LePrevost
400) J. H. Löffler

Pop / Rock / Beat

ARTIST/KÜNSTLER/ARTISTE:

401) 403) Holger Matthies (Photo)
402) Peter Schauman
404) Mary Leonard (Photo)

DESIGNER/GESTALTER/MAQUETTISTE:

401) 403) Holger Matthies
402) William S. Harvey
404) Virginia Team/John Berg

ART DIRECTOR/DIRECTEUR ARTISTIQUE:

401) 403) Christoph Berg
402) William S. Harvey
404) Virginia Team/John Berg

PUBLISHER/VERLEGER/EDITEUR:

401) 403) BASF Musikproduktion, Hamburg
402) Elektra Records, New York
404) Columbia Records, New York

401

401) Cover for a record by a pop group. The same motif is repeated on the back with a four-leaved clover replacing the title.
402) Full-colour inside spread of a record album for the group The Doors.
403) Cover for a recording by the beat group McChurch Soundroom, using a skull covered with candle-wax as an allusion to the title.
404) Cover for a recording by the group The Byrds. Impressions of a face taken in aluminium foil and shown in profile and frontally in blue-grey and silver shades.

401) Vorderseite eines Albums mit progressivem Pop der Gruppe Dies Irae. Schwarzer Rahmen, Stacheldraht über hellgrauem Grund.
402) Geöffnete Innenseite eines Albums der Popgruppe The Doors. Vorwiegend Grüntöne.
403) Umschlag für die Platte *Delusion* der Beatgruppe McChurch Soundroom. Totenkopf mit zerronnenem Wachs als Anspielung auf das Titelstück *Delusion,* in welchem von zerronnenen Hoffnungen und Illusionen die Rede ist.
404) Geöffnete Hülle in Grautönen für Aufnahmen der Gruppe The Byrds. Der Plattentitel *Byrdmaniax* ist ein Wortspiel mit dem Namen der Gruppe und «maniacs» (Verrückte). Impressionen von Gesichtern in Aluminiumfolie geformt und im Profil und von vorn aufgenommen.

401) Pochette pour le disque d'un groupe pop. Le même motif réapparaît au verso avec un trèfle à quatre feuilles à la place du titre.
402) Double page intérieure polychrome d'un album de disques pour le groupe The Doors.
403) Pochette pour l'enregistrement d'un groupe de beat. Le crâne recouvert de cire de bougie renvoie au titre.
404) Pochette d'un disque du groupe The Byrds. Impressions d'un visage reproduit sur feuille d'aluminium et montré de face et de profil; tons gris bleu et argent.

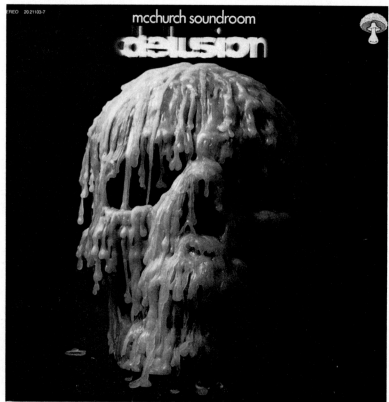

403

402

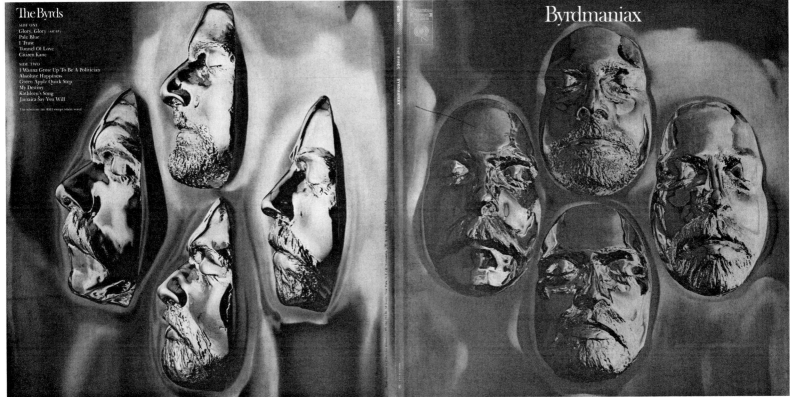

The Byrds

SIDE ONE
Glory, Glory (ASCAP)
Pale Blue
I Trust
Tunnel Of Love
Citizen Kane

SIDE TWO
I Wanna Grow Up To Be A Politician
Absolute Happiness
Green Apple Quick Step
My Destiny
Kathleen's Song
Jamaica Say You Will

The selections are BMI except where noted.

Byrdmaniax

404

405

406

411 a

PHOTOGRAPHER/PHOTOGRAPH/PHOTOGRAPHE:

405) 406) Gene Brownell
407) Wolfgang Heilemann
408) Holger Matthies
409) Jürgen Gesang
410) Klaus Witt
411) 411a) Joschi Jaehnike

DESIGNER/ART DIRECTOR:

405) 406) Dean O. Torrence/Gene Brownell
407) Holger Matthies
408) Holger Matthies/Stefan Böhle
409) Jürgen Gesang/Stefan Böhle
410) Klaus Witt/Wilfried Mannes
411) 411a) Rathin Chattopadhyay/Klaus Dempel/
Wolfgang M. Schmidt

PUBLISHER/VERLEGER/EDITEUR:

405) 406) Prophesy Records, Los Angeles
407) 408) Polydor/Deutsche Grammophon Ges., Hamburg
409) Karussell/Deutsche Grammophon Ges., Hamburg
410) Phonogram, Hamburg
411) 411a) Deutscher Bücherbund/Intercord, Stuttgart

407

408

405) 406) Front and back of cover for a record by a beat group. The colour photography illustrates the title. The chicken was "returned in good health after the photo session".
407) Cover for a record by a beat group, who appear on the cap of the bulb. Blue bulb, pink filament.
408) Cover for a record by a beat group. White mouse, blue cactus, yellow title.
409) Cover for a record by a beat group who claim to be "selling out". An open can appears inside.
410) Cover for a record of West Indian reggae music. Photograph (bars and faces) set in a drawn wall.
411) 411a) Cover and detail for protest songs by a German group.

405) 406) Kücken mit Gasmaske als Symbol für den Plattentitel. Nach Anmerkung auf der Hülle stammt das Kücken aus dem Museum für Wissenschaft und Industrie in Los Angeles und kehrte nach den Aufnahmen gesund wieder zurück.
407) Umschlag für Aufnahmen der Bee Gees. Blauer Grund.
408) Umschlag für die Platte einer Beatgruppe. Weisse Maus auf blauem Kaktus, gelbe Schrift.
409) Umschlagillustration eines Doppelalbums für The Who Sell out (Ausverkauf der Gruppe The Who).
410) Hülle für den neuen westindischen Tanz Reggae.
411) 411a) Plattenhülle und Photo zu Aufnahmen der Gruppe Eulenspygel, deren Songs aktuelle Themen behandeln.

409

410

405) 406) Recto et verso de la pochette d'un disque enregistré par un groupe de beat. Photo couleur illustrant le titre.
407) Pochette de disque pour un groupe de beat représenté sur la douille de l'ampoule bleue. Filament rose.
408) Pour le disque d'un groupe de beat. Souris blanche, cactus bleu, titre jaune.
409) Pochette de disque pour un groupe de beat «en pleines soldes». A l'intérieur, une boîte de conserves entamée.
410) Pochette d'un disque de musique reggae antillaise. Photo (barres et visages) intégrée dans un mur dessiné.
411) 411a) Pochette et détail pour un disque allemand de chansons contestataires.

Pop / Rock / Beat

412) 413) Artwork and complete cover for a recording of music by one of the Beatles.
414) Cover for the selected music of a beat group.
415) Complete cover for a beat group. The polychrome artwork is a play on their name.
416) Complete cover for a beat group playing pieces by V. Vassilieff. Polychrome.
417) Back and front of a cover for music by a rock group, whose name suggests the apple.
418) Complete cover in pop Archimboldo style for renderings by a beat group.

412) 413) Illustration und vollständige Hülle für Aufnahmen eines Mitglieds der Beatles. Die Illustration spielt auf den Titel *Wonderwall Music* an.
414) Hülle für die Platte *Eggplant* (Nachtschattengewächse) der Popgruppe Cream.
415) Geöffnete Plattenhülle für Beatmusik. Die Umschlagillustration wurde durch den Namen der Gruppe inspiriert.
416) Vorder- und Rückseite einer Schallplattenhülle für eine Beatgruppe, die Stücke von V. Vassilieff spielt.
417) Vollständiges Album für die Rock-Gruppe Eden's Children. Roter Apfel – als Anspielung auf den Namen der Gruppe – auf dunkelviolettem Grund.
418) Von Archimboldo inspirierte, im Pop-Stil gehaltene Umschlagillustration der Beatplatte *Jellyroll*. Vorder- und Rückseite in bunten Farben.

412) 413) Composition et pochette complète pour un disque enregistré par l'un des Beatles.
414) Pochette pour une sélection de morceaux d'un groupe de beat avec allusion au titre (Solanacées).
415) Pochette complète pour un groupe de beat. La composition polychrome résulte d'un jeu de mots au sujet du titre.
416) Pochette complète pour un groupe de beat exécutant des œuvres de V. Vassilieff. En polychromie.
417) Recto et verso de la pochette du disque d'un groupe de rock dont le nom évoque l'image de la pomme.
418) Pochette complète de l'enregistrement d'un groupe de beat. Style pop inspiré d'Archimboldo.

412

ARTIST/KÜNSTLER/ARTISTE:

412) 413) Bob Gill
414) Jim Dine
415) Jimmy Grashow
416) Don Weller
417) Norman Trigg (Photo)
418) Ignazio Gomez

DESIGNER/GESTALTER/MAQUETTISTE:

412) 413) Bob Gill
415) Richard Mantel
416) Tom Lazarus
417) William Duevell/Henry Epstein
418) John LePrevost

ART DIRECTOR/DIRECTEUR ARTISTIQUE:

412) 413) Bob Gill
414) Nesuhi Ertegun
415) John Berg
416) 418) John LePrevost

413

414

415

416

418

417

PUBLISHER / VERLEGER / EDITEUR:

412) 413) Apple Records, London
414) Atlantic Recording Corp., New York
415) Epic/Columbia Records, New York
416) Universal City Records, Los Angeles
417) ABC Records, New York
418) Kapp Records, New York

419

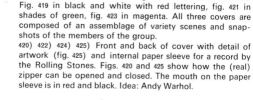

420

421

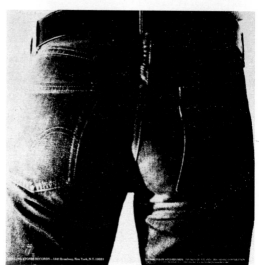

422

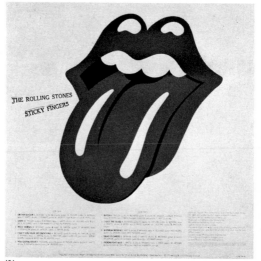

THE ROLLING STONES
STICKY FINGERS

423   424

419) 421) 423) Record cover proper and two internal sleeves for the Rolling Stones' recordings entitled *Exile on Main St.* Fig. 419 in black and white with red lettering, fig. 421 in shades of green, fig. 423 in magenta. All three covers are composed of an assemblage of variety scenes and snapshots of the members of the group.
420) 422) 424) 425) Front and back of cover with detail of artwork (fig. 425) and internal paper sleeve for a record by the Rolling Stones. Figs. 420 and 425 show how the (real) zipper can be opened and closed. The mouth on the paper sleeve is in red and black. Idea: Andy Warhol.

419) 421) 423) Eigentliche Schallplattenhülle und zwei Innenhüllen für *Exile on Main Street* der Rolling Stones. Abb. 419 in Schwarzweiss, Schrift in Magenta, Abb. 421 in Grün und Weiss, Abb. 423 in Magenta und Weiss. Einheitliche Aufmachung der Hüllen mit verschiedenen Schnappschüssen und Variété-Aufnahmen.
420) 422) 424) 425) Verschiedene Ansichten der Plattenhülle von *Sticky Fingers* (Rolling Stones). Abb. 420 und 425 Vorderseite mit halb geöffnetem und geschlossenem Reissverschluss (übrigens ein echter), Abb. 422 Rückseite der Hülle. Abb. 424: Innenhülle in Rot, Weiss und Schwarz. Idee: Andy Warhol.

419) 421) 423) Pochette et deux chemises intérieures pour les enregistrements des Rolling Stones intitulés *Exile on Main St.* 419) Noir et blanc, lettres rouges; 421) tons verts; 423) magenta. Ces trois enveloppes sont illustrées d'un assemblage de scènes de variétés et d'instantanés des divers membres du groupe.
420) 422) 424) 425) Recto et verso de la pochette et détail de la composition (425), ainsi que la chemise intérieure d'un disque des Rolling Stones. 420) et 425) Mode d'emploi de la vraie fermeture éclair de la pochette. Chemise: la bouche est rouge et noir. Idée: Andy Warhol.

ARTIST/KÜNSTLER/ARTISTE:

419) 421) 423) Robert Frank
420) 422) 424) 425) Andy Warhol

DESIGNER/GESTALTER/MAQUETTISTE:

419) 421) 423) John Van Hammersveld/
Norman Seeff
420) 422) 424) 425) Craig Braun

ART DIRECTOR/DIRECTEUR ARTISTIQUE:

419) 421) 423) Robert Frank
420) 422) 424) 425) Andy Warhol/Craig Braun

PUBLISHER/VERLEGER/EDITEUR:

419)–425) Atlantic Recording Corp., New York

Pop / Rock / Beat

THE ROLLING STONES
STICKY FINGERS

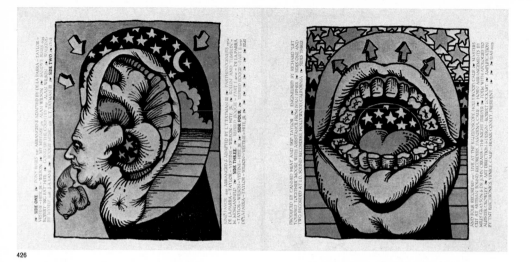

426

427

428

429

426) Inside spread of a double album of blues played by a pop group. The artwork is in shades of brown with orange stars. The same motifs are repeated on a smaller scale on the outside of the record cover.
427) Cover for a record by a pop group. Brown and green shades, white flowers, yellow lettering.
428) Inside spread of a pop blues record. Artwork painted in pastel shades on worm-eaten wooden boards suggested by the title.
429) Cover for a pop blues record by the same group as in fig. 427. Full colour.
430) Cover for a recording by a pop group, with photography suggested by the title.

426) Geöffnete Innenseite eines Doppelalbums für Pop-Blues der Gruppe Canned Heat. Verschiedene helle Brauntöne, orange Sterne. Die gleichen Sujets, etwas kleiner, erscheinen auf der Aussenseite der Hülle.
427) 429) Zwei Plattenhüllen für Aufnahmen von The New Birth. Abb. 427 in Braun, weisse Trompetenblumen, gelbe Schrift. Die ständig grösser werdenden Trompetenblumen beziehen sich auf den Titel: «Es ist nichts Grosses, aber es wächst ständig».
428) Geöffnete Hülle einer Pop-Blues-Platte. Auf Holz gemalte Illustration in hellen Grün- und Brauntönen mit Anspielung auf den Titel.
430) Schallplattenhülle für Aufnahmen einer Popgruppe.

426) Double page intérieure d'un album double de blues joués par un groupe pop. Composition aux tons bruns, étoiles orange. Le même motif se retrouve en format réduit sur la pochette.
427) Pochette pour le disque d'un groupe pop. Tons bruns et verts, fleurs blanches, lettres jaunes.
428) Double page intérieure d'un album de blues pop. Peinture aux tons pastels sur des planches de bois vermoulues évoquant le titre.
429) Pochette d'un disque de blues pop enregistré par le groupe de la fig. 427. En polychromie.
430) Pochette pour l'enregistrement d'un groupe pop. La photo s'inspire du titre.

ARTIST/KÜNSTLER/ARTISTE:
426) Norman Seeff
427) David Wilcox
428) David Anstey
429) David B. Hecht (Photo)
430) Roy Kohara (Photo)

DESIGNER/GESTALTER/MAQUETTISTE:
426) Robert Lockart
427) Acy R. Lehman
428) David Anstey
429) Frank Mulvey
430) Roy Kohara

ART DIRECTOR/DIRECTEUR ARTISTIQUE:
426) Norman Seeff
427) 429) Acy R. Lehman
428) Ralph Moore-Morris
430) George Osaki

PUBLISHER/VERLEGER/EDITEUR:
426) United Artists Records, Los Angeles
427) 429) RCA Records, New York
428) Decca/TELDEC «Telefunken-Decca», London, Hamburg
430) Invictus Records, Hollywood

Pop / Rock / Beat

EREO ST-7305

inside **the glass house**

INVICTUS RECORDS

431

Pop / Rock / Beat

146

432

433

434

435

436

431)–433) Photography, front and inside spread of a cover for a pop blues record.
434) Cover for a selection from the songs of Bob Dylan. Light blue ground.
435) Cover for a recording by a pop group. Title and "gem" in pale blue, green background.
436) Polychrome cover for a record by a pop group.
437) Cover for an album by a pop group.

431)–433) Detail, vollständige Vorderseite und geöffnete Innenseite einer Hülle für eine Pop-Blues-Platte.
434) Schallplattenhülle für die bekanntesten Songs von Bob Dylan. Blauer Grund.
435) Hülle für Aufnahmen einer Popgruppe. Grüner Grund, schwarze Handschuhe, blauweiss schillernde Schrift.
436) Mehrfarbige Hülle für die Popgruppe Stealers Wheel.
437) Vorderseite eines Plattenalbums für die Gruppe May Blitz. Schwarzweiss, Figur links in Farbe.

431)–433) Photo, extérieur et double page intérieure de la pochette réalisée pour un disque de blues pop.
434) Pochette conçue pour un choix de chansons de Bob Dylan. Fond bleu clair.
435) Pochette du disque d'un groupe pop. Titre et «joyau» bleu pâle sur fond vert.
436) Pochette polychrome pour le disque d'un groupe pop.
437) Pochette conçue pour l'album d'un groupe pop.

ARTIST/KÜNSTLER/ARTISTE:

431) 432) Norman Seeff (Photo)
433) Clive Arrowsmith (Photo)
434) Roland Scherman (Photo)
435) Terry Pastor
436) Patrick
437) Tony Benyon

DESIGNER/GESTALTER/MAQUETTISTE:

431)–433) Skip & Jim Taylor
434) John Berg
437) Tony Benyon

ART DIRECTOR/DIRECTEUR ARTISTIQUE:

431)–433) Norman Seeff
434) John Berg
435) 436) Michael Doud
437) Michael Stanford

PUBLISHER/VERLEGER/EDITEUR:

431)–433) United Artists Records, Los Angeles
434) Columbia Records, New York
435) 436) A & M Records, London
437) Vertigo/Phonogram, London

437

438

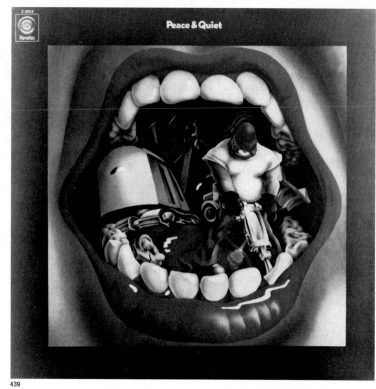

439

440

441

438) Straight archive photography on a cover for a group with a name borrowed from the Chinese.
439) Cover using pictorial elements—earth moving equipment, drill—that are in contrast with the title.
440) Surrealistic collage on a cover for a rock record by the group Moby Grape.
441) Cover for a double album by a blues singer and pianist. The full-colour artwork continues the interior shown on the old sepia photograph.
442) 443) One complete and one front cover for records of blues sung by Bessie Smith.

438) Umschlag für die zweite Platte der Gruppe Kin Ping Meh, deren Name von einem alten chinesischen Roman stammt.
439) Umschlag der Pop-Platte *Peace & Quiet* (Friede und Ruhe). Die Illustration mit Pressluftbohrer, Bagger und schreiendem Maul steht im Kontrast zum Plattentitel.
440) Surrealistische Collage mit überdimensionierter Traube als Symbol des Namens der Rockgruppe Moby Grape.
441) Doppelalbum für den Bluessänger und -pianisten Memphis Slim. Blauer Grund, Photographie in Sepia.
442) 443) Zwei Hüllen für Aufnahmen der Bluessängerin Bessie Smith. Das leere Bett (grünes Bettgestell) in Abb. 442 spielt auf das Titelstück an.

438) Simple photo documentaire pour la pochette d'un groupe ayant choisi un nom chinois.
439) Eléments illustratifs en contradiction avec le titre: matériel de terrassement, marteau pneumatique.
440) Collage surréaliste illustrant la pochette d'un disque de rock du groupe Moby Grape.
441) Pochette d'un album double enregistré par un chanteur de blues et pianiste. La composition polychrome élargit l'intérieur figurant sur la vieille photo bistrée.
442) 443) Pochette complète et recto d'une pochette pour des disques de blues chantés par Bessie Smith.

ARTIST/KÜNSTLER/ARTISTE:

438) Archiv Schapowalow
439) Robert Grossman
440) Bob Cato
441) Jean Lagarrigue
442) 443) Philip Hays

DESIGNER/GESTALTER/MAQUETTISTE:

438) Lipp+Hoffmann
439) Henrietta Condak
440) Bob Cato
441) Claude Caudron
442) 443) John Berg

ART DIRECTOR/DIRECTEUR ARTISTIQUE:

438) Stefan Böhle
439) John Berg/Richard Mantel
440) Bob Cato
441) Alain Marouani
442) 443) John Berg

PUBLISHER/VERLEGER/EDITEUR:

438) Zebra/Deutsche Grammophon Ges., Hamburg
439) 440) 442) 443) Columbia Records, New York
441) Barclay Disques, Neuilly s/Seine

443

442

444

445

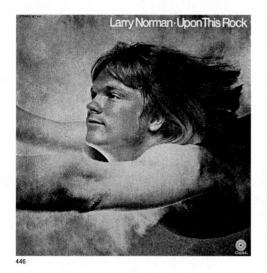

446

447

448

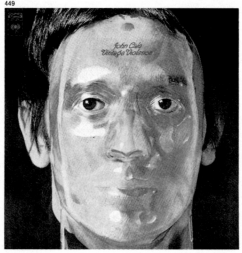

449

450 a

ARTIST/KÜNSTLER/ARTISTE:

444) Bill Imhoff
445) Peter Gowland (Photo)
446) Ed Simpson (Photo)
447) Thomas Höpker
448) Roy Kohara/Ken Veeder/
Rick Rankin (Photo)
449) Isi Valeris (Photo)
450) 450a) Joe Garnet

DESIGNER/ART DIRECTOR:

444) 445) Virginia Team/John Berg
446) Dave Coleman/George Osaki
447) Ulfert Dirichs/Stefan Böhle
448) Roy Kohara/George Osaki
449) Richard Mantel/John Berg
450) 450a) Chuck Beeson/
Roland Young

PUBLISHER/VERLEGER/EDITEUR:

444) 445) 449) Columbia, New York
446) 448) Capitol, Hollywood
447) Polydor/Deutsche Grammophon
450) 450a) A & M, Hollywood

444) 445) Covers for records by a beat group. Fig. 444, blood-red title, blue-green ground; fig. 445, photograph of human body, pink title, blue ground.
446) Photographic cover for religious rock.
447) Cover for the group Epitaph. Red sign, grey-green dunes.
448) Cover for a rock record. Photograph of broken glass, black title red splashes of "blood".
449) For a rock record. Face with plastic mask in shades of pink.
450) 450a) Artwork and complete cover for a rock record.

444) 445) Zwei Hüllen der Rock-Gruppe Sweathog. Abb. 444: Rote Schrift auf hellem Grund. Abb. 445: Rosa Schrift auf Hellblau, vornübergebeugter Körper bläulich.
446) Hülle für Rock-Songs mit religiösem Inhalt. Blau.
447) Dünenlandschaft mit roter Tafel für die Rockgruppe Epitaph.
448) Umschlag einer Rockplatte. Schwarze Schrift, eingeschlagene Scheibe, rote Blutspritzer.
449) Plattenhülle für eine Rockplatte von John Cale. Durchsichtige rosa Gesichtsmaske auf schwarzem Grund.
450) 450a) Plattenhülle für den Rocksänger Gary Wright.

444) 445) Pochettes pour des disques d'un groupe de beat. 444) titre rouge sang, fond bleu vert; 445) photo d'un corps humain, titre rose, fond bleu.
446) Pochette photo pour un disque de rock religieux.
447) Pour le groupe Epitaph. Signe rouge, dunes gris vert.
448) Pochette d'un disque de rock. Photo d'un verre brisé, titre noir, éclaboussures de «sang» rouge.
449) Pochette pour un disque de rock. Visage au masque plastique en divers tons roses.
450) 450a) Composition et pochette complète. Disque de rock.

451) Cover for a rock group, the members of which are shown as cherubs.
452) Black-and-white cover for a recording by a rock group.
453) Cover for an album on the outlaws of the early West.
454) Complete cover for a recording of songs by Claudia Lennear.
455) Cover for a recording of rock music, with a photographic interpretation of the title.
456) Cover for rock music, with a reference to the head of John the Baptist on a charger.
457) Surrealistic cover, with inset in pastel shades, for a rock group.

451) Umschlag einer Folk-Rock-Platte, mit den Mitgliedern der Gruppe als herumfliegende Engel.
452) Schwarzweissumschlag für eine Schallplatte der Popgruppe Grail.
453) Vorwiegend in Grüntönen gehaltene Hülle eines Albums als Dokumentarplatte über die Volks- musik der Banditen des «Wilden Westens» gedacht.
454) Geöffnete Hülle eines Albums für Aufnahmen der Sängerin Claudia Lennear.
455) Umschlag für eine Platte mit bekannten Rock-Aufnahmen. Die Umschlagillustration mit dem das O durchbrechenden Bohrer ist eine photographische Interpretation des Titels.
456) Schallplattenhülle für Aufnahmen einer Rockgruppe. Die Illustration spielt auf Johannes den Täufer an, dessen Kopf König Herodes auf einer Schale präsentiert wurde.
457) Surrealistische Umschlagillustration in matten Farben für die Rockgruppe Epitaph.

451) Pochette pour un groupe de rock représenté sous les traits d'un chœur de chérubins.
452) Pochette noir et blanc pour le disque d'un groupe de rock.
453) Pochette d'un album sur les premiers hors-la-loi de l'Ouest américain.
454) Pochette complète d'un enregistrement de chansons par Claudia Lennear.
455) Pochette d'un disque de rock, avec une interprétation photographique du titre.
456) Pochette pour un disque de rock. Allusion à la tête de saint Jean-Baptiste présentée an Roi Hérode sur un plateau.
457) Pochette surréaliste avec encart aux tons pastels pour un groupe de rock.

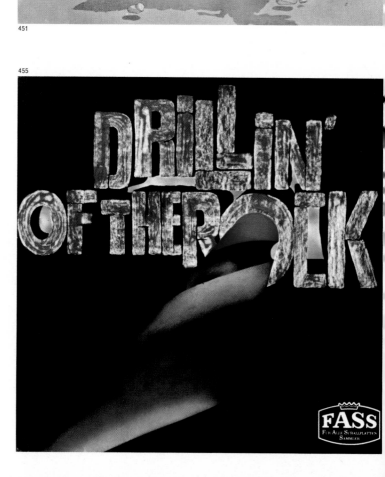

451

ARTIST/KÜNSTLER/ARTISTE:

451) Kim Whitesides
452) Richard Matouschek
453) Henry Parker (Photo)
454) Norman Seeff (Photo)
455) Klaus Witt
456) Fred Marcellino
457) H.J. Löffler

DESIGNER/GESTALTER/MAQUETTISTE:

451) Acy R. Lehman
453) Edwin Lee
454) John Van Hammersveld
456) Fred Marcellino
457) Ulfert Dirichs

ART DIRECTOR/DIRECTEUR ARTISTIQUE:

451) Acy R. Lehman
452) Clemens Krauss
453) Bob Cato/John Berg
454) John Van Hammersveld
455) Wilfried Mannes
456) Allen Davis
457) Stefan Böhle

PUBLISHER/VERLEGER/EDITEUR:

451) RCA Records, New York
452) Metronome Records, Hamburg
453) Columbia Records, New York
454) Warner Bros. Records, Burbank, Ca.
455) Fass/Phonogram, Hamburg
456) Capitol Records, Hollywood
457) Deutsche Grammophon Ges., Hamburg

454

455

452

453

456

457

Pop / Rock / Beat

458 a

ARTIST/KÜNSTLER/ARTISTE:

458) Gene Szafran
458a) William S. Harvey/
      Joel Brodsky (Photo)
459) Art Kane (Photo)
460) H + U Osterwalder
461) M. C. Escher
462) Jim McCrary (Photo)

DESIGNER/GESTALTER/MAQUETTISTE:

458) 458a) William S. Harvey
459) John Berg
460) H + U Osterwalder
461) Milton Glaser
462) Chuck Beeson

ART DIRECTOR/DIRECTEUR ARTISTIQUE:

458) 458a) William S. Harvey
459) John Berg
460) Willy Fleckhaus
461) Milton Glaser
462) Roland Young

PUBLISHER/VERLEGER/EDITEUR:

458) 458a) Elektra Records, New York
459) Columbia Records, New York
460) Twen/Gruner + Jahr, Hamburg
461) Poppy Records, New York
462) A & M Records, Hollywood

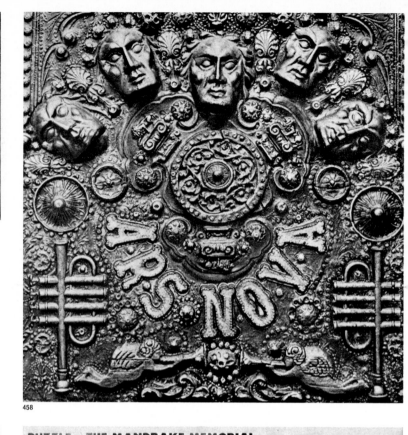

458

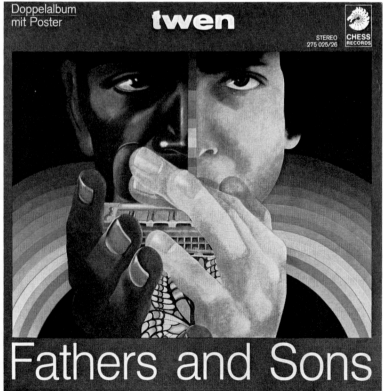

460

461

459

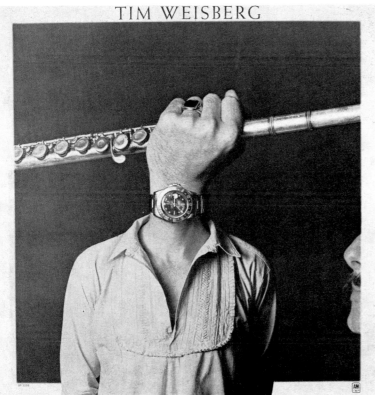

462

458) 458a) Inside page and cover of an album for a rock group. Fig. 458 is a photograph of a coloured relief composition.
459) Complete cover for a rock group, whose name has been cut in the turf.
460) Cover of a blues album which also contained a poster with the same motif. Half of the mouth-organ-player is black, the other half white.
461) Black-and-white cover for a rock group, using an optical illusion drawing by M. C. Escher.
462) Cover for a recording by a flautist "somewhere in between rock and jazz". Colour photograph, green shirt, dark blue ground.

458) 458a) Innenseite und Titelseite eines Plattenalbums der Gruppe Ars Nova. Basrelief auf der Innenseite in verschiedenen dunklen Farbtönen.
459) Geöffnete Hülle mit in die Wiese gepflügtem Namen der Rockgruppe Madura.
460) Hülle eines Doppelalbums, das von der Zeitschrift *Twen* herausgegeben wurde. Der Mund-harmonikaspieler hat eine schwarze und eine weisse Gesichtshälfte.
461) Schwarzweisshülle eines Albums für Aufnahmen der Rockgruppe The Mandrake Memorial. Als Illustration, die auf die Rückseite überläuft, wurde ein Bild M. C. Eschers verwendet.
462) Photographische Interpretation als Umschlagillustration für die Rock-Jazz-Platte des Flötisten Tim Weisberg. Dunkelblauer Grund.

458) 458a) Page intérieure et pochette d'un album enregistré par un groupe de rock. La fig. 458) est la photo d'une composition en relief en couleur.
459) Pochette complète pour un groupe de rock dont le nom a été découpé dans le gazon.
460) Pochette d'un album de blues contenant un poster illustré du même motif. Le joueur d'harmo-nica est représenté moitié blanc, moitié noir.
461) Pochette noir et blanc pour un groupe de rock. Dessin d'illusion optique de M. C. Escher.
462) Pochette pour l'enregistrement d'un flûtiste évoluant «quelque part entre le rock et le jazz». Photo couleur, chemise verte, fond bleu foncé.

463

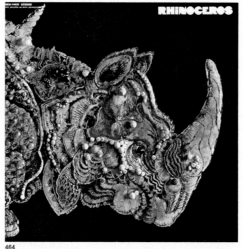

464

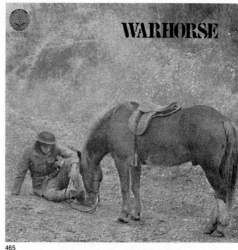

465

466

467

468

ARTIST/KÜNSTLER/ARTISTE:

463) Don Jim
464) Gene Szafran
465) Keef
466) Gretchen Deans (Photo)
467) Bob Prokop (Photo)
469) Pete Smith (Photo)

DESIGNER/ART DIRECTOR:

463) Beverly Parker/Virginia Team
464) William S. Harvey
465) Keef/Sandy Field/Michael Stanford
466) 468) Richard Mantel/John Berg
467) John Craig/Anne Garner
469) Robin Nicol (Design Machine)/
     Michael Stanford

PUBLISHER/VERLEGER/EDITEUR:

463) 466)–468) Columbia Records, New York
464) Elektra Records, New York
465) 469) Vertigo/Phonogram, London

463) Cover for a selection of pieces from the rock opera
     Jesus Christ, Superstar.
464) Cover for a rock record. Polychrome assemblage.
465) Double album in muted colours for a rock group, whose
     name suggested the motif.
466) Cover using polychrome interiors for classical rock.
467) Cover for a folk rock record. The group appears in a
     setting that interprets the title.
468) Cover for a rock group using a genuine old railroad shot
     in which the group has been integrated.
469) Cover for a recording by a rock group whose name
     awakens literary associations.

463) Schallplattenhülle für Aufnahmen aus der Rockoper
     Jesus Christ Superstar.
464) Hülle für die Rockplatte *Rhinoceros.* Mehrfarbige
     Assemblage auf schwarzem Grund.
465) Das Schlachtross als Umschlagillustration soll den
     Namen der Rockgruppe Warhorse symbolisieren.
     Plattenhülle in gedämpften Farben.
466) Hülle für eine Rockplatte von John Cale. Mehrfarbig.
467) Mehrfarbige Plattenhülle für Folk-Rock-Aufnahmen.
468) Handkolorierter Umschlag für die Rockplatte *Pigiron.*
469) Plattenalbum für Aufnahmen von Uriah Heep und
     seiner Rockband.

463) Pochette pour un choix de morceaux tirés de l'opéra
     rock *Jesus Christ Superstar.*
464) Pour un disque de rock. Assemblage polychrome.
465) Album double aux tons mats pour un groupe de rock
     dont le nom a fourni le thème illustratif.
466) Pochette de rock classique. Intérieurs polychromes.
467) Pochette d'un disque de rock populaire. Le décor où
     apparaît le groupe livre une interprétation du titre.
468) Pochette pour un groupe de rock placé dans le décor
     authentique d'un chemin de fer du bon vieux temps.
469) Pochette pour l'enregistrement d'un groupe de rock
     dont le nom fait surgir des associations littéraires.

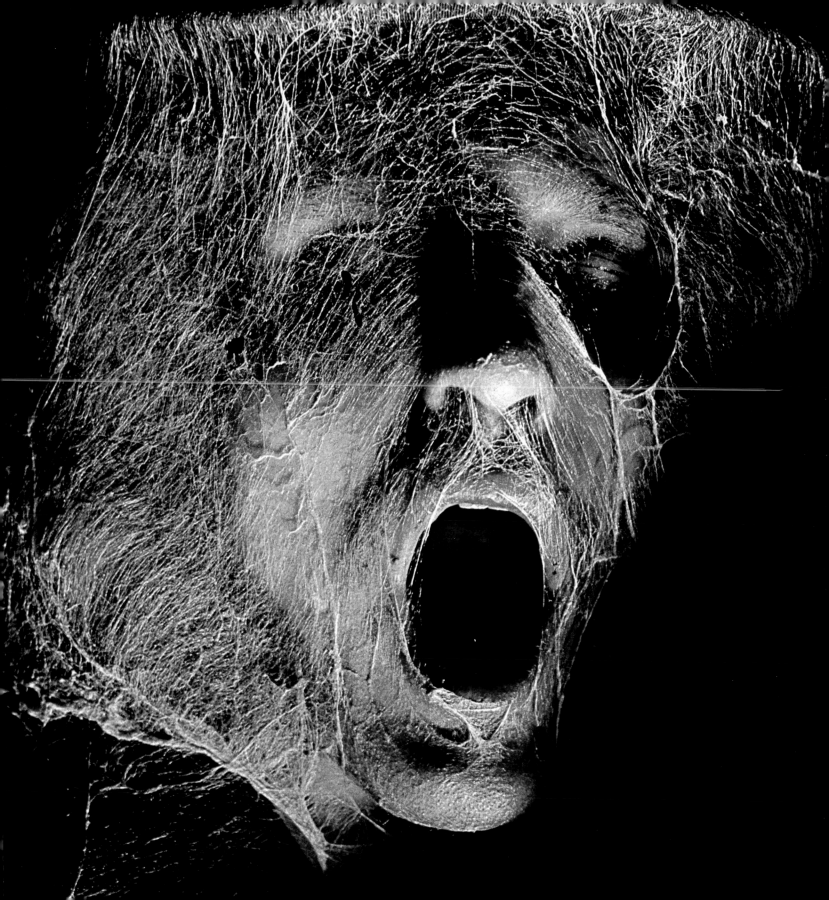

470

470) Two panels of a double album with a live recording of soul at Carnegie Hall.
471) Record cover for a rock group, whose portraits appear on yellow paper through die-cut holes in the pink-and-grey design of the cover.
472) Black-and-white cover for protest songs.
473) Cover for a live recording of a soul band. Polychrome circles on green.
474) Black-and-white design for songs by Lindenberg, whose name suggested the linden and mountain (German *Berg*).
475) Cover in surrealistic vein for a song record.
476) Cover for a record alluding to the American presidential elections of 1972. Flat colours.
477) Record cover for songs by a soul singer.
478) Cover for rock versions of music from the 1920's.
479) Cover for a recording by Paul Williams. Pastel shades.

470) Geöffnete Hülle eines Doppelalbums mit Live-Aufnahmen eines Konzerts der Soulsänger Ike and Tina Turner.
471) Hülle in matten Blautönen für Aufnahmen der Siren. Die gelbschwarze Innenhülle wird im ausgestanzten Kreis, der von einer Rauchwolke durchbrochen wird, sichtbar.
472) Karikierter Bandname mit Gefängnismauer, Atompilz hinter Gitterstäben, Gitarren als Axt und Maschinengewehr.
473) Hülle für Live-Aufnahmen eines Soulkonzerts in Hamburg. Label in verschiedenen Farben auf Grün.
474) Grauweisse Hülle einer Platte mit Songs von Lindenberg.
475) Surrealistische Umschlagillustration für eine Songplatte.
476) Popgruppen spielen für die Präsidentenwahlen in den USA.
477) Hülle für Aufnahmen des Soulsängers Solomon Burke.
478) Jugendstilillustration für Rockmusik mit Themen aus den 20er Jahren.
479) Hülle einer Platte von Paul Williams. Pastellfarben.

470) Deux volets d'un album double avec un enregistrement direct de soul au Carnegie Hall.
471) Pochette de disque pour un groupe de rock dont les portraits apparaissent sur fond jaune après découpe de la composition rose et gris.
472) Pochette noir et blanc pour des chansons contestataires.
473) Pochette pour l'enregistrement direct d'un orchestre de soul. Cercles polychromes sur fond vert.
474) Design noir et blanc pour des chansons de Lindenberg, nom évoquant le tilleul *(Linde)* et la montagne *(Berg)*.
475) Pochette de style surréaliste pour un disque de chansons.
476) Pochette pour un disque faisant allusion aux élections présidentielles de 1972 en Amérique. Couleurs mates.
477) Pochette pour le disque d'un chanteur de soul.
478) Pour des versions rock de la musique des années 20.
479) Pochette pour un disque de Paul Williams. Tons pastels.

477

471

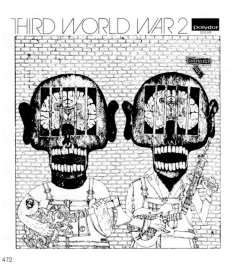

472

473

474

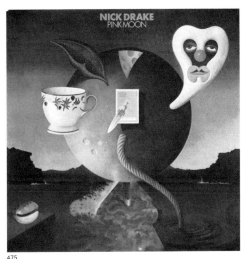

475

476

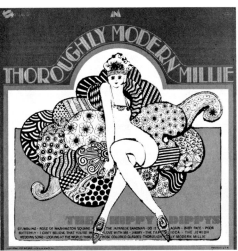

478

479

ART DIRECTOR/DIRECTEUR ARTISTIQUE:

470) Norman Seeff
471) Robert L. Heimall
472) Hartmut Pfeiffer
473) Jochen Hinze
475) Ann Sullivan
476) Chris Whorf
477) Nesuhi Ertegun
478) Paul Hauge/Dwight Frazier
479) Roland Young

PUBLISHER/VERLEGER/EDITEUR:

470) United Artists Records, Los Angeles
471) Elektra Records, New York
472) Polydor/Deutsche Grammophon Ges., Hamburg
473) Karussell/Deutsche Grammophon Ges., Hamburg
474) TELDEC «Telefunken-Decca» Schallplatten, Hamburg
475) Island Records, London
476) Warner Bros. Records, Burbank, Ca.
477) Atlantic Recording Corp., New York
478) Universal City Records, Los Angeles
479) A & M Records, Hollywood

480

480) 481) Complete cover and artwork for a rock record.
482) Complete outside cover for a recording of music by a blind composer. Red cap and robe.
483) Complete outside cover for a rock record.
484) Complete outside cover for a record by a group who are portrayed in the giant's hand.
485) Brightly coloured cover for a soft rock record.
486) Cover for a rock record.
487) Cover for a recording by a rock group. Bright colours, purple beans.
488) Cover interpreting the title. Chiefly green shades.

480) 481) Vollständige Hülle und Illustration für Rockmusik.
482) Für Aufnahmen von Moondog, einer bekannten Gestalt in New Yorks Strassenbild.
483) Riesenvögel zur Illustration des Titels einer Rockplatte.
484) Aufgeklappte Hülle für die Rockplatte der Gentle Giant.
485) Mehrfarbige Hülle für die Rockband November.
486) Hülle für Aufnahmen einer New Yorker Rockgruppe.
487) Überall violette Bohnen zur Illustration des Namens. Hülle in Orange, Grün, Blau für Folk-Rock-Aufnahmen.
488) Umschlag in hellem Grün mit Nachtwandlern in Traumlandschaft als Anspielung auf den Titel.

480) 481) Pochette complète et composition. Disque de rock.
482) Faces externes complètes d'une pochette réalisée pour un compositeur aveugle. Casquette et robe rouges.
483) Recto et verso d'une pochette de rock.
484) Recto et verso d'une pochette conçue pour le groupe montré dans la main du géant.
485) Pochette aux couleurs vives pour un disque de soft rock.
486) Pochette d'un disque de rock.
487) Pochette pour l'enregistrement d'un groupe de rock. Couleurs vives, haricots pourpres.
488) Pochette interprétant le titre. Tons verts prédominants.

481

ARTIST/KÜNSTLER/ARTISTE:

480) 481) Peter Schauman
482) Don Hunstein (Photo)
484) George Underwood
485) Ronald Wolin
486) Ron Coro
487) John Van Hammersveld
488) Graham Wilson

DESIGNER/GESTALTER/MAQUETTISTE:

482) 486) Ron Coro
483) Tony Lane
484) Design Machine
488) John Berg

ART DIRECTOR/DIRECTEUR ARTISTIQUE:

480) 481) 483) John Berg/Tony Lane
482) 486) 488) John Berg
484) Michael Stanford
485) Ronald Wolin
487) John Van Hammersveld/Norman Seeff

160

485

486

482

483

484

487

488

PUBLISHER / VERLEGER / EDITEUR:

480)—483) 486) 488) Columbia Records, New York
484) Vertigo/Phonogram, London
485) A & M Records, Hollywood
487) United Artists Records, Los Angeles

Pop / Rock / Beat

Pop / Rock / Beat

489

490

489) Photographic cover for soul sung by a coloured couple.
490) Black-and-white cover for a recording by a pop composer and singer.
491) Motif suggested by the title with photographic background and brilliant green cabbage.
492) Cover for a pop record in colour photography, using a three-dimensional "sign".
493) 494) Inside spread of a record cover, showing the members of the group in black and white, and front cover. The Churchillian V-for-victory sign has been converted into a three-finger W for war.

489) Vorderseite eines Plattenalbums mit Aufnahmen der Soul-sänger Ike und Tina Turner.
490) Schwarzweisse Plattenhülle für den Popsänger Toussaint.
491) Giftgrüner, überdimensionierter Kohl mitten auf der Strasse als Anspielung auf den Plattentitel *Cabbage Alley.*
492) Mehrfarbige Plattenhülle mit «lachendem Sandwich» auf braunem Brett, für Aufnahmen von Philip Cody.
493) 494) Innenseite mit den Mitgliedern der Gruppe (schwarz-weiss) und Titelseite eines Albums mit Rock-Jazz-Auf-nahmen der Gruppe War. In Anlehnung an Churchills V-Zeichen für Victory (Sieg), sollen die drei ausgestreckten Finger das «W» von War (Krieg) symbolisieren.

489) Pour un disque de soul chanté par un couple.
490) Pochette noir et blanc pour le disque d'un compositeur et chanteur pop.
491) Thème inspiré par le titre (Rue du Chou); fond photo-graphique, chou vert brillant.
492) Pochette pour un disque pop. Photo couleur, «enseigne» tridimensionnel.
493) 494) Double page intérieure d'une pochette montrant les musiciens du groupe en noir et blanc, et recto de la pochette. Le fameux V de Churchill (Victoire) a été trans-formé en W (trois doigts levés) pour «War» = guerre.

491

492

ARTIST/KÜNSTLER/ARTISTE:

489) Herb Krawitz (Photo)
491) Dave Williardson
492) Stan Glaubach/Nick Sangiamo (Photo)
493) 494) Bob Cato/Norman Seeff (Photo)

DESIGNER/GESTALTER/MAQUETTISTE:

489) Ronald Wolin
490) 491) Jon Echevarrieta
492) Steven Bernstein
493) 494) Eric Burdon

ART DIRECTOR/DIRECTEUR ARTISTIQUE:

489) Ronald Wolin
490) 491) Ed Thrasher
492) Steven Bernstein
493) 494) Norman Seeff

PUBLISHER/VERLEGER/EDITEUR:

489) 493) 494) Liberty/United Artists, Los Angeles
490) 491) Warner Bros. Records, Burbank, Ca.
492) RCA Records, New York

493

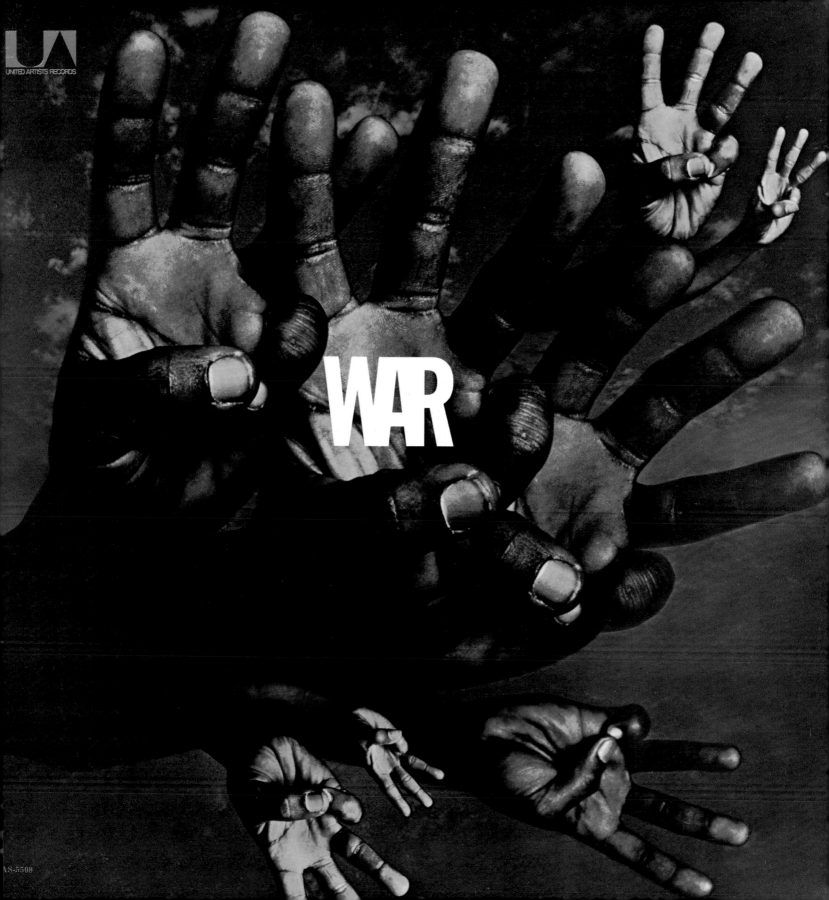

Pop / Rock / Beat

495

496

499

501

500

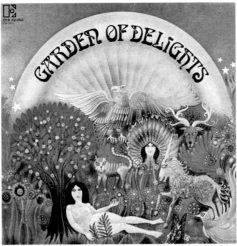

97

498

502

ART DIRECTOR/DIRECTEUR ARTISTIQUE:

495) 499) Mark Schulman
496) M. Chambosse
497) Giannici/Spinelli
498) Robert L. Heimall
500) John Berg
501) Roland Young

PUBLISHER/VERLEGER/EDITEUR:

495) 498) Atlantic Recording Corp., New York
496) Karussell/Deutsche Grammophon Gesellschaft, Hamburg
497) Dischi Numero Uno, Milan
498) Elektra Records, New York
500) Epic/Columbia Records, New York
501) A & M Records, Hollywood
502) Island Records/Ariola-Eurodisc

495) Cover for a record by a soul singer. Head outlined in yellow on red disc.
496) Cover in poppish colours, with cream, for an anthology of music by the group of that name.
497) Front of a record cover for an Italian group (Premiata Forneria Marconi).
498) Polychrome design suggested by the title for a double album with a selection of blues and other songs.
499) Combination of artwork and photography on a cover for a record by a vocalist and pianist.
500) Black-and-white cover for music by a rock group.
501) Photograph of water droplets forming the performer's name used as a cover design.
502) Artwork, mostly in reds and blues, on the front of a record by the King Crimson group.

495) Plattenhülle in dunklen Farbtönen für Aufnahmen des Soulsängers Isaac Hayes.
496) Mit Rahm (cream) garnierte Früchte als Umschlagmotiv für eine Platte der Popgruppe Cream.
497) Mehrfarbige Hülle eines Plattenalbums der italienischen Popgruppe Premiata Forneria Marconi.
498) Hülle des Doppelalbums *Garden of Delights* (Garten der Lüste). Vorwiegend in Grün, Rosa und Blau.
499) In gedämpften Farben gehaltenes Plattenalbum mit graphischen und photographischen Elementen für einen Sänger und Pianisten.
500) Schwarzweisse Plattenhülle für Aufnahmen der Popgruppe Catfish. Der Name bedeutet Katzenwels.
501) Umschlag einer Platte von Renée Armana.
502) Auf die Rückseite überlaufende Illustration des Plattenalbums *In the Court of the Crimson King* mit Aufnahmen der Popgruppe King Crimson. Rot und blau.

495) Pochette pour le disque d'un chanteur de soul. Les contours de la tête sont soulignés en jaune sur un disque rouge.
496) Pochette aux couleurs pop, avec de la crème, pour une anthologie des œuvres du groupe Cream (crème).
497) Recto d'une pochette réalisée pour un groupe italien (Premiata Forneria Marconi).
498) Composition polychrome inspirée du titre de l'album double (recueil de blues et d'autres chansons).
499) Composition mi-graphique mi-photographique pour le disque d'un chanteur-pianiste.
500) Pochette noir-blanc pour un groupe de rock.
501) Pour cette pochette, le nom de l'interprète écrit en goutelettes d'eau a fourni un joli thème de design.
502) Composition pour la pochette d'un disque du groupe King Crimson. Prédominance de tons rouges et bleus.

165

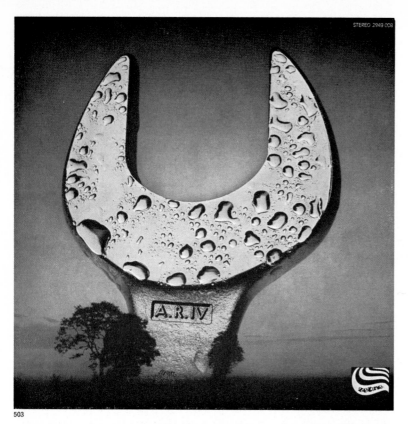

503

503) Cover for music by the Achim Reichel group. Superimposition of two photographs.
504) Cover for a recording by a German group. Figures chiefly in pale pink and blue shades.
505) Complete cover for a record by Ike and Tina Turner. The front cover proper is in red and blue shades, the smaller pictures that frame it can be folded inwards as shown in figs. 505a and 505b.

503) Schallplattenhülle für Aufnahmen von Achim Reichel und seiner Gruppe, mit zwei übereinander kopierten Photographien als Umschlagillustration.
504) Umschlag einer neuen Schallplatte der Gruppe Abacus. Figuren in Hellviolett, Blau, Türki und Schwarz.
505) Vollständig ausgelegte Schallplattenhülle für Aufnahmen von Ike and Tina Turner. Der eigentliche Umschlag ist rot und blau, die kleineren Aufnahmen rundherum können hereingeklappt werden, wie Abb. 505a und 505b zeigen.

503) Pochette pour un disque du groupe Achim Reichel. Surimpression de deux photos.
504) Pochette pour l'enregistrement d'un groupe allemand. Tons rose pâle et bleus prédominants.
505) Pochette complète pour un disque de Ike et Tina Turner. Le recto est imprimé en divers rouge et bleus; les petites images qui l'encadrent peuvent se replier vers l'intérieur, comme le montrent les figures 505a et 505b.

504

ARTIST/KÜNSTLER/ARTISTE:

503) Jacques Schumacher/
     Bert Brüggemann (Photo)
504) Henrike Bröse
505) 505a) 505b) Norman Seeff (Photo)

DESIGNER/GESTALTER/MAQUETTISTE:

503) Fact-Design
504) Ulfert Dirichs
505) 505a) 505b) Norman Seeff/Dave Bhang

ART DIRECTOR/DIRECTEUR ARTISTIQUE:

503) Stefan Böhle
504) Marion Cordes
505) 505a) 505b) Norman Seeff

PUBLISHER/VERLEGER/EDITEUR:

503) 504) Zebra/Deutsche Grammophon
     Gesellschaft, Hamburg
505) 505a) 505b) United Artists Records,
     Los Angeles

505 a

505 b

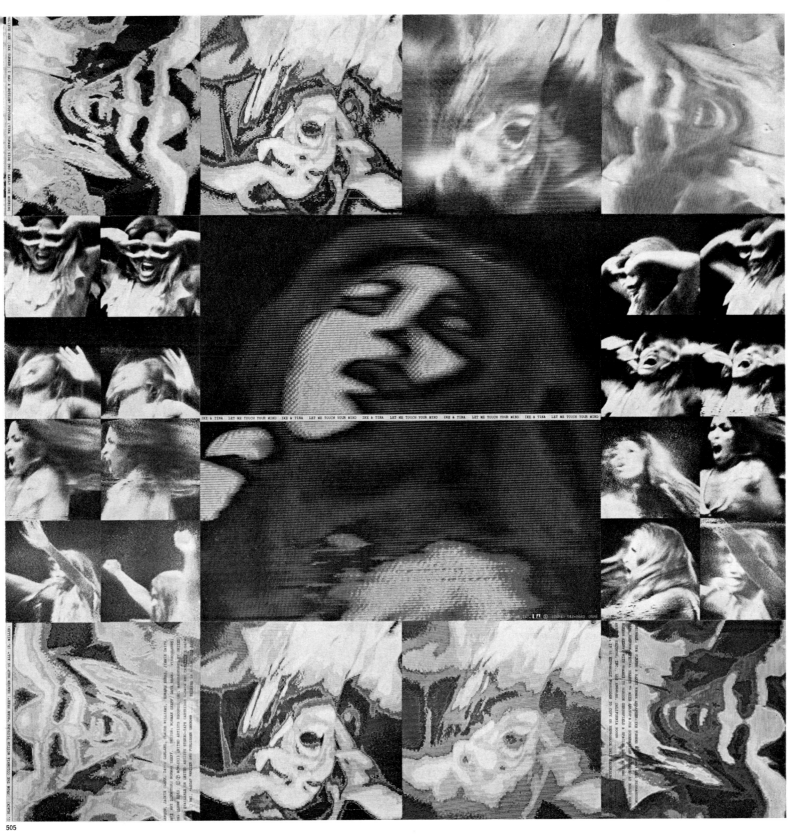

IKE & TINA   LET ME TOUCH YOUR MIND   IKE & TINA   LET ME TOUCH YOUR MIND   IKE & TINA   LET ME TOUCH YOUR MIND   IKE & TINA   LET ME TOUCH YOUR MIND   IKE & TINA   LET ME TOUCH YOUR MIND

Stanley Mason

Since there is no rule without an exception, there are record covers which do not fit into any of the common-or-garden categories. A first group of these is different because its contents are different: not music this time, or at least not music for straight entertainment, but the spoken word, or a course of instruction, or a document of sounds, or even a collection of many forms of audible communication on a given theme. Obvious examples of such records are bedtime tales for children (told better than mummy can usually tell them); readings from poetry, perhaps upgraded by the voice of the poet himself; voices of birds or animals, otherwise so elusive and uncapturable, captured for the nature-lover and student; or courses of music, for instance, in which the various instruments can be made to talk beautifully in turn.

The assignment of the record-cover designer is here often much more clearly defined than in the wide open spaces of musical interpretation. A cover for Beethoven's Ninth or for songs by the Beatles may leave enormous scope for the artist's imagination; but a recording of heart sounds gives him a pretty specific brief. The need to take careful aim is not always a disadvantage to the designer; it sometimes compels him to come up with the incisive idea, as in the covers for a course of creative writing which mark the stages in the solving of a jigsaw puzzle of a typewriter.

A second category of work included in this section is native to Japan and is unusual in so far as the records for which the covers are designed are non-existent. The Asahi and Mainichi newspapers, and the Japan Advertising Artists Club in its day, have organized competitions in which young designers are invited to submit, for instance, cover projects for fictitious records of their choice. Some of these have been so striking in their imaginative approach that they deserve to be reproduced here if only for their inspirational value.

In a last category the record cover ceases to be merely a package, however attractive, for the piece of acoustic communication it encloses and becomes part of a multimedia unit which the buyer acquires. At this point the cover is transformed into a work of creative presentation and begins to live a life of its own. It may unfold ingeniously, have perforations leading to the heart of its mystery, or sport a lid that opens on discoveries. Now the album is art in its own right, and perhaps one day there will be collectors who will keep the cover and throw the record away.

Da es keine Regel gibt ohne Ausnahme, gibt es auch Plattenhüllen, die sich nicht in die üblichen Kategorien einordnen lassen. Eine erste Gruppe ist schon vom Inhalt her verschieden: es handelt sich nicht um Musik, jedenfalls nicht um Musik zur Unterhaltung, es geht hier um das gesprochene Wort, um einen Lehrgang oder ein Tondokument oder sogar um eine Sammlung verschiedener Kommunikationsformen zu einem gegebenen Thema. Als typische Vertreter dieser Gruppe gelten die Gute-Nacht-Geschichten (willkommen für erzählerisch weniger begabte Mütter); literarische Aufzeichnungen, die vielleicht durch die Stimme des Dichters noch aufgewertet werden; Vogel- und Tierstimmen, sonst nur mit Glück oder viel Geduld zu hören, nun für den Naturfreund auf die Platte gebannt; Musiklehrkurse mit den einzelnen Instrumentenstimmen.

Die Aufgabe des Designers wird hier, im Gegensatz zu musikalischen Interpretationen, durch gewisse Richtlinien definiert. Eine Hülle für Beethovens Neunte oder Songs der Beatles lässt der Phantasie des Künstlers sehr viel mehr Spielraum, wogegen eine Aufnahme von Herztönen ihm ziemlich enge, vorgegebene Grenzen setzt. Sich genau an ein bestimmtes Thema halten zu müssen, ist nicht immer ein Nachteil, denn es zwingt den Künstler oft, eine effektvolle Idee zu finden: so zeigt z. B. die Folge von Plattenhüllen für einen Scriptwriter-Kurs die Fortschritte des Lernenden durch das langsam Gestalt annehmende Puzzle einer Schreibmaschine.

Eine zweite Gruppe ist japanischen Hüllen gewidmet, die aussergewöhnlich sind, weil sie für nichtexistierende Platten gestaltet wurden. In Wettbewerben, die die Zeitungen Asahi und Mainichi sowie der frühere Japan Advertising Artists Club organisierten, wurden junge Designer eingeladen, Projekte für fiktive Platten einzusenden. Einige sind graphisch und ideenmässig so gelungen, dass eine Reproduktion auf diesen Seiten ohne Zweifel gerechtfertigt ist.

Zu einer letzten Kategorie gehören Hüllen, die nicht nur als eigentliche Verpackung des musikalischen Inhalts gedacht sind – sie sind Teil einer Multimedia-Einheit, die dem Käufer angeboten wird. Die Hülle wird hier zum Mittel der kreativen Präsentation, sie geht weit über ihre eigentliche Zweckbestimmung hinaus. Sie wird auf ausgeklügelte Weise auseinandergefaltet, hat Öffnungen, die ein geheimnisvolles Inneres enthüllen, oder einen Deckel, der geöffnet werden will und unwahrscheinliche Funde blosslegt. Hier wird die Hülle zur eigenständigen Kunstform, und vielleicht gibt es eines Tages Sammler, die die Hülle aufbewahren und die Platte wegwerfen.

Comme toute règle comporte ses exceptions, il existe toute une série de pochettes de disques qui ne rentrent dans aucune des catégories habituelles. Un premier groupe se définit en raison de son contenu différent: non pas de la musique, du moins pas de la musique destinée au délassement, mais des paroles, ou un cours d'instruction, ou un document sonore, ou même une collection de différentes formes de communication audio pour un thème donné. C'est donc ici que l'on rangera les histoires pour endormir les enfants (la planche de salut des mamans peu douées); les récitations poétiques, parfois magnifiées par la voix du poète; les cris d'animaux, d'oiseaux difficiles à capter dans leur milieu naturel, pour l'ami des bêtes et l'étudiant; les cours de musique qui mettent si bien en relief les divers instruments.

La voie est ici bien mieux tracée au créateur de pochettes que dans le domaine musical général. La Neuvième de Beethoven, un disque des Beatles, voilà des sujets propres à donner des ailes à l'imagination de l'artiste. Un enregistrement des bruits du cœur, par contre, réduit sensiblement la marge de création. Et pourtant, restriction porte richesse, et plus d'une idée convaincante naît dans l'espace de contrainte d'un cours de rédaction créatrice, par exemple, dont les pochettes successives assemblent le puzzle d'une machine à écrire.

Passons à un autre groupe, insolite et japonais cette fois-ci. Les journaux Asahi et Mainichi, le Japan Advertising Artists Club à l'époque, ont organisé à l'intention des jeunes designers des concours de création de pochettes pour disques fictifs. Pochettes sans disques donc, dont certaines sont assez exceptionnelles pour mériter une reproduction.

Le troisième groupe de pochettes inclassables nous fait quitter le domaine de «l'emballage léger» (selon Larousse) plus ou moins séduisant d'un élément de communication acoustique, et nous entraîne dans le domaine des multimedia. La pochette devient alors partie intégrante d'une unité multimedia et se transforme en une œuvre de présentation créatrice qui lui assure une vie propre. On la voit se déplier ingénieusement, proposer un chemin fait de perforations pour accéder au mystère qu'elle recèle, exhiber un couvercle invitant à la découverte. Dans ce genre de pochettes, la création graphique devient un art sui generis propre à plonger dans la béatitude tout designer portant au secret de son cœur les exigences de l'art pour l'art et à lui faire imaginer un instant qu'il se pourrait bien qu'un jour les collectionneurs chevronnés retirent le disque de la pochette pour... le jeter, seule l'enveloppe étant digne d'être conservée.

Miscellaneous Records
Verschiedene Platten
Différents disques

Literary Recordings
Educational Records
Children's Records
Japanese Projects
Special Presentations

Literarische Aufnahmen
Erzieherische Platten
Kinderplatten
Japanische Projekte
Spezielle Präsentationen

Enregistrements littéraires
Disques pédagogiques
Disques pour enfants
Projets japonais
Présentations spéciales

Literary Recordings

506) Cover for a recording of chansons to words by Erich Kästner. Black and green.
507) Three-colour cover for a play recording.
508) Cover for Greek religious poems.
509) For a spoken record ("You won't believe your ears").
510) Cover for a series issued by the Swedish radio, here about Nazi persecution and mass executions.
511) Cover for readings from Goethe and Gerhard Hauptmann.
512) Cover for a documentary record on the attack on Pearl Harbour in 1941. Red "rising sun".
513) 514) From a Greek series about the deeds of Hercules.
515) Cover for readings from the letters of Menachem Mendel. Pastel shades.
516) Cover for a recording of Jewish jokes.

506) Umschlag einer Platte mit 16 Chansons nach Gedichten von Erich Kästner. Schwarzweiss und grün.
507) Dreifarbige Hülle für die Wiedergabe eines Theaterstücks.
508) Plattenhülle für religiöse griechische Gedichte.
509) Für eine Sprechplatte: Sie werden Ihren Ohren nicht trauen.
510) Aus einer Serie des Schwedischen Radios, hier über die Nazi-Verfolgungen und Massenhinrichtungen.
511) Für Lesungen aus Werken von Goethe und Gerhard Hauptmann.
512) Hülle für historische Dokumente zum Überfall auf Pearl Harbour, 1941. Rote «aufgehende Sonne».
513) 514) Aus einer griechischen Serie mit Herkules-Sagen.
515) Pastellfarbener Umschlag für eine Sprechplatte mit Fritz Muliar, der aus Briefen des Menachem Mendel vorliest.
516) Umschlag für eine Platte mit jüdischen Witzen.

506) Pochette pour un disque de chansons pour lesquelles Erich Kästner a livré les paroles. Noir et vert.
507) Pochette trichrome pour l'enregistrement d'une pièce.
508) Pochette pour un choix de poèmes religieux grecs.
509) Pour un disque parlé.
510) Pochette pour un disque sur les persécutions et exécutions massives nazies. Série de la radio suédoise.
511) Pour une récitation de poèmes de Goethe et Hauptmann.
512) Pochette pour un disque documentaire sur l'attaque de Pearl Harbour en 1941. «Soleil levant» rouge.
513) 514) Série grecque consacrée aux travaux d'Hercule.
515) Pochette pour un enregistrement des lettres de Menachem Mendel. Tons pastels.
516) Pochette pour un disque d'humour juif.

ARTIST/KÜNSTLER/ARTISTE:

506) Klempa (Photo)
507) Tomi Ungerer
508) Agni Katzourakis
509) Pierre Jacotin
510) L. E. Frank/T. Bergentz/T. Lenskog/O. Roos
511) Robert Pütz
512) Edwin Lee
513) 514) Hans Keller
515) Walter Schmögner
516) Jürgen Wulff

DESIGNER/GESTALTER/MAQUETTISTE:

506) Holger Matthies
508) Frederick V. Carabott
511) Robert Pütz
512) Edwin Lee

506

507

508

509

510

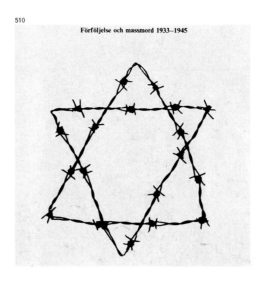

Förföljelse och massmord 1933–1945

511

DEC.7,1941

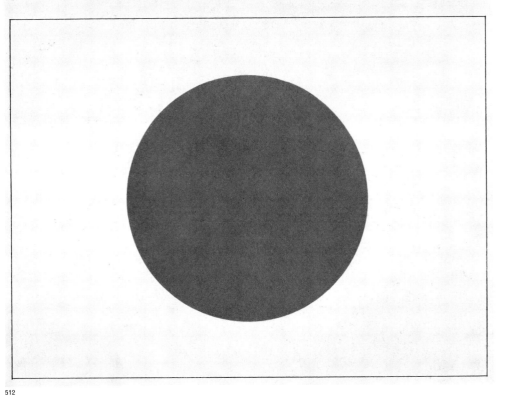

512

515

516

513

ANTEO
DISCESA NEL TARTARO
CATTURA DI CERBERO
DEIANIRA
LA CAMICIA DI NESSO
APOTEOSI DI ERCOLE

RFF-EP 39524

ERCOLE 08

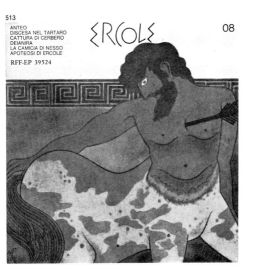

514

L'IDRA DI LERNA
LA CERVA DI CERINEA
IL CINGHIALE DI ERIMANZIO
LA GUERRA
CONTRO I CENTAURI
MORTE DEL
CENTAURO CHIRONE

RFF-EP 39521

ERCOLE 05

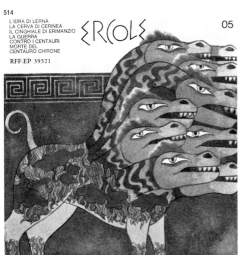

ART DIRECTOR/DIRECTEUR ARTISTIQUE:

506) Holger Matthies
508) Michael Katzourakis
509) Pierre Jacotin
510) Bengt Segerstedt
511) Robert Pütz
512) Edwin Lee
513) 514) Gisela Tobler
516) Willi Mailand

PUBLISHER/VERLEGER/EDITEUR:

506) 516) Deutsche Grammophon Gesellschaft, Hamburg
508) Christian Theater, Athens
509) Dock Remois Familistère, Reims/FRA
510) Sveriges Radio, Stockholm
511) Phonogram, Hamburg
512) The New York Times, New York
513) 514) Ri-Fi, Milan
515) Preiserrecords, Wien

Educational Records
Erzieherische Platten
Disques pédagogiques

517) Cover from a series intended as a training in listening to music. Blue, green and red design on black.
518) Cover for a French course primarily aimed at the American holiday-maker.
519) Cover for a course of music for elementary schools issued by the Japanese Ministry of Education. It also encloses a booklet with text and examples of music.
520) Record cover for a French course.
521)–524) Covers from a series recording the voices of birds and animals: fig. 521, domestic animals; figs. 522 and 523, from a series of birds (showing the wagtail and owl); and fig. 524, from an insect series (showing the grasshopper).
525) Cover for a record about ecological problems in America. Red on white, with the smoke already suggesting the shape of a skull.
526) Cover for the recording of a postgraduate seminar about alcohol withdrawal, issued as a professional service by Pfizer Laboratories Division.
527) Cover for a recording of the sounds made by normal and diseased hearts. Red and black.
528)–532) Covers for five of the six records of an American writing course for radio and television.

517) Aus einer einheitlich gestalteten Serie von Platten zur Musikschulung. Design in Rot, Grün und Blau.
518) Plattenhülle für einen Französischkurs, der vor allem auf das Ferienvokabular ausgerichtet ist.
519) Plattenhülle für einen vom japanischen Erziehungsministerium herausgegebenen Kurs für den Musikunterricht in der Volksschule, mit eingefügtem Textteil und Musikbeispielen.
520) Plattenhülle für einen Französischkurs.
521)–524) Mehrfarbige Schallplattenhüllen aus einer Serie über Vogel- und Tierlaute. Abb. 521: Haustiere; Abb. 522 und 523: Singvögel Europas (mit Bachstelze und Eule als Motiv); Abb. 524: Insekten (mit Heuschrecke).
525) Hülle für eine Platte über Umweltverschmutzung in Amerika. Rot auf Weiss. Der Rauch, der die Form eines stilisierten Totenkopfs annimmt, symbolisiert die Verschmutzung durch Industrieabgase.
526) Plattenhülle mit Auszügen aus einem von Pfizer organisierten Seminar über Alkoholismus.
527) Rot-schwarze Hülle mit Aufnahmen von Herztönen bei gesunden und kranken Herzen.
528)–532) Aus einer Serie von sechs Platten für einen Kurs für Radio- und Fernsehautoren.

517) Pochette bleu, vert, rouge sur noir. Série pédagogique destinée à l'entraînement à l'audition musicale.
518) Pochette d'un cours de français destiné en premier lieu aux touristes américains.
519) Pochette pour un cours de musique à l'intention des écoles élémentaires édité par le Ministère japonais de l'Education Nationale, et comprenant aussi un livret de texte et d'exemples musicaux.
520) Pochette de disque pour un cours de français.
521)–524) Pochettes pour une série de chants d'oiseaux et de cris d'animaux: 521) animaux domestiques; 522) et 523) oiseaux (bergeronnette, hibou); 524) insectes (sauterelle).
525) Pochette d'un disque consacré aux problèmes d'écologie en Amérique. Rouge sur blanc; la fumée déjà évoque les contours d'une tête de mort.
526) Pochette pour l'enregistrement d'un séminaire de recherche sur la désintoxication des alcooliques, édité par la Division Laboratoires de Pfizer et distribué à titre gracieux à la profession médicale.
527) Pochette pour un enregistrement des bruits normaux et anormaux du cœur. Rouge et noir.
528)–532) Pochettes de cinq des six disques d'un cours de rédaction américain pour la radio et la télévision.

517

518

521

522

525

526

519

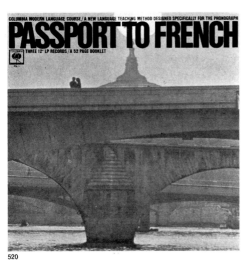

520

523

524

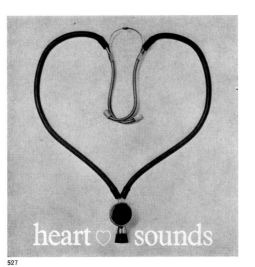

527

528

529-532

533) 534) Covers from a series of readings of German fairy tales for children.
535) 536) Covers for readings of fairy tales, here English tales and those of the Brothers Grimm.
537) Cover for a collection of poems for children. Black and white on deep yellow.
538) Cover for a Dutch collection of songs about Santa Claus, sung by a children's choir.
539) Cover for a collection of stories for children from the Bible, with background music. Bright hues.
540) Cover for a Japanese record of stories for children, in the style of a child's drawing.
541) 542) Detail of the design and complete cover for a record serving for the early musical education of very young children.

533) 534) Aus einer Serie von Märchenplatten für Kinder.
535) 536) Zwei mehrfarbige Hüllen für Märchenplatten, hier für englische Märchen und Märchen der Gebrüder Grimm.
537) Umschlag einer Platte mit Gedichten, die von Max Bolliger für Kinder geschrieben wurden. Gelb, schwarz.
538) Mehrfarbige Hülle für bekannte holländische St.-Niklaus-Lieder, von einem Kinderchor gesungen.
539) Mehrfarbige Plattenhülle für Geschichten aus der Bibel, mit Musik untermalt.
540) Umschlag einer Platte mit japanischen Kindergeschichten. Die Illustration erinnert an eine Kinderzeichnung.
541) 542) Illustration und vollständige Hülle für eine Platte zur Musikerziehung von kleinen Kindern. Die Platte wurde von der Zeitschrift *Eltern* herausgegeben.

533) 534) Pochettes pour une série de disques parlés. Contes de fées allemands.
535) 536) Pochettes pour des enregistrements de contes de fées anglais et allemands (frères Grimm).
537) Pochette pour un recueil de poésies enfantines. Noir et blanc sur jaune orangé.
538) Pochette pour un recueil de noëls hollandais chantés par une chorale enfantine.
539) Pochette pour un disque d'histoires bibliques pour enfants, avec fond musical. Couleurs vives.
540) Pochette pour un disque japonais d'histoires enfantines. Motif imitant un dessin d'enfant.
541) 542) Détail de la composition et pochette complète d'un disque destiné à l'initiation musicale des tout petits.

Children's Records
Kinderplatten
Disques pour enfants

533

534

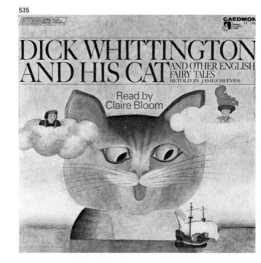

535

537

538

539

ARTIST/KÜNSTLER/ARTISTE:

533) 534) Hella Stolz
535) 536) Etienne Delessert
537) Robert Wyss
538) Toni Giesbergen
539) Simms Taback
540) Makoto Wada
541) 542) Anita Albus

DESIGNER/GESTALTER/MAQUETTISTE:

533) 534) Hella Stolz
535) 536) Etienne Delessert
539) Jack Anesh
540) Makoto Wada
541) 542) Dietmar Meyer

536

540

541

ART DIRECTOR/DIRECTEUR ARTISTIQUE:

533) 534) Hella Stolz
537) Oswald Dubacher
538) Cor Van Tol
541) 542) Dietmar Meyer

PUBLISHER/VERLEGER/EDITEUR:

533) 534) CBS Schallplatten, Frankfurt/M
535) 536) Caedmon Children Classics, New York
537) Ex Libris, Zürich
538) Fontana/Phonogram, Baarn
539) MGM Records, New York
540) Victor Co. of Japan, Tokyo
541) 542) Eltern/Gruner+Jahr, München

542

175

Children's Records
Kinderplatten
Disques pour enfants

ARTIST/KÜNSTLER/ARTISTE:

543)—550) Walter Grieder
551)—553) Heinz Stieger

ART DIRECTOR/DIRECTEUR ARTISTIQUE:

543)—550) Walter Grieder
551)—553) Oswald Dubacher

PUBLISHER/VERLEGER/EDITEUR:

543)—550) Tell Records, Basel
551)—553) Ex Libris, Zürich

543

544

551

Ds Märli vom
Aschenbrödel

Bärndütsch

M. 15

545

Ds tapfere
Schnyderli

Bärndütsch

M. 13

546

Ds Märli vom
gstiflete Kater

Bärndütsch

M. 14

547

König Drosselbart

verzellt vom Roland Keller

M 16

RECORD

548

Die Bremer Stadtmusikanten

verzellt vom Roland Keller

M 16

RECORD

549

Dornröschen

verzellt vom Roland Keller

RECORD

550

d Sylvia Sempert verzellt Märli vom Rotchäppli   vo de Heinzelmännli
                                  vom Dornrösli   vom Wolf und de 7 Geissli
                                  vom Äscheputtel   vo de Sterntaler

552

d Sylvia Sempert
verzellt Märli   d Frau Holle   vom tapfere Schniderli
                  vom Froschkönig   vom Schneewissli und Roserot

553

543)–547) Covers from a series of readings of fairy stories for children. The tales are all by the Brothers Grimm and are read in the Swiss-German dialect.

548)–550) Further examples from the same colourful series as shown in figs. 543 to 547.

551)–553) Colour detail from fig. 552 and two complete covers from another series of tales for children.

543)–547) Aus einer Serie von Märchenplatten für Kinder. Es sind alles Märchen der Gebrüder Grimm, die in schweizerdeutschem Dialekt erzählt werden.

548)–550) Neuere Beispiele aus der farbenfrohen Märchenserie, wie in Abb. 543–547 gezeigt.

551)–553) Detail von Abb. 552 und zwei vollständige Hüllen aus einer anderen Märchenserie für Kinder.

543)–547) Exemples d'une série de pochettes réalisées pour des disques de contes de fées des frères Grimm, enregistrés en dialecte suisse allemand.

548)–550) Nouvelle série d'exemples empruntés à la même collection haute en couleur de disques pour enfants que les pochettes des fig. 543 à 547.

551)–553) Détail en couleur de la fig. 552 et deux pochettes complètes pour une autre série de contes.

d Sylvia Sempert
verzellt Märli

3. Folge

König Drosselbart
Rumpelstilzchen
vom Chätzli und Müsli

vo de Bienekönigin
Hans im Glück
vo de 7 Rabe

554

Kasperlitheater NR. 8
De Giizgnäpper im Pflumewäldli
De flüügend Esel
mit Ines Torelli, Jörg Schneider, Paul Bühlmann

555

Kasperlitheater NR. 7
De Schorsch Gaggo reist uf Afrika
Die siebe Wunderchrüütli
mit Ines Torelli, Jörg Schneider, Paul Bühlmann

557

Children's Records
Kinderplatten
Disques pour enfants

554) Cover in bright colours for Swiss readings of fairy tales. Each rectangle contains a scene from one of the stories related.
555)–558) Covers from a series of children's plays in which the parts are taken by well-known Swiss cabaret performers. All in the Swiss-German dialect.
559) Colourful cover for a collection of bedtime stories for the tiny tots.
560) Cover for a recording of a children's story about a robber, based on a popular book.
561) Full-colour cover from the same series of children's fairy tales as shown in figs. 543–550.

554) Umschlag in fröhlichen Farben für eine Märchenplatte. Jede Illustration zeigt eine Szene aus einem der in Schweizerdeutsch erzählten Märchen.
555)–558) Hüllen aus einer Serie mit Kinderaufführungen. Die einzelnen Rollen, in Schweizerdeutsch, wurden von bekannten Schweizer Cabarettisten gesprochen.
559) Farbenfroher Umschlag einer Platte mit einer Auswahl von Gute-Nacht-Geschichten für kleine Kinder.
560) Hülle einer Platte mit Geschichten aus dem bekannten Kinderbuch *Der Räuber Hotzenplotz*.
561) Mehrfarbige Hülle aus der gleichen, in Abb. 543–550 gezeigten Serie von Märchenplatten für Kinder.

554) Pochette aux couleurs vives pour des enregistrements suisses de contes de fées, dont diverses scènes figurent dans les différents rectangles.
555)–558) Exemples de pochettes pour une série de sketches pour enfants interprétés en dialecte suisse allemand par des fantaisistes suisses bien connus.
559) Pochette haute en couleur pour un recueil d'histoires pour endormir les tout petits.
560) Pochette pour l'enregistrement d'une histoire de brigand pour enfants, d'après un livre populaire.
561) Pochette polychrome figurant dans la même collection de contes de fées que les pochettes 543 à 550.

178

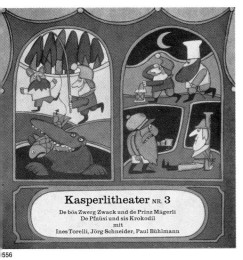

556

559

560

561

558

ARTIST/KÜNSTLER/ARTISTE:

554)–560) Heinz Stieger
561) Walter Grieder

ART DIRECTOR/DIRECTEUR ARTISTIQUE:

554)–560) Oswald Dubacher

PUBLISHER/VERLEGER/EDITEUR:

554)–560) Ex Libris, Zürich
561) Tell Records, Basel

179

562

563

566

564

565

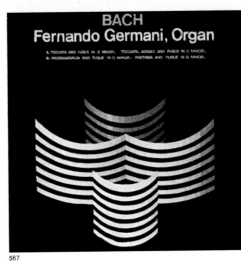

567

572

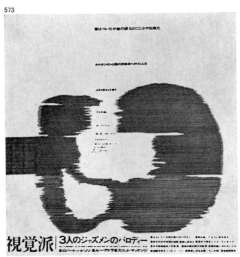

573

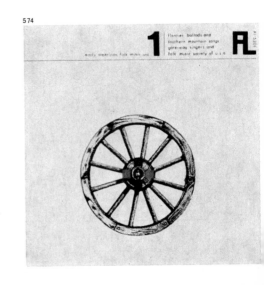

574

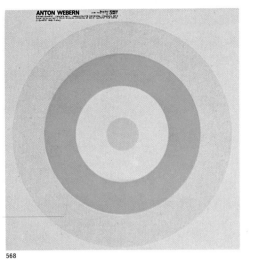

568

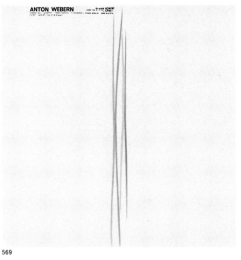

569

570

571

575

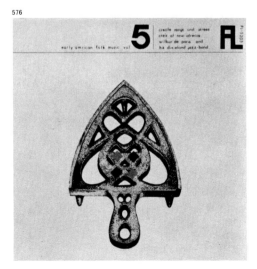

576

562)–565) Projects for a series of record covers for French and Italian chansons.
566) 567) Projects for record covers from a series for organ music by Bach.
568)–571) From a series of projects for record covers for the music of Anton von Webern.
572) 573) Projects for record covers for modern jazz, here suggesting banjo and guitar.
574)–576) Projects for an album of early American folk music, here ballads, college and Creole songs.

562)–565) Entwürfe für eine Serie von Plattenhüllen für französische und italienische Chansons.
566) 567) Aus einer Serie von Umschlagentwürfen für Orgelkonzerte von J.S. Bach.
568)–571) Entwürfe für eine Serie von Schallplatten mit Werken des Komponisten Anton von Webern.
572) 573) Umschlagentwürfe für eine Serie von Platten mit Modern-Jazz-Stücken. Die Motive zeigen stilisierte Instrumente, hier ein Banjo und eine Guitarre.
574)–576) Umschlagentwürfe für eine Serie von Schallplatten mit Aufnahmen früher amerikanischer Volksmusik, hier Balladen, Studentenlieder und kreolische Songs.

562)–565) Etudes de pochettes pour des disques de chansons françaises et italiennes.
566) 567) Etudes de pochettes pour une série de disques de Bach (musique pour orgue).
568)–571) Etudes de pochettes pour des disques du compositeur autrichien Anton von Webern.
572) 573) Maquettes de pochettes pour du jazz moderne, évoquant un banjo et une guitare.
574)–576) Maquettes pour la pochette d'un album de musique populaire américaine ancienne: ballades, chansons de campus et chants créoles.

ARTIST/KÜNSTLER/ARTISTE:

562)–565) Sonoko Arai
566) 567) Kimihisa Nakamura
568)–571) Mitsuo Funakoshi
572) 573) Koji Morisaki/Kiyoshide Yamamoto
574)–576) Tohru Takimoto/Hatsuko Tanaka

ARTIST/KÜNSTLER/ARTISTE:

577) 578) 583)–585) Toshiki Ohashi
579)–582) Koji Ito
586)–591) Koji Morisaki/Kiyoshi Wakusi

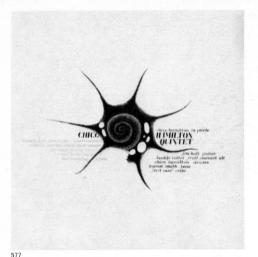

577

578

579

580

577) 578) Projects for a series of covers of records by the Chico Hamilton Quintet.
579)–582) Projects for record covers for French chansons.
583)–585) Projects for covers from a series of recordings by the jazz musician Dave Brubeck.
586)–591) Projects for a series of record covers for American folk music.

577) 578) Umschlagentwürfe für Platten mit Aufnahmen des Chico Hamilton Quintets.
579)–582) Beispiele aus einer Serie von Entwürfen für französische Chansons.
583)–585) Umschlagentwürfe für eine Serie von Aufnahmen des Jazzmusikers Dave Brubeck.
586)–591) Entwürfe für eine Serie von Schallplattenhüllen für amerikanische Volksmusik.

577) 578) Etudes de pochettes pour des disques du Chico Hamilton Quintet.
579)–582) Etudes de pochettes pour des disques de chansons françaises.
583)–585) Etudes de pochettes pour une série d'enregistrements de Dave Brubeck.
586)–591) Etudes de pochettes pour une série de disques de musique populaire américaine.

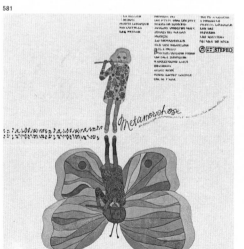

581

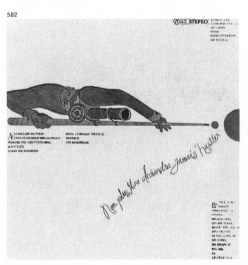

582

Japanese Projects
Japanische Projekte
Projets japonais

DAVE BRUBECK RECORD ALBUM

583

DAVE BRUBECK RECORD ALBUM

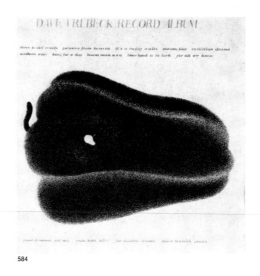

584

DAVE BRUBECK RECORD ALBUM

585

586

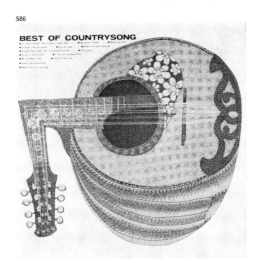

BEST OF COUNTRYSONG

587

BEST OF COUNTRYSONG

588

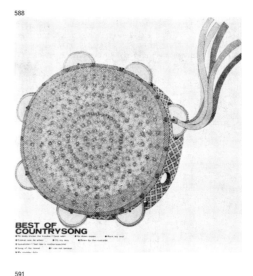

BEST OF COUNTRYSONG

589

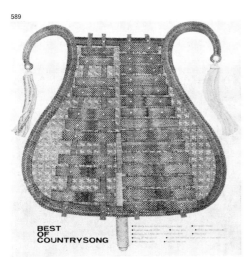

BEST OF COUNTRYSONG

590

BEST OF COUNTRYSONG

591

BEST OF COUNTRYSONG

592

593

594

592)–594) Three cover projects in colour for recordings of organ music by Bach.
595)–597) Projects for record covers for children's songs.
598)–603) Projects for covers of recordings of classical music from the Western world in an American composers series. The copy mostly consists of imaginary names.
604) Project for a cover for music by a quintet. See also figs. 577 and 578.

592)–594) Drei mehrfarbige Umschlagentwürfe für Aufnahmen von Orgelmusik von Bach.
595)–597) Entwürfe für Platten mit Kinderliedern.
598)–603) Umschlagentwürfe für Aufnahmen klassischer Musik aus dem Westen, als Teil einer Serie über amerikanische Komponisten. Die Namen sind erfunden.
604) Umschlagentwurf für Aufnahmen eines Quintets. Siehe auch Abb. 577 und 578.

592)–594) Trois maquettes de pochettes couleur pour des disques de Bach (musique pour orgue).
595)–597) Maquettes de pochettes pour des chansons enfantines.
598)–603) Maquettes de pochettes pour des disques de musique classique occidentale. Série de compositeurs américains. Texte composé en majeure partie de noms fantaisistes.
604) Maquette de pochette pour le disque d'un quintette instrumental. Cf. aussi les fig. 577 et 578.

595

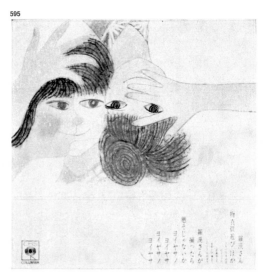

596

597

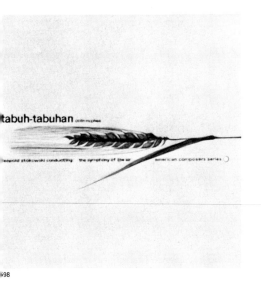

tabuh-tabuhan

leopold stokowski conducting   the symphony of the air   american composers series

marion bauer:
suite
for string
orchestra

marion bauer:
prelude
and fugue
for flute
and strings
mary howe:
stars
mary howe:
sand
the vienna orchestra
william strickland
conductor

american composers series

sylvia marlowe
harpsichord with claude monteux.flute:harry shulman.oboe
bernard greenhouse.cello

john lessard:toccata
arthur berger:bagatelle
virgil thomson:sonata
arthur berger:intermezzo
vittorio rieti:sonata all'antica
harold shapero:sonta no.1 in d major
virgil thomson:cantabil:a portrait of nicolas de chatelain
ben weber:serenade:op39,for flute.oboe.cello and harpsichord
american composers series

carl ruggles:
lilacs
carl ruggles:
portals
douglas moore:
cotillion suite
the juilliard string orchestra:
frederick prausnitz
conductor

american composer sereis

maro and anahid
ajemian
piano and violin

charles ives:
sonata no.4
for violin and piano
"children's day
at the camp meetng"
wallingford riegger:
sonata
for violin and piano
roger sessions:
from my diary
american composers series

CHICO HAMILTON QUINTET

ARTIST/KÜNSTLER/ARTISTE:

592)–594) Eiko Ishioka
595)–597) Tsunehiko Yanagimachi/Setsuko Majima
598)–603) Yoko Nishikido
604) Toshiki Ohashi

Japanese Projects
Japanische Projekte
Projets japonais

605

606

607

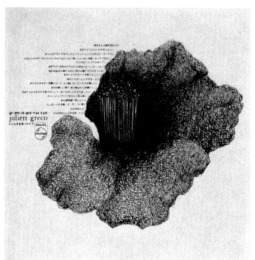

609

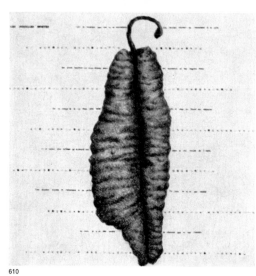

610

611

613

614

615

608

612

616

ARTIST/KÜNSTLER/ARTISTE:

605)–608) Masao Yuwamoto
609)–612) Shoko Kumazaki/Hazuyuki Gotoh
613)–616) Kyoko Matsumoto/Yasuo Terakado

605)–608) Projects for a series of covers for jazz music, this time using the names of famous performers. Designs in full colour.
609)–612) Projects for record covers from a series of French chansons, sung by Juliette Gréco and other well-known chansonniers.
613)–616) Projects for record covers from a series of folk songs from Spain and other parts of Europe.

605)–608) Umschlagentwürfe für eine Serie von Platten mit Aufnahmen berühmter Jazzmusiker, hier mit den wirklichen Namen. Design in Farbe.
609)–612) Umschlagentwürfe für eine Serie von Schallplatten mit französischen Chansons, gesungen von Juliette Gréco und andern bekannten Chansonniers.
613)–616) Aus einer Serie von Entwürfen für Aufnahmen von Volksliedern aus Spanien und andern Teilen Europas.

605)–608) Etudes de pochettes pour une série de disques de jazz, utilisant ici les noms d'interprètes célèbres. Compositions polychromes.
609)–612) Etudes de pochettes pour une série de disques de chansonniers français de renom, dont Juliette Gréco.
613)–616) Etudes de pochettes de disques pour une série de chansons populaires européennes (Espagne et autres pays).

617) 618) Record cover designed to look like a set of transparencies of musician John Cale, and view with the cover sheet raised to show the photographs below.

619) Record cover made to appear like a police file. Songs by Roman Murray. Beige, red lettering.

620) For songs sung by Canadians. Round red, white and blue paper sleeve in a square transparent cover.

621) 622) Blind-embossed plastic covers for texts spoken to the music of an ensemble. Fig. 621 magenta with yellow label, fig. 622 black with white label.

623) 624) Cover with two die-stamped fold-outs for a recording by a group called Bread, who are shown in colour.

625) 626) Cover in the form of a garbage can for the Eloy group. In fig. 625 the "lid" is lifted.

627) 628) Plastic cover containing a paper wrapper, shown in fig. 628 with the corners raised to reveal the record.

617) 618) Vorderseite mit Dia-Serie vom Interpreten John Cale und Ansicht mit leicht angehobenem Deckblatt, durch dessen ausgestanzte Fenster die Photos sichtbar werden.

619) Vom Titel (Busted = Singverbot) inspirierte Plattenhülle, die an eine Polizeiakte erinnert. Aufnahmen von Roman Murray. Beige mit roter Schrift, schwarzweisses Photo.

620) Blau-rot-weisse Papierhülle in transparenter Plastiktasche. Für bekannte, von Kanadiern gesungene Melodien.

621) 622) Kunststoffhüllen mit Blindprägung für Platten mit *electric music*. 621: *Kluster zwei Osterei*, himbeerrot, gelbes Label; 622: *Klopfzeichen*, schwarz, weisses Label.

623) 624) Hülle mit zwei auslegbaren Teilen, beide mit ausgestanzter Fensteröffnung. Für Aufnahmen der Gruppe Bread.

625) 626) Als Kehrichteimer aufgemachte Hülle (Abb. 625 «enthüllt» dessen Inhalt) für die Gruppe Eloy.

627) 628) In transparenter Plastikhülle steckender Packpapierumschlag. Abb. 628 mit leicht angehobenen Ecken.

617) 618) Pochette conçue de manière à évoquer une série de diapositifs du musicien John Cale, et vue ouverte montrant les photos disposées sous la feuille de couverture.

619) Pochette en forme de dossier de police. Chansons de Roman Murray «interdit de chanter». Beige, lettres rouges.

620) Disque de chanteurs canadiens. Chemise papier ronde, rouge/blanc/bleu, dans pochette carrée transparente.

621) 622) Pochettes plastiques gaufrées pour des textes récités avec accompagnement de musique par un ensemble. 621) Magenta, étiquette jaune; 622) noir, étiquette blanche.

623) 624) Pochette avec deux encarts dépliants découpés pour un disque du groupe Bread, présenté en couleurs.

625) 626) Pochette en forme de poubelle pour le groupe Eloy. La fig. 625 montre la poubelle ouverte.

627) 628) Pochette plastique contenant un emballage papier, dont les bords relevés dévoilent le disque (fig. 628).

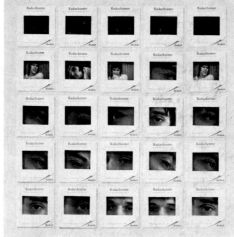

617

618

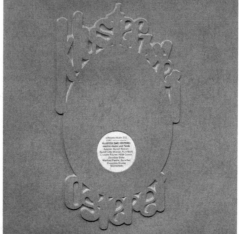

621

622

625

626

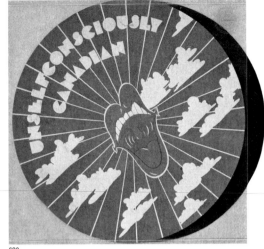

Special Presentations
Spezielle Präsentationen
Présentations spéciales

ARTIST/KÜNSTLER/ARTISTE:

617) 618) Ed Thrasher (Photo)
619) Norman Seeff (Photo)
620) Mauro Cotechini
621) Peter M. Kretzmann
622) Peter M. Kretzmann/Karl Seifert
623) 624) Robert L. Heimall (Photo)
625) 626) Juligan Studio (Photo)
627) 628) Dieter Bläser

DESIGNER/GESTALTER/MAQUETTISTE:

617) 618) Andy Warhol
619) Jon Echevarrieta
620) Mauro Cotechini
623) 624) Robert L. Heimall

ART DIRECTOR/DIRECTEUR ARTISTIQUE:

617) 618) Ed Thrasher
619) Norman Seeff
620) Mauro Cotechini
621) 622) Leo Werry
623) 624) Robert L. Heimall
625) 626) Wilfried Mannes
627) 628) Erdmann & Kohnen

PUBLISHER/VERLEGER/EDITEUR:

617) 618) Reprise/Warner Bros. Records,
        Burbank, Ca.
619) United Artists Records, Los Angeles
620) CBC Records, Edmonton/CAN
621) 622) 627) 628) L. Schwann Verlag,
        Düsseldorf
623) 624) Elektra Records, New York
625) 626) Phonogram, Hamburg

629) 630) Cover for pieces about animals played by a quintet. When the cover is raised, three-dimensional animals appear in folded board.
631) Full-colour label for Poppy Records.
632) Black-and-white label for the Black Sabbath group.
633) 634) Cover designed to look like a fruit crate, opening (fig. 634) on red apples packed in purple paper.
635) 636) Cassette-type album (set-up box with hinged lid) for a *Porgy and Bess* recording. Photograph of riveted sheet-iron in grey shades, die-stamped openings revealing colour portraits of singers.
637)–639) Cover for the Alice Cooper record *School's out.* Fig. 638 shows how the much-initialled "desk-top" lifts to reveal the record in a genuine pair of blue panties. Below the record appear (fig. 639) the chaotic desk contents.

630

629

629) 630) Geschlossene und aufgeklappte Hülle (Aufsteller mit farbigen Tieren) für Aufnahmen eines Jazz-Quintets.
631) Mehrfarbiges Label für Poppy Records.
632) Schwarzweiss-Label für eine Platte von Black Sabbath.
633) 634) Als Versandkiste aufgemachte Hülle der Rockband Magna Carta für Songs aus Wasties Obstgarten. Rote Äpfel in violettem Papier.
635) 636) Plattenkassette (zusammengenietete Blechplatten) mit ausgestanztem P & B für *Porgy and Bess.*
637)–639) Hülle für Alice Coopers *School's out.* 637: Vorderseite mit verkritzeltem Pultdeckel; 638: angehobener Deckel und Platte mit echtem wegwerfbaren Damenslip; 639: Ansicht der im Pult verstauten Sachen.

629) 630) Pochette pour un quintette. Soulevée, elle révèle des maquettes d'animaux (le thème de la musique).
631) Etiquette polychrome pour Poppy Records.
632) Etiquette noir-blanc pour un disque des Black Sabbath.
633) 634) Pochette en forme de cageot de fruits et ouvrant sur des pommes rouges dans du papier pourpre (634).
635) 636) Album-coffret pour un enregistrement de *Porgy and Bess.* Photo d'une tôle rivée grise. Les ouvertures gaufrées font entrevoir les chanteurs.
637)–639) Pochette pour *School's out,* d'Alice Cooper. Le pupitre aux nombreux graffiti se soulève, révélant le disque emballé dans un vrai slip de femme.

631

632

633

634

635

636

637

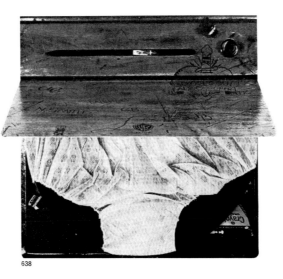

638

639

640

640) Transparent plastic cover with a tuck-in flap and embossed title *Clear Spot*. Band name printed on a white cardboard stiffener, brown record label.

641)–644) Front and back of a commemorative album cover for songs by Marilyn Monroe, and two double spreads from a twelve-page book insert with black-and-white shots of the star. Cover in full colour.

640) Transparente Plastikhülle mit Einstecklasche und blindgeprägtem Titel – *Clear Spot*. Bandname in Schwarz auf weissem Karton; Platte mit braunem Label.

641)–644) Mehrfarbige Vorder- und Rückseite eines Plattenalbums für bekannte Songs von Marilyn Monroe und zwei Doppelseiten aus einem 12seitigen Beihefter mit Schwarzweissphotos von verschiedenen Photographen.

640) Pochette plastique transparente avec rabat et titre gaufré *Clear Spot*. Le nom de l'orchestre est imprimé sur un carton blanc. Etiquette de disque en brun.

641)–644) Recto et verso d'une pochette pour un album commémoratif de chansons de Marilyn Monroe, et deux doubles pages d'une brochure intercalaire de 12 pages, avec des photos noir-blanc de la vedette. Pochette polychrome.

ARTIST/KÜNSTLER/ARTISTE:

640) Jim McCrary (Photo)
641)–644) G. Barris, J. Bryson, A. de Dienes, M. Greene, P. Halsman, T. Kelley, D. Kirkland, Magnum Photos, Inc., A. Newman, L. Schiller/ W. R. Woodfield, S. Shaw, B. Stern, B. Willoughby

DESIGNER/GESTALTER/MAQUETTISTE:

640) John+Barbara Casado
641)–644) Paul Bruhwiler/Gloria L. Clark

ART DIRECTOR/DIRECTEUR ARTISTIQUE:

640) Ed Thrasher
641)–644) Paul Bruhwiler

PUBLISHER/VERLEGER/EDITEUR:

640) Reprise/Warner Bros., Burbank, Ca.
641)–644) 20th Century Records, Los Angeles

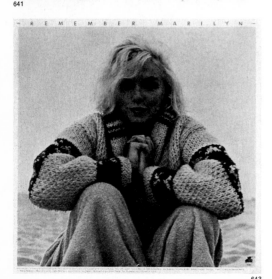

641

642

643

644